Innovative Approaches
Implementation

M0001113385

Multilevel governance systems like the European Union (EU) calibrate integration with member state discretion in order to implement common, yet context-sensitive solutions to shared policy problems. Research on implementation in the EU typically focuses on legal compliance with EU policy. However, this focus gives us an incomplete picture of EU implementation, its diversity and practice. The contributions of this collection represent a shift toward a more performance-oriented perspective on EU implementation as problem-solving. They approach implementation fundamentally as a process of interpretation of superordinate law by actors who are embedded within multiple contexts arising from the coexistence of dynamics of Europeanization, on the one hand, and what has been termed 'domestication', on the other. Moving beyond legal compliance, the contributions provide new evidence on the diversity of domestic responses to EU policy, the roles and motivations of actors implementing EU policy, and the 'black box' of EU law in action and its enforcement. By reassessing the relative importance of EU policy and domestic factors and actors for the outcomes of EU implementation, the results give insight into on the nuanced interplay between Europeanization and domestication forces, useful for both EU researchers and practitioners.

The chapters in this book were originally published in a special issue of the *Journal of European Public Policy*.

Eva Thomann is a political scientist specialized in Public Policy and Public Administration. She is a senior lecturer in the Department of Politics at the University of Exeter, UK. Her research about the implementation of public policies in multilevel systems and at the frontline was published, amongst others, in the *European Journal of Political Research, Policy Sciences, Public Administration, Governance*, and the *Journal of Public Policy*. Her article 'Customizing Europe: transposition as bottom-up implementation' appeared in the *Journal of European Public Policy* in 2015. A single-authored book about the customization of European Union (EU) food safety policy is forthcoming in Palgrave Macmillan's International Series on Public Policy.

Fritz Sager is professor of Political Science and member of the Executive Board of the KPM Center for Public Management at the University of Bern, Switzerland. He is specialized in policy research and evaluation, administrative studies and theory, organizational analysis, and Swiss politics. His research has been published in the *European Journal of Political Research, Public Administration Review, Governance, Public Administration, Journal of Public Policy*, and the *European Political Science Review*, among others. His most recent books are "The Political Economy of Capital Cities" with Heike Mayer, David Kaufmann and Martin Warland (Routledge/Taylor and Francis, 2017), "Policy-Analyse in der Schweiz" with Karin Ingold and Andreas Balthasar (NZZ libro, 2017) and "Evaluation im politischen System der Schweiz" edited with Thomas Widmer and Andreas Balthasar (NZZ libro, 2017). His research has won several awards.

Journal of European Public Policy Series

Edited by
Jeremy Richardson, *Nuffield College, Oxford University, UK, and National Centre for Research on Europe, University of Canterbury, New Zealand*

Berthold Rittberger, *International Relations, Geschwister Scholl Institute of Political Science, University of Munich, Germany*

This series seeks to bring together some of the finest edited works on European Public Policy. Reprinting from special issues of the *Journal of European Public Policy*, the focus is on using a wide range of social sciences approaches, both qualitative and quantitative, to gain a comprehensive and definitive understanding of public policy in Europe.

For a complete list of books in this series please visit https://www.routledge.com/Journal-of-European-Public-Policy-Special-Issues-as-Books/book-series/JEPPSPIBS.

The European Union as a Global Regulator
Edited by Alasdair Young

Ideas, Political Power, and Public Policy
Edited by Daniel Béland, Martin B. Carstensen and Leonard Seabrooke

Political Budgeting Across Europe
Edited by Christian Breunig, Christine S. Lipsmeyer and Guy D. Whitten

Federal Challenges and Challenges to Federalism
Edited by John Erik Fossum and Markus Jachtenfuchs

The European Union at an Inflection Point
(Dis)integrating or the new normal
Edited by Alasdair Young

Governance by International Public Administrations
Bureaucratic influence and global public policies
Edited by Christoph Knill and Michael Bauer

European Union Enlargement and Integration Capacity
Edited by Tanja Börzel, Antoaneta L. Dimitrova and Frank Schimmelfennig

Transforming Food and Agricultural Policy
Post-exceptionalism in public policy
Edited by Carsten Daugbjerg and Peter Feindt

Innovative Approaches to EU Multilevel Implementation
Moving beyond legal compliance
Edited by Eva Thomann and Fritz Sager

Innovative Approaches to EU Multilevel Implementation

Moving Beyond Legal Compliance

Edited by
Eva Thomann and Fritz Sager

Routledge
Taylor & Francis Group

LONDON AND NEW YORK

First published 2018 by Routledge

2 Park Square, Milton Park, Abingdon, Oxfordshire OX14 4RN
52 Vanderbilt Avenue, New York, NY 10017

Routledge is an imprint of the Taylor & Francis Group, an informa business

First issued in paperback 2020

Chapter 3 © 2018 Ellen Mastenbroek. Originally published as Open Access.
Chapter 5 © 2018 Nora Dörrenbächer. Originally published as Open Access.
Chapter 6 © 2018 Miroslava Scholten. Originally published as Open Access.
Chapters 1–2, 4 & 7–8 © 2018 Taylor & Francis

All rights reserved. No part of this book may be reprinted or reproduced or utilised in any form or by any electronic, mechanical, or other means, now known or hereafter invented, including photocopying and recording, or in any information storage or retrieval system, without permission in writing from the publishers.

Notice:
Product or corporate names may be trademarks or registered trademarks, and are used only for identification and explanation without intent to infringe.

British Library Cataloguing in Publication Data
A catalogue record for this book is available from the British Library

ISBN 13: 978-0-8153-6000-1 (hbk)
ISBN 13: 978-0-367-51961-2 (pbk)

Typeset in MyriadPro
by diacriTech, Chennai

Publisher's Note
The publisher accepts responsibility for any inconsistencies that may have arisen during the conversion of this book from journal articles to book chapters, namely the possible inclusion of journal terminology.

Disclaimer
Every effort has been made to contact copyright holders for their permission to reprint material in this book. The publishers would be grateful to hear from any copyright holder who is not here acknowledged and will undertake to rectify any errors or omissions in future editions of this book.

Contents

CONTENTS

Citation Information

The chapters in this book were originally published in the *Journal of European Public Policy*, volume 24, issue 9 (2017). When citing this material, please use the original page numbering for each article, as follows:

Chapter 1

Moving beyond legal compliance: innovative approaches to EU multilevel implementation
Eva Thomann and Fritz Sager
Journal of European Public Policy, volume 24, issue 9 (2017) pp. 1253–1268

Chapter 2

Moving beyond (non-)compliance: the customization of European Union policies in 27 countries
Eva Thomann and Asya Zhelyazkova
Journal of European Public Policy, volume 24, issue 9 (2017) pp. 1269–1288

Chapter 3

Guardians of EU law? Analysing roles and behaviour of Dutch legislative drafters involved in EU compliance
Ellen Mastenbroek
Journal of European Public Policy, volume 24, issue 9 (2017) pp.1289–1307

Chapter 4

Policy implementation through multi-level governance: analysing practical implementation of EU air quality directives in Germany
Judith A.M. Gollata and Jens Newig
Journal of European Public Policy, volume 24, issue 9 (2017) pp. 1308–1327

CITATION INFORMATION

Chapter 5

Europe at the frontline: analysing street-level motivations for the use of European Union migration law
Nora Dörrenbächer
Journal of European Public Policy, volume 24, issue 9 (2017) pp. 1328–1347

Chapter 6

Mind the trend! Enforcement of EU law has been moving to 'Brussels'
Miroslava Scholten
Journal of European Public Policy, volume 24, issue 9 (2017) pp. 1348–1366

Chapter 7

Strategies in multilevel policy implementation: moving beyond the limited focus on compliance
Eva G. Heidbreder
Journal of European Public Policy, volume 24, issue 9 (2017) pp. 1367–1384

Chapter 8

Toward a better understanding of implementation performance in the EU multilevel system
Eva Thomann and Fritz Sager
Journal of European Public Policy, volume 24, issue 9 (2017) pp. 1385–1407

For any permission-related enquiries please visit:
http://www.tandfonline.com/page/help/permissions

Notes on Contributors

Nora Dörrenbächer is a PhD candidate and researcher at the Institute for Management Research, Radboud University in Nijmegen, the Netherlands.

Judith A.M. Gollata is scholar at the Faculty of Sustainability at Leuphana University of Lüneburg, Germany.

Eva G. Heidbreder is professor of European Multilevel Governance at the Otto von Guericke University of Magdeburg, Germany.

Ellen Mastenbroek is professor of European Public Policy at the Institute for Management Research, Radboud University, the Netherlands.

Jens Newig is professor of Governance and Sustainability at Leuphana University of Lüneburg, Germany.

Fritz Sager is professor of Political Science and member of the Executive Board of the KPM Center for Public Management at the University of Bern, Switzerland.

Miroslava Scholten is an associate professor of EU Law at Utrecht University, the Utrecht Centre for Regulation and Enforcement in Europe (RENFORCE), the Netherlands.

Eva Thomann is a political scientist specializing in Public Policy and Public Administration. She is a senior lecturer in the Department of Politics at the University of Exeter, UK.

Asya Zhelyazkova is a political scientist specializing in European Union politics and is currently a research fellow at the School of Management of Radboud University Nijmegen, the Netherlands.

Moving beyond legal compliance: innovative approaches to EU multilevel implementation

Eva Thomann and Fritz Sager

ABSTRACT
Research on implementation in the European Union (EU) is characterized by a strong focus on legal conformance with EU policy. However, this focus has been criticized for insufficiently accounting for the implications of the EU's multilevel governance structure, thus providing an incomplete picture of EU implementation, its diversity and practice. The contributions of this collection represent a shift towards a more performance-oriented perspective on EU implementation as problem-solving. They approach implementation fundamentally as a process of interpretation of superordinate law by actors who are embedded within multiple contexts arising from the coexistence of dynamics of Europeanization, on the one hand, and what has been termed 'domestication', on the other. Moving beyond legal compliance, the contributions provide new evidence on the diversity of domestic responses to EU policy, the roles and motivations of actors implementing EU policy, and the 'black box' of EU law in action and its enforcement.

Introduction

This collection moves beyond legal compliance in European Union (EU) multi-level implementation research to shed light on alternative responses to super-ordinate law, practical implementation patterns and mechanisms to ensure compliance in the EU. In response to increasingly complex and transboundary shared regulatory challenges, multilevel governance systems like the EU centralize steering tasks and delegate decision-making and/or execution competencies to different levels of territorial tiers – supranational (global and regional), national, regional (domestic) and local (Levi-Faur 2011: 11; Majone 1999). As Thatcher and Coen (2008: 806) point out, the 'implementation of public policies always raises questions of discretion and diversity'. Multilevel systems calibrate integration with member state discretion in order to implement common solutions to shared policy problems, tailor-made to specific local contexts (Kissling-Näf and Wälti 2007; Pülzl and Treib 2007). This in turn should enhance the acceptance of centralized policies and, possibly, member state performance (Börzel and Hosli 2003; Elmore 1979; Keman 2000). The impact of such multilevel structures on policy outputs, outcomes and impacts is the subject of multilevel implementation research ever since Pressman and Wildavsky (1974) studied '[h]ow Great Expectations in Washington Are Dashed in Oakland'. Its currently dominant line is the rich body of literature on implementation in the EU and Europeanization.

In the quest to connect EU and domestic politics, seminal works on multilevel governance in the EU have amply scrutinized the EU's problem-solving capacity in terms of the impact of the EU on domestic institutions and policies at the national and local level (e.g., Featherstone and Radaelli 2003; Graziano and Vink 2008; Héritier 1999; Richardson 2012; Scharpf 1997). This collection contributes to this discussion. Its basic premise lies in understanding implementation as a core process in the problem-solving cycle. Hence, what is of interest here is the actual solutions to shared problems in the EU regulatory space (Knill and Tosun 2012). Implementation research has always held contradictory views on the role of discretion for policy success (Knill 2015; Pülzl and Treib 2007; Thomann *et al.* 2016). Accordingly, the question of what constitutes successful problem-solving is approached very differently by top–down and bottom–up implementation perspectives (Hill and Hupe 2014).

On the one hand, 'conformance implementation' refers to the degree to which the centrally decided blueprint is implemented from top to bottom (Barrett and Fudge 1981). This top–down school, which dominates Europeanization research, is primarily interested in comparing the intended and actually achieved outcomes of implementation, where the degree of the goal attainment serves as an indicator for implementation success (Knill 2015). Implicitly or explicitly, top-down perspectives tend to view discretion and the resulting deviations from the centrally decided rule as a control problem (Thomann *et al.* 2016). Alternatively, 'performance implementation' denotes whether a policy achieves outcomes that resolve the original policy problem at stake (Barrett 2004; Barrett and Fudge 1981; Mastop and Faludi 1997). This process-oriented bottom–up perspective emphasizes the role of policy implementers as problem-solvers, whose closeness to the source of the policy problem enhances their ability to achieve policy success (Elmore 1979). Hence, it is expected that policy instruments and goals may undergo context-sensitive modifications during the process of policy implementation. Implementers should have flexibility and autonomy for adjustment to facilitate learning, capacity-building and support-building in order to address policy problems. Ultimately, effective implementation is measured by the extent to which the perceived outcomes correspond with the preferences of the actors involved in the implementation process (Knill 2015). From this perspective, diverse approaches of problem-solving are actually an intended result of the decentralized implementation structures of multilevel systems (Joachim *et al.* 2007: 7).

However, we have very little systematic knowledge about this diversity of policy solutions (see, however, recently Bondarouk and Liefferink 2016; Sager *et al.* 2014; Thomann 2015a). Multilevel implementation research – in the EU and beyond – retains a strong top–down focus on member state compliance with central state decisions. A telling illustration is the title of a recent study which reads: 'You Can't Make Me Do It' (Haeder and Weimer 2013; see also Whitford 2007). This holds especially for Europeanization research, which is in its vast majority concerned with the question of whether EU directives are transposed into domestic law as required (see Angelova *et al.* 2012; Töller 2010; Toshkov 2010; Treib 2014). Accordingly, the past 25 years of EU compliance research have produced a fair amount of knowledge on the full or partial (non-) compliance with EU directives, the timeliness and correctness of transposition, the amount of non-compliance and transposition rates (Angelova *et al.* 2012; Töller 2010; Treib 2014). While undoubtedly relevant, several insights suggest that research on legal compliance gives us an incomplete picture of EU implementation.

Indeed, the emphasis on conformance implementation in EU research faces increasing critiques as it 'insufficiently captures the implications of member states being part of a multilevel system' (Schmidt 2008: 299), and 'tends to prejudge the EU as the main source of domestic change' (Börzel and Risse 2012: 2). As Knill (2015) highlights, this perspective relies on a highly simplified model of political steering and insufficiently takes into account the role, relevance and capacities of actors involved in the execution of a certain policy programme. The compliance concept captures the degree of conformance implementation, but does not necessarily help us to understand performance (Thomann 2015a). Or, as Bondarouk and Liefferink (2016: 2) put it, the 'approach, by which compliance is juxtaposed to noncompliance, masks potentially great variance in responses between authorities and does not tell much about the extent of the domestic efforts to implement the policy'. In fact, there is growing evidence that under certain circumstances, legal compliance with EU law may be unrelated to its practical application (Falkner *et al.* 2005; Versluis 2003, 2007; Zhelyazkova *et al.* 2016). Accordingly, Treib (2014: 29) highlights that 'we have as yet comparatively little evidence on the extent to which there is non-compliance beyond transposition and on the factors that are conducive to effective application and enforcement'. However, if we accept the notion that any policy is only as good as its practical implementation (Hill and Hupe 2014; Thomann 2015b), then this leaves us with unsatisfactory knowledge about the actual problem-solving capacity of the EU (Scharpf 1997).

In summary, after decades of legal compliance research, much is known about the conformance at the legislative stage in the EU, but much less is known about performance in practice. Analysing multilevel implementation beyond legal compliance has a high practical relevance, not least because in the vein of economic modernization and globalization, policy problems have become increasingly complex transboundary and cross-sectoral. This has resulted both in an increased demand for regulation and in a blurring of the distinction between the global and the national (Levi-Faur 2011). Take, for instance, the enormous transformation of EU regulation in the past 20 years (Richardson and Mazey 2015). The latter has considerably expanded from a concentration on competition policy to coverage of many sectors (Thatcher and Coen 2008), and toward 'softer' governance modes (Newig and Koontz 2014; Radulova 2007). Notwithstanding the growing empirical relevance of EU rules, many aspects of EU implementation remain a black box, and 'the tendency to neglect issues of enforcement and application has even increased' (Treib 2014: 15). Against this background, it is vital to gain better empirical and theoretical understanding of the degree to which such multilevel systems are actually able to address the problems they are intended to solve *in practice* (Sparrow 2000). Not only Europeanization scholars, but also practitioners can benefit from such insights to improve policy outcomes.

Contribution to the state of the art

To fill these gaps, this collection presents innovative approaches to EU implementation that follow recent quests to move beyond legal compliance (Schmidt 2008). Therefore, the studies in this collection scrutinize other stages of the implementation cycle and adopt a more performance-oriented approach to EU implementation, from various angles. What unites them is their reassessment of the relative importance of EU policy, on the one hand, and domestic factors and actors, on the other, in explaining the outcomes of EU implementation. Rather than focusing on compliance, they embrace the notion put forward by Bugdahn (2005: 177) that

> the implementation of EU policies is best conceptualized as a blend of effective EU influence over domestic policy choices in a given policy area – defined as Europeanization – and of domestic choices of non-prescribed or non-recommended policy options in the same policy area – which is termed domestication.

The contributions of this collection understand Europeanization and domestication as complementary forces, which jointly explain the multiple embeddedness of actors (Beyers 2005) involved in EU implementation. In this sense, the interplay between Europeanization and domestication is a central explanation for performance implementation. Furthermore, the contributions have as their entry point the notion that the 'transposition of European Economic Community directives is – to a very large extent –an act of interpretation' (Voermans 2009: 81). Emphasizing problem-solving and performance, these studies hence analyse implementation fundamentally as a process of interpretation of superordinate law by actors who are embedded within distinct and multiple contexts. In this vein, the collection addresses three closely intertwined sets of salient questions that research on legal compliance has left unaddressed.

A first crucial interest of this collection is to gain a better understanding of the *different responses to superordinate law in the complex EU multilevel systems, apart from legal compliance*. This entails two aspects: transposition outcomes other than conformance; as well as the question of how policy-makers address the complexity of this system when deciding over implementation modes. Beyond legal compliance, very little is known about other possible transposition outcomes. Recent research suggests that member states differ notably in the substantial similarity of domestic policies (e.g., Bondarouk and Liefferink 2016; Steunenberg 2007; Sager *et al.* 2014) and that fully compliant member states go beyond the minimum requirements of superordinate law (Voermans 2009). Thomann (2015a) highlights the prevalence of the legitimate 'customization' of EU law and its implications for understanding member states as bottom–up problem-solvers. However, we still lack a systematic picture of the diversity of the 'European experience' (Majone 1999) – not least because research has hitherto invested little in the systematic conceptualization and operationalization of such transposition outcomes. It is only then that we can find out: what are the more fine-grained patterns of implementation in Europe, and can we identify underlying logics in this diversity (Thomann and Zhelyazkova 2017)?

Analysing the diversity of EU implementation is crucial in order to understand trade-offs between the well-explored conformance implementation and the more neglected performance implementation. This is all the more important as a single model of implementing structure does not exist in the EU (Peters 2014: 136; Richardson and Mazey 2015). Capturing the possible facets of multilevel implementation outcomes requires an analytic focus on the management of and responses to the complexity of such systems (Hooghe and Marks 2003; Sanderson 2006). While this 'multi-layer problem' (Hill and Hupe 2003) has long been recognized by implementation research, analytical solutions to it still need further development. In this context, several contributions have emphasized the potential for cross-fertilization between theoretical perspectives on EU implementation, on the one hand, and on policy implementation and comparative federalism, on the other (e.g., Barrett 2004; Börzel and Hosli 2003; Hill and Hupe 2014; Hooghe and Marks 2003; Keman 2000; Kissling-Näf and Wälti 2007; Knill 2015; Knill and Tosun

2012; Ongaro *et al.* 2010; Pülzl and Treib 2007; Sabatier and Mazmanian 1980; Whitford 2007; Winter 2003). Notwithstanding this, attempts at connecting Europeanization theory with policy implementation theory are still rare (see recently Knill 2015). Taking this agenda further, Heidbreder (2017) draws from implementation theory in order to identify different implementation types that are responsive to the complexity of the EU multilevel setting, depending on functional characteristics of the policy and the domestic setting at hand (Heidbreder 2011; Matland 1995).

After shifting the focus to performance at the legislative stage of implementation, the second interest of this collection lies in moving further down the implementation chain and *opening the 'black box' of EU law in action* (Versluis 2003, 2007). As individuals implementing public policies effectively act as decision-makers in their own right, understanding domestication implies to look at the practical implementation and enforcement of EU policy (Hill and Hupe 2014; Lipsky 1980/2010; Thomann 2015b). Our present knowledge on the practical implementation of EU law is scattered (e.g., Beunen *et al.* 2013; Falkner *et al.* 2005; Hartlapp and Falkner 2009; Héritier 1999; Versluis 2007). The most conclusive result so far is that the 'law in the books' is not necessarily the same as the 'law in action' (Treib 2014: 16; Versluis 2003) – a lesson which is also drawn in federalist settings (Kissling-Näf and Wälti 2007; Sager 2007). Previous results suggest that legal compliance levels sometimes tell us little about the degree and quality of the practical implementation of centralized law (Beunen *et al.* 2013; Falkner *et al.* 2005; Hartlapp and Falkner 2009; Zhelyazkova *et al.* 2016). This insight has important implications for practical implementation in terms of the patterns, mechanisms and actors involved that need exploration. However, accounting for practical implementation adds additional layers of complexity to implementation analyses, and implies a focus on the interaction of different governance levels (Egeberg and Trondal 2009; Exadaktylos and Radaelli 2012; Hill and Hupe 2003; Knill and Tosun 2012; Kuhlmann and Wayenberg 2016; Mavrot and Sager 2016). It also requires a systematic policy evaluation, which is resource-intensive, underdeveloped in many countries and needs improvement in the EU (Knoepfel *et al.* 2011; Mastenbroek *et al.* 2016; Sabatier and Mazmanian 1980; Treib 2014). As a result of these obstacles, a crucial question remains to be explored: How does practical implementation – in terms of conformance and/or performance – look like in the EU multilevel system, and how can we explain it?

The current state of the art suggest that there are situations in which member states might decide to resolve problems independently of superordinate law (Barrett and Fudge 1981; Mastop and Faludi 1997). How do they perform such shifts from Europeanization to domestication in practice? To tackle this question, Dörrenbächer (2017) analyses the frontline implementation of EU immigration policy and uses insights from the behavioural public administration literature (Grimmelikhuijsen *et al.* 2017; Lipsky 1980/ 2010). Moreover, we hardly know how varying capacities for resilience determine member states' responses to problems, specifically if the latter are pronouncedly transboundary, such as air pollution which lack 'spatial fit' (Young 2002). While the potential of multilevel governance for improving policy implementation (rather than being an obstacle to it, see Leventon [2015]) has been acknowledged in implementation theory (Hooghe and Marks 2003), the empirical question of whether this is actually the case on the ground has hardly been addressed in the EU literature. As Gollata and Newig (2017) demonstrate, understanding these capacities implies taking a closer look at the horizontal and vertical co-operation and co-ordination between different levels of governance, with additional layers of governance being added in a federalist setting (see also Kuhlmann and Wayenberg 2016; Mathieu *et al.* 2016).

Jensen (2007) highlights that the effective practical implementation of EU policy is also a question of oversight and enforcement (Sager 2009). Simultaneously, as the EU has traditionally delegated these tasks to member states (Jans *et al.* 2015; see also Joachim *et al.* 2007; Perkins and Neumayer 2007), monitoring and enforcement can be expected to be a major source of domestication. The scarce existing evidence suggests that (the possibility of) oversight and enforcement is crucial for practical application in the EU, and that its absence leads to compliance deficits (Garoupa 2012; Jensen 2007; König and Mader 2014; Zhelyazkova and Yordanova 2015). Scholten and Ottow (2014) also made first, sector-specific steps toward a typology of EU enforcement mechanisms (see also Heidbreder 2015). However, Tosun (2012: 445) highlights the 'need for detailed descriptions of how these activities are actually pursued'. One reason why this is still missing is that the EU traditionally lacks enforcement competencies, and hence little encompassing data are available (Jans *et al.* 2015). Interestingly, however, recent years have witnessed a growing focus on the role of EU agencies and networks for improving the practical implementation of EU law, who formulate implementation guidelines for national agencies, inspect the implementation practices of national agencies, and provide training to national inspectors (see e.g., Egeberg and Trondal 2009; Groenleer *et al.* 2010; Versluis and Tarr 2013). Scholten (2017) points to an ongoing trend toward Europeanization in this regard. The growing role of the EU in the field of direct enforcement can be explained by the problems that indirect enforcement faces; if the 'traditional' implementation of regulation by national authorities is failing, enforcement at the community level is likely to follow in the same policy area (Scholten and Scholten 2016).

In order to understand the mechanisms underlying patterns of diversity, practical implementation and enforcement, it is necessary to address a third question, namely that of the *different roles and motivations of national actors implementing EU policy.* Europeanization theory has a long tradition of assuming different logics of action – rationalist or norm-driven – underlying implementing actors' behaviour (Jupille *et al.* 2003; Mastenbroek and Kaeding 2006; March and Olsen 1998). Concurrently, it has been noted that actors implementing EU policy are also multi-hatted (Egeberg and Trondal 2009) in that they are expected to be loyal both to EU policy and to national policy. The discussion about a European administrative space has given rise to the question of whether there is such figure as the European public servant (Sager and Overeem 2015). As Mastenbroek (2017) notes,

> individual politicians and civil servants involved in compliance processes may vary in their propensity to comply with EU law … These individuals' stances towards EU law are likely to have consequences for their behaviour, and thus for the functioning of the larger political-legal system in which they operate – in this case the European Union.

National implementation processes often serve the purpose to correct for what implementers perceive to be an inadequate balance between the two (e.g., Thomson 2010).

However, little is known about how the multiple embeddedness of actors in the EU multilevel system (Beyers 2005) creates diverse identities and problem perceptions, affects the interplay of these logics, and ultimately leads actors to lend different priorities to Europeanization and domestication respectively. Part of the problem is that the focus on legal compliance in EU implementation research has also implied that the processes of administrative rule-making, as well as the frontline implementation of EU rules, have been neglected (Treib 2014). As a result, our empirical knowledge about the importance of EU policy for implementing actors, relative to domestic policy, is limited. Empirical analyses of actors' motivations in the practice of EU implementation are urgently needed for a better understanding of the potentials and limits of Europeanization (Woll and Jacquot 2010). In this vein, Mastenbroek (2017) analyses an often neglected category of actors, namely legislative drafters and other EU-related legislative tasks, and the considerations that may or may not lead them to act as 'guardians' of EU law. Dörrenbächer (2017) looks at the different motivations driving actors in referring to EU policy and domestic law respectively when implementing EU migration policy at the frontline.

This collection explicitly seeks to move beyond the 'universe' of Europeanization research (Treib 2014) in order to benefit from the insights from different strands of literature. We intend to show that doing so can contribute importantly to overcoming the lack of cumulative, generalizable theoretical knowledge on the problem-solving capacity of multilevel systems (Hill and Hupe 2014; Pülzl and Treib 2007). In this vein, the contributions of this collection draw from neighbouring fields, including general frontline and multilevel implementation theory (Dörrenbächer, 2017; Heidbreder 2017), the literatures on regulatory change (Thomann and Zhelyazkova 2017), legislative ethics (Mastenbroek 2017), social psychology (Dörrenbächer 2017), multilevel governance (Gollata and Newig 2017) and regulation (Scholten 2017). Finally, the empirical studies presented here not only involve cross-sectoral comparison (Mastenbroek 2017; Thomann and Zhelyazkova 2017), they also explore neglected policy areas beyond environmental and social policies (Treib 2008; Töller 2010; Angelova *et al.* 2012), namely immigration policy (Dörrenbächer 2017) and air quality policy (Gollata and Newig 2017).

Structure and content of the collection

Following the different stages of the policy cycle, the collection begins by *moving beyond legal compliance as a transposition outcome.* Thomann and Zhelyazkova (2017) set the stage by discussing conceptual considerations and empirical challenges facing researchers engaging in the systematic comparative analysis of the 'customization' of EU law to depict diverse interpretations of EU rules beyond compliance. By conceptualizing this as a phenomenon of vertical regulatory change, they propose a generalized definition of customization and offer a flexible scheme for measuring customization, both in quantitative and qualitative comparative settings. Their empirical analysis provides the first large-scale mapping of the customization of EU environmental and justice and home affairs policies in 27 member states. Next to revealing the considerable diversity of compliant transposition, they find that customization follows pronounced policy-specific EU regulatory logics.

The contribution by Mastenbroek (2017) sheds light on the roles and strategies of administrative actors responsible for EU compliance. She scrutinizes the multiple roles of legislative drafters who are responsible for preparing the transposition of EU directives at the national level, and guarding the compatibility with 'autonomous' national legislation with EU legal injunctions. Specifically, she analyses how these actors deal with their multiple roles resulting from their double-hattedness as guardians of EU law, on the one hand, and politically loyal national civil servants, on the other. Based on qualitative interviews with legislative drafters and their superiors in diverse Dutch ministries, she paints a nuanced picture of the role conceptions of these actors which guide their reinterpretation of EU law so as to integrate EU legal requirements with national policy objectives, and prioritize one over the other in case of incompatibilities.

The next two contributions deal with the *practical implementation of EU policy.* Gollata and Newig (2017) empirically test the proposition underlying theories of polycentric governance, that multilevel governance is conducive to effective policy-making and delivery. This expectation is based on the arguments about the role of decentralization, spatial fit and participation, combined with a central planning and oversight mandate also known as 'mandated participatory planning'. Using the understudied case of the implementation of EU air quality legislation, they study all 137 air quality and action plans established since 2004 in German municipalities and agglomerations, as a case of a transboundary policy with a lack of spatial fit. Their analysis highlights the horizontal and vertical co-operation between different levels of government and administrative layers within the same policy arena. While this case does not suggest that multilevel governance improved policy delivery, it points to learning and capacity building between local implementers.

Moving further down the implementation chain, Dörrenbächer (2017) 'zooms in' on individuals. Using concepts from social psychology, her analysis specifically focuses on the question what instrumental and normative motivations drive frontline bureaucrats to use EU law to solve the legal ambiguity arising from placing implementers between domestic and EU regulatory frameworks. Drawing on qualitative interviews with 21 frontline bureaucrats in 10 German immigration agencies, Dörrenbächer's analysis provides rare insights into the concrete interplay of Europeanization and domestication when EU law is practiced next to national law. Her results suggest that these actors use EU law in situations when national regulations remain unclear. This reliance on EU law at the frontline can even correct for problematic transposition.

The contribution by Scholten (2017) shows that while the power to enforce EU law has traditionally been the responsibility of EU member states, the enforcement stage of the EU policy cycle has been moving towards 'Brussels' via the proliferation of EU entities with direct enforcement powers, EU enforcement networks and the use of EU hard, soft and case law. As Scholten highlights, this development raises the question of what role there is to play for the EU in the traditionally national field of EU enforcement. She discusses the implications for the EU's problem-solving capacity, as well as challenges posed for the legitimacy, accountability and practical effectiveness of EU enforcement.

The final contribution by Heidbreder (2017) adopts a conceptual, bird's eye perspective that connects the dots between the complexity of EU implementation beyond compliance and general implementation research. Drawing on the distinction between top–down and bottom–up implementation and Hooghe and Mark's (2003) two types of multilevel governance, Heidbreder identifies four implementation types with distinct logics in the EU multilevel system: centralization; agencification; convergence; and networking. Based on Matland's (1995) ambiguity–conflict model of policy implementation, this enables her to derive causal expectations about which implementation type is functionally linked with strategic choices of policy-makers. Based on empirical illustrations, she discusses the descriptive and integrative capacity of her framework to systematically structure the different implementation practices in the EU and gain a better understanding of the potential pitfalls of its multilevel structure.

In the end, we wrap up the findings of the different studies and discuss their implications in view of the benefits of turning toward a more performance-oriented perspective on EU implementation as done in this collection (Thomann and Sager 2017). We draw preliminary conclusions about the interplay between Europeanization and domestication beyond compliance, while also formulating scope conditions, avenues for future research, and implications for practitioners.

Acknowledgements

The impetus for this collection was born at the panel 'Innovative approaches to multilevel implementation research: moving beyond legal compliance' at the 2nd International Conference on Public Policy in Milano, Italy, in July 2015. We are very grateful to all the participants, discussants and the referees for their valuable comments, and to the editors of *Journal of European Public Policy* for their advice and support in making this happen.

Disclosure statement

No potential conflict of interest was reported by the authors.

Funding

Eva Thomann gratefully acknowledges financial support by the Schweizerischer Nationalfonds zur Förderung der Wissenschaftlichen Forschung [grant numbers P2BEP1-162077 and P300P1_171479].

References

Angelova, M., Dannwolf, T. and König, T. (2012) 'How robust are compliance findings? A research synthesis', *Journal of European Public Policy* 19(8): 1269–91.

Barrett, S.M. (2004) 'Implementation studies: time for a revival? Personal reflections on 20 years of implementation studies', *Public Administration* 82(2): 249–62.

Barrett, S. and Fudge, C. (1981) *Policy and Action: Essays in the Implementation of Public Policy*, London: Methuen.

Beunen, R., Van Assche, K. and Duineveld, M. (2013) 'Performing failure in conservation policy: the implementation of European Union directives in the Netherlands', *Land Use Policy* 31: 280–88.

Beyers, J. (2005) 'Multiple embeddedness and socialization in Europe: the case of council officials', *International Organization* 59: 899–936.

Bondarouk, E. and Liefferink, D. (2016) 'Diversity in sub-national EU implementation: the application of the EU ambient air quality directive in 13 municipalities in the Netherlands', *Journal of Environmental Policy & Planning*, DOI:10.1080/1523908X.2016.1267612.

Börzel, T.A. and Hosli, M.O. (2003) 'Brussels between Bern and Berlin: comparative federalism meets the European Union', *Governance* 16(2): 179–202.

Börzel, T.A. and Risse, T. (2012) 'From Europeanisation to diffusion: introduction', *West European Politics* 35(1): 1–19.

Bugdahn, S. (2005) 'Of Europeanization and domestication: the implementation of the environmental information directive in Ireland, Great Britain and Germany', *Journal of European Public Policy* 12(1): 177–99.

Dörrenbächer, N. (2017) 'Europe at the frontline: Analyzing street-level motivations for the use of European Union migration law', *Journal of European Public Policy*, doi:10.1080/13501763.2017.1314535

Egeberg, M. and Trondal, J. (2009) 'National agencies in the European administrative space: government driven, commission driven or networked?', *Public Administration* 87(4): 779–790.

Elmore, R.F. (1979) 'Backward mapping: implementation research and policy decisions', *Political Science Quarterly* 94(4): 601–616.

Exadaktylos, T. and Radaelli, C.M. (2012) *Research Design in European Studies: Establishing Causality in Europeanization*, Chippenham and Eastbourne: Palgrave Macmillan.

Falkner, G., Treib, O., Hartlapp, M. and Leiber, S. (2005) *Complying with Europe: EU Harmonisation and Soft Law in the Member States*. New York: Cambridge University Press.

Featherstone, K. and Radaelli, C.M. (2003) *The Politics of Europeanization*. Oxford: Oxford University Press.

Garoupa, N. (2012) 'An economic analysis of legal harmonization: the case of law enforcement within the European Union', in T. Eger and H.B. Schäfer (eds.), *Research Handbook on the Economics of European Union Law*. Cheltenham and Northampton: Edward Elgar Publishing, pp. 279–88.

Gollata, J.A.M. and Newig, J. (2017) 'Policy implementation through multi-level governance: analysing practical implementation of EU air quality directives in Germany', *Journal of European Public Policy*, doi:10.1080/13501763.2017.1314539

Graziano, P. and Vink, M.P. (2008) *Europeanization: New Research Agendas*, Basingstroke: Palgrave Macmillan.

Grimmelikhuijsen, S., Jilke, S., Olsen, A.L. and Tummers, L. (2017) 'Behavioral public administration: combining insights from public administration and psychology', *Public Administration Review* 77(1): 45–56.

Groenleer, M., Kaeding, M. and Versluis, E. (2010) 'Regulatory governance through agencies of the European Union? The role of the European agencies for maritime and aviation safety in the implementation of European transport legislation', *Journal of European Public Policy* 17(8): 1212–30.

Haeder, S.F. and Weimer, D.L. (2013) 'You can't make me do it: state implementation of insurance exchanges under the affordable care act', *Public Administration Review* 73 (s1): S34–47.

Hartlapp, M. and Falkner, G. (2009) 'Problems of operationalization and data in EU compliance research', *European Union Politics* 10(2): 281–304.

Heidbreder, E.G., (2011) 'Structuring the European administrative space: policy instruments of multi-level administration', *Journal of European Public Policy* 18(5): 709–727.

Heidbreder, E.G., (2015) 'Multilevel policy enforcement: innovations in how to administer liberalized global markets', *Public Administration* 93(4): 940–55.

Heidbreder, E.G. (2017) 'Strategies in multilevel policy implementation: moving beyond the limited focus on compliance', *Journal of European Public Policy*, doi:10.1080/13501763.2017.1314540

Héritier, A. (1999) *Policy-making and Diversity in Europe: Escape from Deadlock*, Cambridge: Cambridge University Press.

Hill, M. and Hupe, P. (2003) 'The multi-layer problem in implementation research', *Public Management Review* 5(4): 471–90.

Hill, M. and Hupe, P. (2014) *Implementing Public Policy*. London: Sage publications.

Hooghe, L. and Marks, G. (2003) 'Unraveling the central state, but how? Types of multi-level governance', *American Political Science Review* 97(2): 233–43.

Jans, J.H., de Lange, R., Prechal, S. and Widdershoven, R.J.G.M. (2015) *Europeanisation of Public Law*, Groningen: Europa Law Publishing.

Jensen, C.B. (2007) 'Implementing Europe: a question of oversight', *European Union Politics* 8(4): 451–77.

Joachim, J., Reinalda, B. and Verbeek, B. (2007) *International Organizations and Implementation: Enforcers, Managers, Authorities?*, Abingdon: Routledge.

Jupille, J., Caporaso, J.A. and Checkel, J.T. (2003) 'Integrating institutions: rationalism, constructivism, and the study of the European Union', *Comparative Political Studies* 36(1-2): 7–40.

Keman, H. (2000) 'Federalism and policy performance. A conceptual and empirical inquiry', in U. Wachendorfer-Schmidt (ed.), *Federalism and Political Performance*. London: Routledge, pp. 196–227.

Kissling-Näf, I. and Wälti, S. (2007) 'The Implementation of Public Policies', in U. Klöti, P. Knoepfel, H. Kriesi, W. Linder, Y. Papadopoulos and P. Sciarini (eds.), *Handbook of Swiss Politics. 2nd Completely Revised Edition*, Zurich: NZZ, pp. 501–24.

Knill, C. (2015) 'Implementation', in J. Richardson und S. Mazey (eds.), *European Union: Power and Policy-making*, London und New York: Routledge, pp. 371–97.

Knill, C. and Tosun, J. (2012) 'Governance institutions and policy implementation in the European Union', In J. Richardson (ed.), *Constructing A Policy-Making State? Policy Dynamics in the EU*, Oxford: Oxford University Press, pp. 309–33.

Knoepfel, P., Larrue, C., Varone, F. and Hill, M. (2011) *Public Policy Analysis*, Bristol: Policy Press.

König, T. and Mäder, L. (2014) 'The strategic nature of compliance: an empirical evaluation of law implementation in the central monitoring system of the European Union', *American Journal of Political Science* 58(1): 246–63.

Kuhlmann, S. and Wayenberg, E. (2016) 'Institutional impact assessment in multi-level systems: conceptualizing decentralization effects from a comparative perspective', *International Review of Administrative Sciences* 82(2): 233–54.

13

Leventon, J. (2015) 'Explaining implementation deficits through multi-level governance in the EU's new member states: EU limits for arsenic in drinking water in Hungary', *Journal of Environmental Planning and Management* 58(7): 1137–53.

Levi-Faur, D. (2011) 'Regulation and regulatory governance', in *Handbook on the Politics of Regulation*, Cheltenham and Massachusetts: Edward Elgar, pp. 1–25.

Lipsky, M. (1980/2010) *Street-Level Bureaucracy: The Dilemmas of the Individual in Public Services*, New York: Russell Sage Foundation.

Majone, G. (1999) 'Regulation in comparative perspective', *Journal of Comparative Policy Analysis: Research and Practice* 1(3): 309–24.

March, J.G. and Olsen, J.P. (1998) 'The institutional dynamics of international political orders', *International Organization* 52(4): 943–69.

Mastenbroek, E. (2017) 'Guardians of EU law? Analyzing roles and behavior of Dutch legislative drafters involved in EU compliance', *Journal of European Public Policy*, doi:10.1080/13501763.2017.1314537

Mastenbroek, E. and Kaeding, M. (2006) 'Europeanization beyond the goodness of fit: domestic politics in the forefront', *Comparative European Politics* 4(4): 331–54.

Mastenbroek, E., van Voorst, S. and Meuwese, A. (2016) 'Closing the regulatory cycle? A meta evaluation of ex-post legislative evaluations by the European Commission', *Journal of European Public Policy* 23(9): 1329–48.

Mastop, H. and Faludi, A. (1997) 'Evaluation of strategic plans: the performance principle', *Environment and Planning B: Planning and Design* 24: 815–32.

Mathieu, E., Verhoest, K. and Matthys, J. (2016) 'Measuring multi-level regulatory governance: organizational proliferation, coordination, and concentration of influence', *Regulation & Governance*, DOI:10.1111/rego.12127.

Matland, R.E. (1995) 'Synthesizing the implementation literature: the ambiguity-conflict model of policy implementation', *Journal of Public Administration Research and Theory* 5(2): 145–74.

Mavrot, C. and Sager, F. (2016) 'Vertical epistemic communities in multilevel governance', *Policy & Politics*, DOI: 10.1332/030557316X14788733118252.

Newig, J. and Koontz, T.M. (2014) 'Multi-level governance, policy implementation and participation: the EU's mandated participatory planning approach to implementing environmental policy', *Journal of European Public Policy* 21(2): 248–67.

Ongaro, E., Massey, A., Wayenberg, E. and Holzer, M. (2010) *Governance and Intergovernmental Relations in the European Union and the United States: Theoretical Perspectives*, Cheltenham and Northampton: Edward Elgar Publishing.

Perkins, R. and Neumayer, E. (2007) 'Implementing multilateral environmental agreements: an analysis of EU Directives', *Global Environmental Politics* 7(3): 13–41.

Peters, B.G. (2014) 'Implementation structures as institutions', *Public Policy and Administration* 29(2): 131–44.

Pressman, J.L. and Wildavsky, A.B. (1974) *Implementation. How Great Expectations in Washington Are Dashed in Oakland*, Berkeley: University of California Press.

Pülzl, H. and Treib, O. (2007) 'Implementing public policy', in F. Fischer, G.J. Miller and M.S. Sidney (eds.), *Handbook of Public Policy Analysis: Theory, Politics, and Methods*, Boca Raton, FL: CRC Press/Taylor and Francis, pp. 89–107.

Radulova, E. (2007) 'The OMC: an opaque method of consideration or deliberative governance in action?', *Journal of European Integration* 29(3): 363–80.

Richardson, J. (2012) *Constructing a Policy-making State? Policy Dynamics in the EU*, Oxford: Oxford University Press.

Richardson, J. and Mazey, S. (2015) *European Union: Power and Policy-making*, London and New York: Routledge.

Sabatier, P. and Mazmanian, D. (1980) 'The implementation of public policy: a framework of analysis', *Policy Studies Journal* 8(4): 538–60.

Sager, F. (2007) 'Making transport policy work: polity, policy, politics and systematic review', *Policy & Politics* 35(2): 269–88.

Sager, F. (2009) 'Governance and coercion', *Political Studies* 57: 537–558.

Sager, F. and Overeem, P. (eds.). (2015) *The European Public Servant: A Shared Administrative Identity?*, Colchester: ECPR Press.

Sager, F., Thomann, E., Zollinger, C. and Mavrot, C. (2014) 'Confronting theories of European integration: a comparative congruence analysis of veterinary drug regulations in five countries', *Journal of Comparative Policy Analysis: Research and Practice* 16(5): 457–74.

Sanderson, I. (2006) 'Complexity, "practical rationality" and evidence-based policy making', *Policy & Politics* 34(1): 115–32.

Scharpf, F. (1997) 'Introduction: the problem-solving capacity of multilevel governance', *Journal of European Public Policy* 4(4): 520–38.

Schmidt, S.K. (2008) 'Beyond compliance: the Europeanization of member states through negative integration and legal uncertainty', *Journal of Comparative Policy Analysis: Research and Practice* 10(3): 299–308.

Scholten, M. (2017) 'Mind the trend! enforcement of EU law has been moving to "Brussels"', *Journal of European Public Policy*, doi:10.1080/13501763.2017.1314538

Scholten, M. and Ottow, A. (2014) 'Institutional design of enforcement in the EU: the case of financial markets', *Utrecht Law Review* 10(5): 80–91.

Scholten, M., and Scholten, D. (2016) 'From regulation to enforcement in the EU policy cycle: a new type of functional spillover?', *JCMS: Journal of Common Market Studies*, doi: 10.1111/jcms.12508.

Sparrow, M.K. (2000) *The Regulatory Craft: Controlling Risks, Solving Problems and Managing Compliance*, Washington, DC: Brookings Institution Press.

Steunenberg, B. (2007) 'A policy solution to the European Union's transposition puzzle: interaction of interests in different domestic arenas', *West European Politics* 30(1): 23–49.

Thatcher, M. and Coen, D. (2008) 'Reshaping European regulatory space: an evolutionary analysis', *West European Politics* 31(4): 806–36.

Thomann, E. (2015a) 'Customizing Europe: transposition as bottom-up implementation', *Journal of European Public Policy* 22(10): 1368–87.

Thomann, E. (2015b) 'Is output performance all about the resources? A fuzzy-set qualitative comparative analysis of street-level bureaucrats in Switzerland', *Public Administration* 93(1): 177–94.

Thomann, E., Lieberherr, E. and Ingold, K. (2016) 'Torn between state and market: private policy implementation and conflicting institutional logics', *Policy and Society* 35(1): 57–69.

Thomann, E. and Sager, F. (2017) 'Toward a better understanding of implementation performance in the EU multilevel system', *Journal of European Public Policy*, doi:10.1080/13501763.2017.1314542

Thomann, E. and Zhelyazkova, A. (2017) 'Moving beyond (non-)compliance: the customization of European Union policies in 27 countries', *Journal of European Public Policy*, doi:10.1080/13501763.2017.1314536

Thomson, R. (2010) 'Opposition through the back door in the transposition of EU Directives', *European Union Politics* 11(4): 577–96.

Töller, A.E. (2010) 'Measuring and comparing the Europeanization of national legislation: a research note', *JCMS: Journal of Common Market Studies* 48(2): 417–44.

Toshkov, D. (2010) 'Taking stock: a review of quantitative studies of transposition and implementation of EU law', *Institute for European Integration Research*, Working paper No. 01/2010.

Tosun, J. (2012) 'Environmental monitoring and enforcement in Europe: a review of empirical research', *Environmental Policy and Governance* 22: 437–48.

Treib, O. (2014) 'Implementing and complying with EU governance outputs', *Living Reviews in European Governance* 9(1): 1–46.

Versluis, E. (2003) *Enforcement matters. Enforcement and Compliance of European Directives in Four Member States*, Delft: Eburon.

Versluis, E. (2007) 'Even rules, uneven practices: opening the 'black box' of EU law in action', *West European Politics* 30(1): 50–67.

Versluis, E. and Tarr, E. (2013) 'Improving compliance with European Union law via agencies: the case of the European railway agency', *JCMS: Journal of Common Market Studies* 51(2): 316–33.

Voermans, W. (2009) 'Gold-plating and double banking: an overrated problem?', in H. Snijders and S. Vogenauer (eds.), *Content and Meaning of National Law in the Context of Transnational Law*, Munich: Sellier European Law Publishers, pp. 79–88.

Whitford, A. (2007) 'Decentralized Policy Implementation', *Political Research Quarterly* 60(1): 17–30.

Winter, S.C. (2003) 'Implementation perspectives: status and reconsideration', in B.G. Peters and J. Pierre (eds.), *Handbook of Public Administration*, Thousand Oaks: Sage, pp. 212–22.

Woll, C. and Jacquot, S. (2010) 'Using Europe: strategic action in multi-level politics', *Comparative European Politics* 8(1): 110–26.

Young, O.R. (2002) *The Institutional Dimensions of Environmental Change: Fit, Interplay, and Scale*, Cambridge and London: MIT press.

Zhelyazkova, A. and Yordanova, N. (2015) 'Signalling 'compliance': the link between notified EU directive implementation and infringement cases', *European Union Politics* 16(3): 408–28.

Zhelyazkova, A., Kaya, C. und Schrama, R. (2016) 'Decoupling practical and legal compliance: analysis of member states' implementation of EU policy', *European Journal of Political Research* 55(4): 827–46.

Moving beyond (non-)compliance: the customization of European Union policies in 27 countries

Eva Thomann and Asya Zhelyazkova

ABSTRACT

Europeanization research often neglects that the implementation of European Union (EU) policy results in diverse national outcomes, even if member states comply with EU law. Such fine-grained Europeanization patterns have been explored as 'gold-plating' and 'customization'. This contribution builds and expands on this research to propose a general conceptualization and measurement of customization as the changes that provisions of EU Directives undergo in their regulatory density and restrictiveness during legal transposition. Using unique data on the customization of EU directive provisions from two policy areas in 27 countries, our empirical analysis reveals distinct changes in density and restrictiveness, pronounced policy-specific and state-level customization patterns. The findings illustrate how national customization strategies often follow specific EU regulatory logics in different integration contexts. We outline implications for future research on the causes and consequences of the inherent diversity of EU implementation regarding dimensions of customization, issues of legitimacy and effectiveness.

Introduction

This contribution lays the conceptual basis for systematic comparative research on the 'customization' of European Union (EU) policy, and explores empirical customization patterns across member states and policy sectors. Multilevel governance systems calibrate legal and economic integration with member state discretion in implementation (Hooghe and Marks 2003; Majone 1999; Windhoff-Héritier 2001). In Europeanization research, this discretion has mainly been studied in terms of legal compliance (Treib 2014). Yet case study evidence suggests that even the compliant implementation of EU policy entails divergent national outcomes, frequently as a result of

Supplemental data for this article can be accessed at doi:10.1080/13501763.2017.1314536.

high levels of EU policy ambiguity (e.g. Falkner *et al.* 2005; Shapiro 1999; Versluis 2003). Such differences co-exist with incentives of national authorities to comply with the EU directives (Mastenbroek 2017; Steunenberg 2007).

Consider how the EU guarantees that motor vehicles are properly checked and maintained while in use (Davidson 2006: 23–5). Council Directive 91/328/EC requires a roadworthiness test to be carried out every other year from the car's fourth year onwards. However, the Directive allows for bringing forward the date of the first test, and/or shortening the interval between two successive tests. As to 2006, member states complied with this EU rule in strikingly diverse ways. Only 9 out of 25 countries transposed the EU rule literally. Fourteen member states required an earlier first inspection; and 10 countries, annual follow-up inspections. Car owners face very differing demands, depending on how the respective country interprets the EU rule. Research on 'gold-plating' and 'customization' (Thomann 2015) scrutinizes such interpretations.

However, we know remarkably little about the extent, reasons and implications of this fine-grained diversity in EU implementation (Thomann and Sager 2017). This is unfortunate for three intertwined reasons. First, national authorities strive to avoid infringement costs while choosing the most appropriate strategies to implement EU policies (Steunenberg 2007). These strategies have potentially far-reaching implications for how common policy problems are resolved in practice in the EU (Scharpf 1997), but go unnoticed by analysing legal compliance. Second, a growing body of evidence suggests that, under certain circumstances, legal compliance with EU law may be unrelated to its practical application (Falkner *et al.* 2005; Versluis 2003, 2007; Zhelyazkova *et al.* 2016). Therefore, third, studying legal compliance without considering adaptations of EU policy to domestic circumstances provides an incomplete picture of EU implementation. Yet, conceptual and empirical obstacles have hindered the accumulation of systematic, cumulative knowledge on this phenomenon.

Conceptually, diversity in EU transposition has primarily been linked with issues of unintended competitive distortions (e.g. Davidson 2006; Jans *et al.* 2009; Morris 2011; Voermans 2009). Thomann (2015) then proposed a more fine-grained conceptualization of member states' customization of the density and restrictiveness of EU rules. We build on this earlier work to refine and generalize the customization concept in three ways. First, we assume that customization is a phenomenon of *vertical regulatory change* irrespective of (non-)compliance. Second, different aims and manifestations of EU law in contexts of positive and negative integration allow for *different directions of change* (Lowi 1972; Scharpf 1997; Vink 2002). Third, we link the concept more explicitly to the regulatory output literature to specify the *meaning, distinctness and interrelation of the two dimensions of change,* density and restrictiveness (Adam *et al.* 2015; Bauer and Knill 2014; Knill *et al.* 2012; Schaffrin *et al.* 2015).

Empirically, existing knowledge on these phenomena is still limited to a few case studies of selected policies and countries. Without broader comparative studies, the empirical relevance of these insights and their contingency upon selection bias, sectoral and national specificities remain unclear (Angelova *et al.* 2012; Toshkov 2010; Treib 2014). To remedy such biases and enable cumulative research, we propose a comprehensive and differentiated scheme to measure customization. Applying a subset of the proposed comprehensive conceptualization, we ask: What empirical customization patterns do we observe across EU member states and policy areas? What is the relationship between different dimensions of customization? We scrutinize how 27 member states customize separate provisions from 31 EU directives from two policy areas: justice and home affairs (JHA) (10) and environment (21).

This descriptive and explorative analysis illustrates pronounced policy-specific differences in customization that often conform to EU regulatory logics. Furthermore, our study shows that the relationship between different dimensions of customization differs across policy areas: the number of rules added to or taken away from an EU requirement (*customized density*) may not necessarily tell us about more substantive changes of EU policies through levels of *restrictiveness* in national legislation. Previous research has neglected this distinction. Next, we discuss the conceptualization and measurement of customization. After introducing the data and methods, we present and discuss our results. We outline theoretical implications and trajectories for future research.

Understanding diversity in multilevel implementation

Europeanization scholars highlight that the inherent ambiguity of EU rules result in different degrees of flexibility and legal uncertainty, leading to different interpretations by member states and implying that implementation is dominated by national politics (Schmidt 2008; Windhoff-Héritier 2001). Additionally, relatively long-lasting policy, regulatory or administrative traditions or styles 'predispose [countries] to formulate and implement public policies in certain distinct ways' (Adam *et al.* 2015: 2; Richardson *et al.* 1982).

These concepts resonated in Europeanization research, for example, as 'worlds of compliance' (Falkner *et al.* 2005) and non-literal interpretations of EU law (Steunenberg 2007). Situations when member states go beyond the minimum requirements of EU law have been referred to as voluntary over-implementation (Falkner *et al.* 2005) or gold-plating. Gold-plating denotes all instances:

when implementation goes beyond the minimum necessary to comply with a Directive, by:

- extending the scope, adding in some way to the substantive requirement, or
- substituting wider domestic legal terms for those used in the Directive; or
- not taking full advantage of any derogations which keep requirements to a minimum (e.g. for certain scales of operation, or specific activities); or
- providing sanctions, enforcement mechanisms and matters such as burden of proof which go beyond the minimum needed (e.g. e.g., as a result of picking up the existing criminal sanctions in that area); or
- implementing early, before the date given in the Directive. (Voermans 2009: 8)

Only a few case studies have addressed this phenomenon, suggesting that countries have different approaches toward gold-plating. For example, the United Kingdom (UK) and Spain are rather literal transposers, while the Netherlands sometimes add extra rules (Davidson 2006; Lugt 1999: 132; Versluis 2003: 17, 19). Tendencies towards over-implementation were found in the power sector in Germany and Sweden (Padgett 2003) and regarding social policies in certain old and new member states (Falkner *et al.* 2005). The Netherlands and the UK rarely engage in the gold-plating of environmental directives (Jans *et al.* 2009; Morris 2011; Voermans 2009). The literature often treats gold-plating as a potentially problematic transposition outcome that can conflict with compliance (Mastenbroek 2005), associated with red tape 'resulting in unnecessary burdens and competitive disadvantages for domestic businesses' (Voermans 2009: 8; see also Davidson 2006). However, this view 'insufficiently captures the implications of member states being part of a multi-level system' (Schmidt 2008: 299).

Thomann (2015: 1370) proposes to think of EU member states as problem-solvers who use their leeway to adapt – that is, customize – EU rules to local contexts. While building on the gold-plating concept, Thomann (2015) seeks to separate the question of diversity in implementation from questions of non-compliance. Therefore, she analyses only cases of correct transposition, where compliant member states go beyond market-correcting EU minimal standards. Moreover, she uses the concrete categories that have been fruitfully applied to measure changes of regulatory, (re-)distributive and morality policies (Adam *et al.* 2015; Bauer and Knill 2014; Knill *et al.* 2012; Schaffrin *et al.* 2015). These changes occur on two distinct, although typically interrelated dimensions, namely regarding the amount of rules (density) and their content (intensity). Hence, Thomann refines the gold-plating notion by accounting for *degrees* to which the domestic regulations complement an EU rule with *more* or *stricter* rules than required, and adding these into a combined customization index. Gold-plating scholars have not clearly distinguished these two change dimensions: some, like Versluis (2003: 48), emphasize the 'adding of extra requirements' (density), whereas others like

Lugt (1999: 132) emphasize 'the laying down of stricter requirements' (stringency). Yet, as we illustrate below, the two dimensions of density and restrictiveness illuminate countries' distinct customization strategies. For example, the UK often added exemptions to EU food safety rules (customized density) to maintain regulations that remain as liberal as possible (no customized restrictiveness) (Thomann 2015).

However, previous studies may exaggerate idiosyncratic country differences, by often focusing on only one policy area (Treib 2014). Member states could exhibit completely different transposition patterns regarding other policies. How exactly these changes occur across a wider range of policies and countries remains unclear. To enable systematic cumulative research on the phenomenon, we now refine and generalize the definition of customization.

How do EU rules change during transposition?

Thomann's (2015) customization concept presupposes compliant transposition. Note, however, that customization and compliance are two distinct phenomena: the tailoring of rules to local circumstances may occur within the scope of discretion granted by an EU rule (compliance), or outside (non-compliance). Which of them is the focus of analysis depends on the specific research interest. Furthermore, the requirement of assessing member states' compliance first may unnecessarily complicate the measurement of customization. Especially ambiguous EU provisions do not provide a clear yardstick defining (non-)compliant behaviour (Schmidt 2008), so 'differences in degree' may more adequately capture varying responses. But even if directives contain very clear yardsticks, establishing compliance may be a contentious process. Confining the analysis to instances of clear-cut compliance may hence result in a loss of substantively interesting and important cases of customization.

Furthermore, previous studies refer to situations when member states *add to* EU provisions. Indeed, often domestic rules *go beyond the necessary minimum* set out by EU rules, especially when these aim at positive integration to correct common market problems – such as the safety of motor vehicles – through (re-)regulation (Vink 2002: 3). While countries have to regulate at least as much as the EU prescribes, more ambitious domestic policies – for example, more frequent roadworthiness tests – help correct the problem (Jans *et al.* 2009; Scharpf 1996). However, implementers adapt non-standardizing EU rules in differing directions, depending on their specific nature and purpose. Particularly in contexts of negative integration, EU rules often set out a regulatory limit that member states must not exceed (Scharpf 1996). Such rules may serve to avoid restrictions of freedoms or rights or distortions of the common market, such as barriers to trade (Vink 2002: 2). Customized domestic rules that *go below the EU provision,* for example lower pricing than maximally allowed by the EU, can result from a regulatory 'race to the bottom'. Many EU rules also provide a *range of acceptable regulation* (Steunenberg 2007). For example, EU copyright legislation provides a 'menu' of exemptions to the limits of reproduction rights of right-holders. National legislators should *at the very least* allow 'temporary acts of reproduction'; beyond the defined range of possible exemptions, they also cannot include *additional* exemptions. However, this ideal-typical distinction is often not clear-cut in practice, especially for ambiguous EU rules, and does not necessarily correlate with positive or negative integration contexts (Scharpf 1997: 522; Schmidt 2008). Researchers should therefore always explicitly account for situations in which transposing countries both add to or take away from EU rules.

Finally, the existing toolbox to measure regulatory change highlights the relevance of the two dimensions of density and restrictiveness. Schaffrin *et al.* (2015) differentiate changes in policy outputs according to six substantive categories: objectives; scope; integration; budget; implementation; and monitoring. Overall customization patterns consist of the extent of the changes in these categories of EU rules along the two dimensions of density and restrictiveness. An aggregated customization index may add up the values (Thomann 2015) or calculate their average, where larger deviations both in positive or negative directions indicate more extensive customization levels. Yet distinguishing the two dimensions is not obsolete. Although they are logically connected, they refer to distinct aspects of state action and illuminate a differentiation of variation in national adaptation strategies that can be insightful (Knill *et al.* 2012). So far, the implications of the distinctness and interrelation of these dimensions for understanding the differences in the national transposition of EU legislation have not been studied systematically.

Regulatory density tells us about the formal extent and breadth to which governmental activities address a certain policy area. It captures the amount of government activity, as one aspect of government size and growth (Bauer and Knill 2014). *Customized density* refers to changes in the degree of regulatory penetration, complexity and internal differentiation (Knill *et al.* 2012). Member states may or may not apply optional EU rules, concretize, amend, differentiate or specify exemptions to especially broadly formulated EU rules. Often, more customized density leads to more restrictive rules. However, sometimes the opposite happens. For example, the Directive 2003/4/EC allows member states to refuse public access to environmental information if such disclosure would adversely affect intellectual property rights. Yet Slovenia specifies that intellectual property rights is not a ground for refusal (less restrictive) by adding that the applicant can still review a copy of the requested information (more density than the EU provision).

This example shows that simply counting outputs may not do adequate justice to the content of rules, which can be adapted in its intensity.

Customized restrictiveness captures how EU rules change in the scope and level of state intervention to influence target group behaviour through the extent of the substantial freedom left to policy addressees or the generosity of the services or resources provided (Bauer and Knill 2014: 33; Knill *et al.* 2012: 430; Schaffrin *et al.* 2015).[1] This dimension reflects different answers of member states to 'the question of how to resolve the tension between citizens' individual freedoms and public intervention in order to reach political goals' (Adam *et al.* 2015: 19). Depending on the importance or significance governments attach to certain measures, domestic rules represent a tightening (adds restrictiveness) or loosening (removes restrictiveness) of the EU rules. For instance, we have seen that member states added different degrees of restrictiveness to the EU's roadworthiness test requirement to ensure the continued safety of motor vehicles. Restrictiveness also captures different state traditions representing deeply institutionalized norms specifying the relationship between state and society. Liberal member states generally tend to minimally intervene into individual and collective freedom, while others are traditionally more interventionist (Adam *et al.* 2015; Richardson *et al.* 1982). For example, Germany adopts a regulatory strategy to reduce antibiotic resistance through severe restrictions of the use of antibiotics for livestock; conversely, the UK has more lenient rules and resorts to private self-regulation and codes of good practice instead (Thomann 2015).

Increases in density often imply increases in restrictiveness, and vice versa. For instance, unlike Directive 2003/35/EC, Latvian law does not limit the scope of the public entitled to challenge decisions related to public participation in environmental plans and programmes (less density). Any natural and legal entity has the right to challenge a respective decision (less restrictiveness). Changes in one dimension usually affects the other – but not inherently in the same direction. For example, many member states adopted less restrictive conditions for acquisition of European Community (EC) long-term resident status than minimally required by Directive 2003/109/EC (less restrictiveness). Doing so also entailed defining the categories of persons to which these conditions should apply (more density). Nevertheless, member states' transposition outcomes were still more favourable to EU refugees than the EU directive. While modifications in density may increase or decrease levels of restrictiveness, they can also serve definitional or other purposes, such as concretizing EU rules to enhance legal certainty, or integrating the particular concerns of specific interest groups.

Our main point is that by only focusing on one of the two dimensions or simply merging them, one may miss interesting variation (Schaffrin *et al.* 2015). By analogy, body size and weight are also closely interconnected. Nonetheless, only by looking at both can we make meaningful comparisons of people's physical appearance. While their relevance and implications for customization is subject to future research, the two dimensions have proven useful for describing policy change (Bauer and Knill 2014; Knill *et al.* 2012) and regulatory styles (Adam *et al.* 2015).

We thus expand and refine existing concepts and define customization as the changes that EU rules undergo in their density and restrictiveness during legal transposition *independent from assessments of (non-)compliance*, along the different categories of policy content (objectives, scope, integration, budget, implementation and monitoring) and the dimensions of density (formal) and restrictiveness (content). This definition includes scenarios of transposing rules *adding to or removing* density or restrictiveness from an EU provision.

Measuring customization

Figure A1 in the Online Appendix resumes our proposed conceptualization and measurement of customization, which can be adopted partly or fully to fit any specific research setting. We apply a subset of the scheme for comparing customization across 27 member states (excluding Croatia) and two policy areas: justice and home affairs (10 Directives) and environment (21 Directives).

Data

The EU Commission sometimes mandates legal experts to craft evaluation or monitoring reports that can be used as secondary data sources (Mastenbroek *et al.* 2016). Our own analysis uses conformity reports that share the same structure and contain so-called concordance tables (TOCs) that include the directive provision, the domestic transposition measure, and an explicit evaluation of the latter's level of conformity by a national legal expert (see Tables A1–A3 in the Online Appendix). While prepared for assessing compliance, these expert assessments also provide invaluable information about customization and gold-plating. The experts discussed the detailed nature of transposition outcomes and whether these 'went beyond' the requirements of the directive.

Casing

Domestic regulations of single EU provisions constitute the relevant units of analysis for customization (Zhelyazkova 2013). Relevant provisions can be identified by stakeholders and experts (Thomann 2015), or as single paragraphs of articles of an EU directive (Franchino 2007: 109). TOCs, as used here, provide a pre-determined separation of articles and sub-articles. In decentralized countries, customization occurs in both national and subnational legislation. EU rules differ widely in their relevance, length and substantial richness, and might hence have to be weighted according to these criteria (Toshkov 2010). To partly remedy this issue, this study includes only substantive provisions that required implementation and have implications for the national legislation and administrative practice.

Measurement

Establishing degrees and directions of customization becomes particularly challenging as ambiguous EU rules do not establish clear benchmarks (Schmidt 2008). Comparing the wording of the EU and transposing provisions is highly time and resource intensive. Instead, we closely scrutinized and matched the expert evaluations of each provision to the two customization dimensions. Our sample hence only includes those state-provision dyads that contain explicit expert evaluations about customization. This procedure pragmatically addresses the issue of ambiguity, but excludes those provisions that are so broad or unclear that evaluating customization is difficult. Conformity assessments hence systematically under-represent the actual extent of customization. Expert evaluations with no information about customization do not imply equivalent transposition of the EU provisions. The legal expert may not have reported minor cases of customization particularly with compliant national measures. Hence, the set of cases of customization captured by our analysis is neither complete nor representative. Therefore, we can only compare relative customization levels across member states and policy areas. Yet we can still explore the relationship between the dimensions of density and restrictiveness across member states and issue areas.

Customized density refers to the amount/number of rules (policies and/or instruments) that are added to or removed from the EU provision (e.g. scope restrictions, concretizations, requirements, conditions, exemptions or specifications added or taken away). In our analysis, a domestic transposing rule customizes the directive provision with more density, if it adds at least one element to the latter. Alternatively, a member state may remove density by omitting an element of or not transposing an EU provision. We counted the times that an expert mentioned an addition to (coded as 1) or an omission (coded as −1) from a specific EU provision. Density levels range between −2 and 4.

Customized restrictiveness occurs along an instrument's personal, substantive and/or temporal scope of application. The personal scope depicts the types of individuals or organizations addressed. Customized restrictiveness here indicates that a domestic requirement or restriction is valid for a larger target group than the EU provision; or that a freedom, resource or service is granted to a smaller set of addressees. The substantive scope refers to the activities (behavioural boundaries, cases, constellations, services, resources) covered by an instrument (Knill *et al.* 2012: 429, 431). More restrictive instruments seek to minimize certain behaviours, resources or services, or prescribe requirements that considerably limit individual freedom, as compared to the EU provision (Adam *et al.* 2015: 6). In temporal terms, activities, services or resources can be restricted to, granted or required for longer or shorter time periods.

The experts' evaluations neither distinguish the three levels of scope, nor assess degrees of customized restrictiveness. Instead, we relied on expert assessments that identified transposition outcomes as either more restrictive (coded as 1) or less restrictive (–1; hence, more favourable to the relevant addresses) than the respective EU provision. For example, the experts mentioned that some member states implemented more flexible requirements for asylum applications or granted more rights to refugees (e.g. healthcare exceeding emergency cases). Other member states requested additional documents for asylum applications or further restricted refugees' rights relative to the JHA Directives. Customized restrictiveness amounts to 0, if a provision was neither assessed as more restrictive nor as less restrictive than the EU provision. The most obvious manifestation of limited customization is literal or identical (equivalent) transposition. Note that customization can also result from *non-changes* in domestic policies (Bauer and Knill 2014: 33; Thomann 2015: 1370). In this case, differences between the EU and the domestic rule are decisive.

Results

Comparing transposition in 27 member states across two policy areas facilitates a comprehensive assessment of customization patterns. The JHA directives define the conditions for obtaining a refugee status, the treatment of third-country nationals (TCNs) and their families. Many of these often controversial JHA provisions do not allow for more restrictive conditions that lower the standards for TCNs or refugees residing in the EU. Instead, the environment directives impose technical requirements regarding, for example, emissions trading and environmental assessments of waste management plans. These EU environmental rules frequently restrict the behaviour of sellers, producers, consumers, etc., and allow the member states to impose stricter conditions on domestic products.

After excluding all missing cases, our data-set contains 750 and 894 observations regarding member-state customization of specific EU provisions for JHA and environment directives respectively.[2] Fourteen per cent of the latter 894 provision-state dyads represent sub-national transposition. As customization hence varied within Belgium, the UK and some regions in Spain, Austria and Finland, the number of observations in environmental policy is higher than in JHA policy, despite the lower number of assessed provisions.

Figure 1 presents the average member-state differences in customized restrictiveness and density, separately for JHA and environment EU provisions.

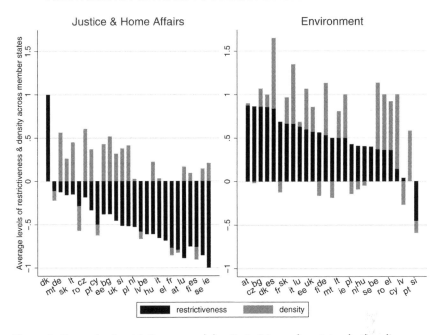

Figure 1. Customized restrictiveness and density in 27 member states, both policy areas.

The figure indicates significant differences in customization across the two policy areas that follow the regulatory logic of the EU policy. Most member states transposed JHA provisions *less* restrictively than prescribed by the EU directives (74 per cent of the observations). For example, Provision 27(2) of Directive 2004/83/EC requires that member states treat refugees in the same way as other TCNs. Beyond that, countries like Bulgaria, Finland, Hungary, Ireland, Poland and Sweden grant adults with refugee or subsidiary protection status access to the general education system under the same conditions as nationals. Denmark is the only exception. Even though it generally participates in Schengen legislation, general unwillingness to abandon its restrictive immigration policy made Denmark opt out of Title IV provisions of the Amsterdam Treaty covering free movement, immigration and asylum. While we do not analyse the rationale behind member states' consistent tendencies to transpose immigration directives less restrictively here, note that these decisions were taken prior to the recent refugee crisis.

Conversely, the transposition of environment directives – typical for positive integration – is on average *more* restrictive for sellers, producers and the public than the EU requires (63 per cent of all assessed cases). For example, Article 9(2) of Directive 2001/18/EC mandates member states to make all information about releases of genetically modified organisms (GMOs) publicly available. Italy included an additional obligation for those who cultivate GMOs to install adequate cartels clearly indicating the presence of GMOs. Slovenia's flexible transposition of Directive 2003/4/EC is an exception: it loosens the EU's conditions for publicly requesting and receiving environmental data, even if such information is protected by intellectual property rights.

In short, customization appears to be largely driven by the nature of the EU provisions and the direction of flexibility for which they allow. By contrast, customized density does not exhibit pronounced cross-country or policy-specific differences. The member states included additional rules to 28 per cent of the JHA policies, and to 48 per cent of the EU environmental provisions. Only very rarely did member states remove rules from environment directives.

Rather than pragmatically focusing only on the density or the restrictiveness dimension or simply combining them into one index, we seek to gain a fuller understanding about the relationship between these two aspects of customization (see Figure A2 in the Online Appendix). We find a strong positive relationship between customized restrictiveness and density in the JHA area, where restrictiveness is often removed from EU provisions by reducing the amount of rules during transposition (97 per cent of all cases reducing density; Pearson $r = 0.49$). To facilitate a favourable treatment of refugees, many EU member states chose not to transpose exemptions that would impose stricter requirements for obtaining refugee status. Article 17(3) of Directive 2004/83/EC, for instance, allows the member states to exclude a TCN or a stateless person from being eligible for subsidiary protection if that person has committed one or more crimes prior to admission to the member state. Austria, Belgium, Cyprus, Finland, France, Germany, Greece, Hungary, Italy, Lithuania, Netherlands, Portugal and Romania did not transpose this provision (less density, less restrictiveness). Sometimes, density and restrictiveness were also added. While Directive 2001/51/EC provides alternatives for financial penalties on carriers transporting illegal immigrants, Poland and Spain even introduced all three alternatives (more density), making national provision more restrictive for carriers.

Conversely, there is no significant relationship between density and restrictiveness in the environment sector (Pearson $r = -0.04$). Whereas member states included additional rules to EU provisions, many of them were neither more nor less restrictive than the EU provisions (44 per cent of cases with increased density). For example, Flanders (Belgium) transposed Directive 2004/3/EC on public access to environmental information by adding that 'information officers' should be designated. This concretization does not necessarily affect levels of restrictions to obtaining access to environmental information. Furthermore, in 73 per cent of the cases in which the member states removed rules from an EU provision, national transposition was more, rather than less, restrictive than the EU requirements. For example, Directive 2000/76/EC on the incineration of waste specified that the emission limit value for nitrogen oxides does not apply to plants only co-incinerating hazardous waste until 1 January 2007. Hungary, however, did not transpose this exemption (less density). This rendered the Hungarian provision more stringent than the EU provision, as the emission limits apply immediately.

In sum, the relationship between restrictiveness and density varies across policy areas. Whereas the two dimensions co-vary in JHA policy, adding more rules is not associated with more restrictive outcomes in environmental policy. This suggests that information about customized density is not sufficient to understand domestic alterations of EU provisions. Even in the JHA area the relationship is not perfect. Directive 2001/51/EC, for instance, requires that member states ensure penalties to carriers of illegal immigrants. Art. 4(2) specifies that this requirement should not interfere with member states' obligations in cases where a third country national seeks international protection. However, Italy, Malta, the Netherlands, Portugal, Romania and Slovenia did not transpose this provision (less density), such that sanctions are applied regardless of whether asylum is sought or granted (more restrictive to carriers). In other cases, density was added to remove restrictiveness. For example, going beyond Art. 15 (1)(a) of Directive 2001/55/EC, the Czech legislation explicitly allows family reunification of a parent of a minor under 18 (more density, less restrictiveness).

These findings imply that patterns of customized restrictiveness relatively consistently follow the direction of flexibility indicated by EU legislation. Only by specifying 'what' – density or restrictiveness – was added to or taken away from the EU provision do we adequately understand customization patterns. Thus, Figure 1 reveals differences that remain hidden when combining both dimensions into one customization index, as country-level density and restrictiveness could sometimes go in the opposite direction.

Whereas regulatory change could lead to non-compliance with EU rules, most of the instances of customization reported by experts also occurred when transposition was compliant (Figure A4 in the Online Appendix). We therefore 'zoom in' to consider the divergence of only those adaptations that met the EU requirements. Figure 2 compares the average levels and variation of compliant customized restrictiveness across member states for both policy areas (see Figure A5 in the Online Appendix for customized density).

The analysis reveals the considerable diversity of compliant transposition in the EU that remains hidden by only distinguishing (non-)compliance. For example, Bulgaria, Austria, the Czech Republic and France transposed the EU environment provisions significantly more restrictively than other countries such as Slovenia, Portugal, Latvia and Belgium. Although the country differences are less pronounced in the JHA area, Cyprus, Ireland, Luxembourg and Romania generally transposed the EU provisions less restrictively relative to most other member states. In short, customization patterns do vary significantly across compliant member states. Yet national authorities

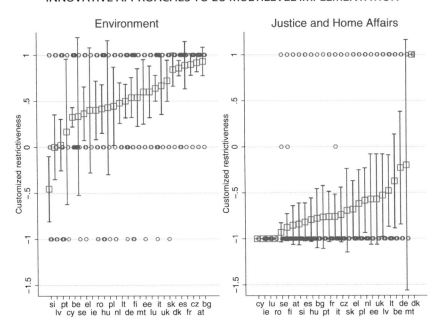

Figure 2. Customized restrictiveness across member states for compliant national laws.

Note: Bars = customized restrictiveness, capped lines = confidence intervals, hollow circles = individual cases.

respond differently to EU requirements depending on the policy sector. These patterns could indicate that domestic politics matter more for customization than country-specific transposition styles.

Discussion

In several respects, this study significantly enhances our knowledge about the diversity of transposition outcomes beyond legal compliance in the EU (Schmidt 2008). Building on earlier work on gold-plating and Thomann (2015), we have proposed a general but flexible conceptualization and measurement scheme that can travel across contexts to guide systematic comparative research on the customization of EU directives. By partly applying the scheme to the transposition of EU directives in two policy areas and 27 member states, this study paints the very first comprehensive – although descriptive and broad – picture of customization in the EU. Our large-N data-set differentiates neither different substantive categories of regulatory change, scopes of application nor degrees of customized restrictiveness on a continuous scale (Schaffrin *et al.* 2015). Relying on expert evaluations limited the scope of our results and made it impossible to identify absolute levels of customization. An internally more valid analysis requires considerable case knowledge and implies relatively high costs for data collection and coding (Adcock and Collier 2001; Hartlapp and Falkner 2009; Mastenbroek *et al.* 2016). Future research should comprehensively address the analytic challenge of identifying customization in face of legal ambiguity. When EU rules are very ambiguous, it might make more sense to compare countries' implementation with each other, rather than against an EU template (e.g. Sager *et al.* 2014). The results nonetheless provide preliminary, but solid evidence for the added value of analysing customization.

Systematically distinguishing customized density and restrictiveness and allowing for different directions in which EU rules are changed helped us to illuminate different strategies of how member states interpret EU provisions, and the remarkable extent to which these adaptations follow sectoral EU regulatory logics. Contrary to previous case studies, our large-N comparison does not conclusively indicate distinct country-specific styles of gold-plating or customizing EU directives (Falkner *et al.* 2005; Jans *et al.* 2009; Morris 2011; Thomann 2015; Versluis 2003; Voermans 2009). Rather, pronounced policy-specific differences and domestic politics seem to characterize customization patterns – which resonates with compliance findings (Steunenberg 2007; Treib 2014). Depending on the nature and purpose of EU policies, member states not only add, but sometimes also remove density and/or restrictiveness from EU provisions. Accordingly, we find that member states often provide less restrictive conditions to TCNs than those defined in JHA directives. Instead, environmental directives are routinely customized to further restrict the behaviour of target groups.

Our findings also suggest that member states simultaneously strive to achieve compliance, and adapt EU policies to their local contexts. The resulting diversity in compliant transposition remains concealed when only looking at legal compliance. Moving beyond legal compliance to account for the customization of EU directives therefore obviously provides substantive complementary insights into the diversity of transposition outcomes. But why should we bother about this diversity anyway?

Conclusions: Implications for Europeanization research

EU implementation patterns beyond legal compliance are to a large extent unknown territory (Heidbreder 2017; Treib 2014). Reducing discretionary deviations from centrally decided provisions to a control problem neglects bottom–up views emphasizing that local implementers' closeness to the source of the policy problem enhances their ability to achieve policy success (Elmore 1979; Knill and Tosun 2012). Member states as problem-solvers with an informational advantage may improve EU policies, by adapting them to heterogeneous contexts and integrating local policy positions (Hooghe and Marks 2003: 235; Whitford 2007). This can facilitate context-sensitive solutions of the original policy problem at stake and increase the likelihood of effective and broadly accepted policy solutions at the point where the problem is most immediate (Keman 2000; Matland 1995). By introducing a bottom–up notion of member state discretion to Europeanization research, research on customization helps address salient questions.

First, rising levels of Euroscepticism and recent events such as Brexit highlight how European integration is increasingly perceived as a loss of sovereignty over national policies. The customization phenomenon relativizes the extent of this loss of control. It illuminates how member states use transposition as an opportunity to modify EU law and regain control. For example, Europeanization scholars could inquire how member states make use of different dimensions of customization to satisfy domestic interests during implementation (e.g. Thomson 2010). They could investigate to what extent more or less restrictive interpretations of EU rules enhance the legitimacy and acceptance of EU law 'on the ground' (Dörrenbächer 2017).

Second, policy problems are only effectively resolved once EU policies are put into practice (Treib 2014). Legal compliance levels have a limited capacity to explain the practical application of EU law (Zhelyazkova *et al.* 2016). Conversely, the customization of EU policy is likely to result in different national practical application, enforcement and compliance practices (Versluis 2003, 2007). Customization patterns may prove a major missing link for gaining a better understanding of the EU's problem-solving capacity (Scharpf 1997). For example, customized restrictiveness and density could have a different impact on practical implementation. Studying restrictiveness helps Europeanization scholars understand the freedom of manoeuvre national laws grant to implementing actors at the stage of practical implementation. This should generally influence the extent to which implementing actors can accommodate the ambiguous EU directives in a way that also fits local objectives. Conversely, adding more rules can complicate the practical implementation process. Whereas such conjectures need to undergo empirical scrutiny, our analyses showed that customized restrictiveness and density are distinct yet interrelated aspects of Europeanization processes.

Finally, the customization concept contributes to the fundamental theoretical debates surrounding the use of discretion in general multilevel implementation research (Thomann *et al.* 2016). Our results illustrate the interaction between centralized control and decentralized flexibility (Whitford 2007). Studies in comparative politics have long investigated the conditions under which national authorities increase or decrease the leeway of domestic implementing actors, mostly in the United States (US) federal system (Epstein and O'Halloran 1999; Huber and Shipan 2002). Especially customized restrictiveness could provide a useful yardstick for comparing discretionary freedoms across different member states and issue areas.

Much remains to be done to further explore such fine-grained Europeanization patterns, their explanation and implications for the practical application, effectiveness and acceptance of EU law. Future research should definitively strive for a more in-depth coding of customization, analyse its empirical relevance, and expand these insights to new policy areas. Our conceptualization and proposed measurement of customization should help Europeanization researchers to cumulatively paint a more complete picture of what Majone (1999: 309) famously termed the 'European experience'.

Notes

1. Additionally, *formal intensity* depicts domestic enforcement measures, administrative and procedural capacities that influence the probability of effectively achieving substantial requirements and the consequentiality of non-compliant behaviour (Adam *et al.* 2015; Knill et al. 2012). Customization occurs during legal transposition. Changes in formal intensity are therefore only captured if the EU directive explicitly contains respective provisions, and measured in their restrictiveness at the legal transposition stage.
2. The member states vary in the number of EU provisions based on which customization is evaluated. For example, customization in Italy was evaluated for 95 Environment provisions, but only for seven environment provisions in Poland and Cyprus.

Acknowledgements

We thank Tetty Havinga, Eva Heidbreder, Ellen Mastenbroek, Jale Tosun and the anonymous referees for their excellent comments.

Disclosure statement

No potential conflict of interest was reported by the authors.

Funding

Eva Thomann gratefully acknowledges financial support by the Schweizerischer Nationalfonds zur Förderung der Wissenschaftlichen Forschung [grant numbers P2BEP1-162077 and P300P1_171479].

References

Adam, C., Hurka, S. and Knill, C. (2015) 'Four styles of regulation and their implications for comparative policy analysis', *Journal of Comparative Policy Analysis: Research and Practice*, doi:10.1080/13876988.2015.1082262.

Adcock, R. and Collier, D. (2001) 'Measurement validity: a shared standard for qualitative and quantitative research', *American Political Science Review* 95(3): 529–546.

Angelova, M., Dannwolf, T. and König, T. (2012) 'How robust are compliance findings? A research synthesis', *Journal of European Public Policy* 19(8): 1269–1291.

Bauer, M.W. and Knill, C. (2014) 'A conceptual framework for the comparative analysis of policy change: measurement, explanation and strategies of policy dismantling', *Journal of Comparative Policy Analysis: Research and Practice* 16(1): 28–44.

Davidson, N. (2006) '*Davidson review: Implementation of EU legislation*', Retrieved online from http://www.cabinetoffice.gov.uk/regulation/reviewing_regulation/davidson_review/index.asp [last accessed 7.3.2016].

Dörrenbächer, N. (2017) 'Europe at the frontline: analyzing street-level motivations for the use of European Union migration law', *Journal of European Public Policy*, doi:10.1080/13501763.2017.1314535

Elmore, R.F. (1979) 'Backward mapping: implementation research and policy decisions', *Political Science Quarterly* 94(4): 601–616.

Epstein, D. and O'Halloran, S. (1999) *Delegating Powers: A Transaction Cost Politics Approach to Policy Making under Separate Powers*, Cambridge: Cambridge University Press.

Falkner, G., Treib, O., Hartlapp, M. and Leiber, S. (2005) *Complying with Europe: EU harmonisation and soft law in the member states*, New York: Cambridge University Press.

Franchino, F. (2007) *The Powers of the Union: Delegation in the EU*, Cambridge: Cambridge University Press.

Hartlapp, M. and Falkner, G. (2009) 'Problems of operationalization and data in EU compliance research', *European Union Politics* 10(2): 281–304.

Heidbreder, E.G. (2017) 'Strategies in multilevel policy implementation: moving beyond the limited focus on compliance', *Journal of European Public Policy*, doi:10.1080/13501763.2017.1314540

Hooghe, L. and Marks, G. (2003) 'Unraveling the central state, but how? Types of multilevel governance', *American Political Science Review* 97(2): 233–243.

Huber, J. and Shipan, C. (2002) *Deliberate Discretion? The Institutional Foundations of Bureaucratic Autonomy*, Cambridge, UK: Cambridge University Press.

Jans, J.H., Squintani, L., Aragão, A., Macrory, R. and Wegener, B.W. (2009) '"Gold plating" of European environmental measures?' *Journal of European Environmental Planning Law* 6(4): 417–435.

Keman, H. (2000) 'Federalism and policy performance. A conceptual and empirical inquiry', in U. Wachendorfer-Schmidt (ed.), *Federalism and political performance*, London: Routledge, pp. 196–227.

Knill, C., Schulze, K. and Tosun, J. (2012) 'Regulatory policy outputs and impacts: exploring a complex relationship', *Regulation and Governance* 6(4): 427–444.

Knill, C. and Tosun, J. (2012) 'Governance institutions and policy implementation in the European Union', in J. Richardson (ed.). *Constructing a Policy-Making State? Policy Dynamics in the EU*, Oxford: Oxford University Press, pp. 309–333.

Lowi, T.J. (1972) 'Four systems of policy, politics, and choice', *Public Administration Review* 32(4): 298–310.

Lugt, M. (1999) *Enforcing European and National Food Law in the Netherlands and England*, Lelystad: Koninklijke Vermande.

Majone, G. (1999) 'Regulation in comparative perspective', *Journal of Comparative Policy Analysis: Research and Practice* 1(3): 309–324.

Mastenbroek, E. (2005) 'EU compliance: still a "black hole"?' *Journal of European Public Policy* 12(6): 1103–1120.

Mastenbroek, E. (2017) 'Guardians of EU law? Analysing roles and behavior of Dutch legislative drafters involved in EU compliance', *Journal of European Public Policy*, doi:10.1080/13501763.2017.1314537

Mastenbroek, E., van Voorst, S. and Meuwese, A. (2016) 'Closing the regulatory cycle? A meta evaluation of ex-post legislative evaluations by the European Commission', *Journal of European Public Policy* 23(9): 1329–1348.

Matland, R.E. (1995) 'Synthesizing the implementation literature: the ambiguity-conflict model of policy implementation', *Journal of Public Administration Research and Theory* 5(2): 145–174.

Morris, R.K.A. (2011) 'The application of the Habitats Directive in the UK: compliance or gold plating?', *Land Use Policy* 28(1): 361–369.

Padgett, S. (2003) 'Between synthesis and emulation: EU policy transfer in the power sector' *Journal of European Public Policy* 10(2): 227–245.

Richardson, J., Gustafsson, G. and Grant, J. (1982) 'The concept of policy style', in J. Richardson (ed.), *Policy styles in Western Europe*, Winchester: George Allen & Unwin, pp. 1–16.

Sager, F., Thomann, E., Zollinger, C. and Mavrot, C. (2014) 'Confronting theories of European integration: a comparative congruence analysis of veterinary drugs regulations in five countries', *Journal of Comparative Policy Analysis: Research and Practice* 16(5): 457–474.

Schaffrin, A., Sewerin, S. and Seubert, S. (2015) 'Toward a comparative measure of climate policy output', *Policy Studies Journal*, doi:10.1111/psj.12095.

Scharpf, F. (1996) 'Negative and positive integration in the political economy of European welfare states', In G. Marks, F.W. Scharpf, P.C. Schmitter and W. Streeck (eds), *Governance in the European Union*, London: Sage, pp. 15–39.

Scharpf, F. (1997) 'Introduction: the problem-solving capacity of multi-level governance', *Journal of European Public Policy* 4(4): 520–538.

Schmidt, S.K. (2008) 'Beyond compliance: the Europeanization of member states through negative integration and legal uncertainty', *Journal of Comparative Policy Analysis: Research and Practice* 10(3): 299–308.

Shapiro, M. (1999) 'Implementation, discretion and rules', in J.A.E. Vervaele (ed.), *Compliance and Enforcement of European Community law*, The Hague: Kluwer Law International, pp. 27–34.

Steunenberg, B. (2007) 'A policy solution to the European Union's transposition puzzle: interaction of interests in different domestic arenas', *West European Politics* 30(1): 23–49.

Thomann, E. (2015) 'Customizing Europe: transposition as bottom-up implementation', *Journal of European Public Policy* 22(10): 1368–1387.

Thomann, E., Lieberherr, E. and Ingold, K. (2016) 'Torn between state and market: private policy implementation and conflicting institutional logics', *Policy and Society* 35(1): 57–69.

Thomann, E. and Sager, F. (2017) 'Moving beyond legal compliance: Innovative approaches to EU multilevel implementation', *Journal of European Public Policy*, doi:10.1080/13501763.2017.1314541

Thomson, R. (2010) 'Opposition through the back door in the transposition of EU Directives', *European Union Politics* 11(4): 577–96.

Toshkov, D. (2010) 'Taking stock: a review of quantitative studies of transposition and implementation of EU law', *Institute for European Integration Research*, Working paper No. 01/2010.

Treib, O. (2014) 'Implementing and complying with EU governance outputs', *Living Reviews in European Governance* 9(1): 1–30.

Versluis, E. (2003) *Enforcement Matters. Enforcement and Compliance of European Directives in Four Member States*, Delft: Eburon.

Versluis, E. (2007) 'Even rules, uneven practices: Opening the 'black box' of EU law in action', *West European Politics* 30(1): 50–67.

Vink, M.P. (2002) 'Negative and positive integration in European Immigration Policies', *European Integration Online Papers* 6(13).

Voermans, W. (2009) 'Gold-plating and double banking: an overrated problem?' in H. Snijders and S. Vogenauer (eds), *Content and Meaning of National Law in the context of Transnational Law*, Munich: Sellier European Law Publishers, pp. 79–88.

Whitford, A. (2007) 'Decentralized policy implementation', *Political Research Quarterly* 60(1): 17–30.

Windhoff-Héritier, A. (2001) *Differential Europe: The European Union Impact on National Policymaking*. Oxford: Rowman & Littlefield.

Zhelyazkova, A. (2013) 'Complying with EU Directives' requirements: the link between EU decision-making and the correct transposition of EU provisions', *Journal of European Public Policy* 20(5): 702–721.

Zhelyazkova, A., Kaya, C., and Schrama, R. (2016) 'Decoupling practical and legal compliance: analysis of member states' implementation of EU policy', *European Journal of Political Research* 55(4): 827–846.

🔓 OPEN ACCESS

Guardians of EU law? Analysing roles and behaviour of Dutch legislative drafters involved in EU compliance

Ellen Mastenbroek

ABSTRACT

By drafting statutes and delegated acts, national legislative drafters play a crucial role in European Union (EU) compliance. Given their extensive legal training, they can be expected to operate as 'guardians of EU law' and thus correct national non-compliant tendencies. Yet, they also have a role as politically loyal civil servants, responsive to national political demands. This conntribution answers the question of to what extent Dutch legislative drafters fulfil a role of 'guardian of EU law'. Using in-depth interviews, the paper analyses legislative drafters' role conceptions and their strategies in case national political demands prove incompatible with EU legal requirements. It finds that most Dutch legislative drafters try to reconcile EU law with their ministers' political demands, if necessary by reinterpreting EU law. When this proves unfeasible, most respondents prioritize political loyalty over EU legality. Ultimately, therefore, legislative drafters do not form an insurmountable normative factor in EU compliance.

Introduction

The European Union (EU) has a Janus-faced system of implementation. Whereas policies are made at the EU level, implementation is largely member states' responsibility. This institutional feature has attracted great academic attention in the last decades (Angelova *et al.* 2012; Treib 2014). The consensus amongst compliance researchers is that the institutional setup of the EU offers ample leeway for 'politics of compliance' (Mastenbroek 2005).

So far, most theories on EU compliance have been rationalist in nature. Several authors view domestic transposition and implementation as

This is an Open Access article distributed under the terms of the Creative Commons Attribution-NonCommercial-NoDerivatives License (http://creativecommons.org/licenses/by-nc-nd/4.0/), which permits non-commercial re-use, distribution, and reproduction in any medium, provided the original work is properly cited, and is not altered, transformed, or built upon in any way.

processes in which various domestic stakeholders must agree on a particular outcome (Dimitrova and Steunenberg 2000; Kaeding 2008; Mastenbroek and Kaeding 2006; Steunenberg 2006). Central to these rationalist accounts are the preference constellations of alleged preference-maximizing domestic actors. Compliance then revolves around the question 'who gets what, how, and when' (Kaeding 2008: 116).

This rationalist position disregards normative factors promoting compliance. Just like individual citizens (Gibson and Caldeira 1996), individual politicians and civil servants involved in compliance processes may vary in their propensity to comply with EU law (Burcu Bayram 2017; Wockelberg 2014). These variant stances towards EU law are likely to have consequences for administrators' compliance behaviour, and thus for the functioning of the larger political–legal system in which they operate – the EU.

It could be argued that domestic actors' normative stances towards EU law may be affected by their involvement at the EU level (Quaglia *et al.* 2008; Beyers 2010). However, the general conclusion from the research on EU socialization has been that national civil servants involved in EU decision-making at most develop a weak EU loyalty, which coexists with national identity (Quaglia *et al.* 2008: 160). National administration 'remains the key point of reference for national officials … [who] continue to classify themselves as national agents, although they perform both national and European roles' (Connaughton 2015: 201–2). To quote Egeberg (1999: 461): 'most obligations, expectations, information networks, incentives and sanctions are connected to the institutions that employ them nationally'.

This sobering conclusion may partly result from selection bias, i.e., the focus on civil servants involved in EU negotiations. Although these officials closely engage with counterparts from other member states and the EU institutions, socialization may not materialize. That is, these civil servants have as their key role the articulation and defence of national policy preferences, underpinned by rigid negotiation mandates and advanced negotiation skills aimed at maximizing national utilities. Hence, it should not surprise us that national negotiators have been found not to develop strong EU loyalties.

This contribution studies a more likely case for the development of normative factors conducive to EU compliance, by studying Dutch *legislative drafters*. These civil servants, who typically hold university legal degrees, have as their core task the provision of legal input in the process of drafting bills and delegated legislation (Tholen and Mastenbroek 2013: 489). They typically carry out several EU-related tasks: drafting bills and measures that transpose EU directives; guarding the compatibility of national law with EU requirements flowing from directly binding legislation; and ensuring the compatibility of 'autonomous' bills- i.e., regular national proposals for new legislation – with EU law.

Crucially, these legislative drafters can be argued to be 'double hatters' (Egeberg and Trondal 2009: 779): actors with roles related to both their national operating context and the European context. Just like national judges, they may have obtained a 'Community mantle' (Maher 1994: 234). First, their role is first and foremost to guard legality (Tholen and Mastenbroek 2013: 489) – which comprises EU legal requirements (Veerman 2007). Second, this role conception is underpinned by a strong professional identity, which may counterbalance political loyalty (Van den Berg and Dijkstra 2015: 253). Third, this role conception is transmitted through extensive university-level education and postdoctoral training.[1] This group is fully aware of the key principles of EU law, such as supremacy, autonomy of EU law and Community loyalty. Fourth, in line with their standing as conscience of the *rechtsstaat*, Dutch legislative drafters have a rather autonomous organizational position, mostly separated from so-called *policy officials*, who work in substantive policy divisions (*cf.* Page 2003: 654). Fifth, as EU compliance is a highly specialized job, they are likely to have a great knowledge advantage over their minister. Not surprisingly, the Dutch legislative drafting profession has been criticized on several counts for its inflexible stance *vis-à-vis* policy demands (Mastenbroek 2007: 149–50). Finally, the Netherlands is known for its strong rule of law (Gibson and Caldeira 1996: 70), which further increases the chances of identifying a normative counterweight to purely political processes of compliance.

In sum, national legislative drafters may be seen as a more, if not most, likely case[2] for the prioritization of EU law over incompatible national political demands. Crucially, this contribution addresses the question of to what extent these legislative drafters indeed prioritize EU legal requirements over (incompatible) policy demands by their minister – thus providing a normative counterweight to the national politics of EU compliance. More specifically, the study analyses to what extent these drafters heed their role of 'guardians of EU law' and how they balance this role with that of a politically loyal civil servant – like any national civil servant, they also are expected to be responsive to their minister's political preferences.

To analyse the EU-related roles of legislative drafters, the study develops a typology based on cross-fertilization between Christensen's (1991) typology of bureaucratic role conceptions with the literature on the ethics of legislative drafting (Purdy 1987; MacNair 2003) and executive branch legal interpretation (Moss 2000; Luban 2006). Three role conceptions are distinguished. The first conceives of the legislative drafter as a politically loyal *translator* driven by the minister's policy demands; legal requirements only being involved in terms of risk assessment. The second role is that of the guardian of EU law. Driven by notions of professional autonomy, the drafter is to develop the best view of EU law, steering clear of political influence. The third role is an integrating position, according to which legislative drafters must do justice to both domestic political demands and EU legal requirements. After sketching legislative drafters' role conceptions concerning EU compliance and their ways of integrating EU legal requirements with national political demands, the contribution further explores the strategies used by those drafters in cases of irresolvable incompatibilities.

By analysing role conceptions and strategies of legislative drafters, the present study adds to the literature on EU compliance. First, it goes beyond the somewhat dichotomous understanding typical to EU transposition studies (for exceptions, see Thomann 2015; Bondarouk and Mastenbroek forthcoming). Instead of tracing compliance with EU rules from the top–down, it analyses the attitudes and behaviour of civil servants involved in EU compliance in a bottom–up manner. By studying whether and how legislative drafters integrate EU legal requirements with national political demands, this contribution hence adopts a 'performance' view on compliance (Thomann and Sager 2017). Second, the contribution adds to the literature on EU socialization. Crucially, given the importance of education as a 'transmission belt' for socialization (Trondal 2004: 8), legislative drafters are an interesting group to study. If we find no clear EU loyalty amongst this group of civil servants deeply trained and instructed in the fact that EU law should prevail over national political demands, where else are we to find this sense of loyalty?

Roles of legislative drafters in an EU context

A role is 'the behavior expected of an actor in a specific social situation' (Beyers 2005: 902; see also Rizzo *et al.* 1970). A distinction can be made between external role expectations and internal role conceptions, or 'those norms, rules, expectations and prescriptions of appropriate behavior perceived by individual officials' (Beyers and Trondal 2004: 920).

Christensen (1991) argued that the central tension in the work of civil servants is that between *political loyalty* and *professional autonomy*. According to the former principle, civil servants must be loyal to their political superiors. Beyers and Trondal (2004: 923–4), in line with Wahlke *et al.* (1962), called this the 'imperative model of representation'. The principle of *professional autonomy* (Christensen 1991: 310), by contrast, implies that civil servants have their own professional obligations. This position corresponds with the 'liberal model' of Beyers and Trondal (2004: 923–4), according to which bureaucrats are independent experts. These two general bureaucratic roles can be used to derive two different EU-related role conceptions (*cf.* Wockelberg 2014), tailored to the work of legislative drafters working on EU matters. While the first role is driven by national political loyalty, the second role is driven by professional autonomy – in this case meaning the prioritization of EU legal requirements.[3]

First, national civil servants involved in EU affairs could be seen as loyal to their national minister.[4] In legal ethics, this is known as the *translator*[5] position (Purdy 1987: 80). Drafters-as-translators should transform their political superiors' instructions into legal terminology (MacNair 2003: 145). Crucially, drafters in this role conception should act 'non-judgmentally' and 'as directed' (Purdy 1987: 79, 95). Legal considerations may enter the equation – but not for an intrinsic, deontological reason. To fully effectuate the principle of political loyalty, the drafter should not automatically transform all political instructions. Instead, they should also advise on the risks of a desired course of action, thus protecting their political superiors' interests, such as staying in office. In this view, it is a drafter's duty to fully inform their superiors on the consequences of their actions (Purdy 1987: 100).

Alternatively, extending the principle of professional autonomy (Christensen 1991: 310), legislative drafters can be viewed as *autonomous professionals*. In this view, drafters should prioritize their profession-specific expertise. A drafter's cardinal duty, according to the legislative ethics literature, is to ensure the rule of law (MacNair 2003: 145), while working for a political principal. In the words of legal ethicist Wendel (2005: 6): '[governmental] lawyers[6] may not treat the law instrumentally, as an obstacle to be planned around, but must treat legal norms as legitimate reasons for political action in their practical deliberation'.

A similar view can be gleaned from Moss (2000). Under his 'neutral expositor model', the government lawyer must act as a judge instead of an advocate, steering clear from political influence. They should work from the 'best view of the law' (Moss 2000: 1306) and deliver advice that is 'objective and not colored by the exigencies of a particular circumstance or policy goal' (*ibid.*: 1310). They should tell their client 'what the law *is* … , regardless of what the client *wishes it to be*' (Luban, 2005). This position seems highly relevant for understanding the role of legislative drafters working on EU matters. As a result of the EU legal principles of autonomy, supremacy and Community Loyalty, member states cannot autonomously decide whether or not to comply with EC law: they have voluntarily and irreversibly transferred certain legislative powers to the Community and are obliged to comply with the legal provisions arising from the use of these powers (Kapteyn and VerLoren van Themaat 1998: 81). Drafters involved in EU compliance can thus be seen as *guardians of EU law*.[7]

The previous two role conceptions are each guided by one normative principle. However, we can also conceive of an integrated role conception (Hall 1972), which does justice to both principles. In the legal ethics literature, Moss (2000) developed such an integrated role conception. According to this conception, the drafter is to proffer 'any reasonable argument, in support of his client's policy objectives'. This role is modelled on that of an advocate, who may zealously present his client in the most favourable light

(Luban [2006]: 69), while staying within legal limits. According to this position, which we will call the *integrating professional*, democratically elected political superiors are responsible for political decisions, while having to remain within legal bounds. Integrating professionals are expected to base their actions and choices on both their superior's policy objectives and EU legal requirements.

This integrating position may be tenable in many circumstances: political loyalty and professional expertise may very well coexist (Christensen 1991: 315). However, if national political demands are irreconcilable with EU legal requirements, the integrating position may result in mutually incompatible behavioural prescriptions for a civil servant, a situation denoted as *role conflict* (Driscoll 1981: 179). Such situations are characterized by the absence of an institutionalized formula for reconciling the opposed demands (Toby 1952: 326). This situation is endemic to the work of legislative drafters, as argued by Veerman (2007: 83), a renowned Dutch specialist on legislative drafting:

> If a particular policy is deemed necessary by a politician but undesirable by legislative drafters, it is seldom possible to bring these diametrically opposed points of view in equilibrium using a yardstick that is relevant for both 'politics' and 'law'.

Accordingly, the role of the integrating professional is intrinsically unstable. When legal limits and political demands are incompatible, the drafter must make a difficult choice. According to the legal ethics perspective, the drafter eventually must prioritize the legal and constitutional limitations over political demands. The key here is with the term 'reasonable argument,' (Purdy 1987: 85). When a drafter cannot come up with a reasonable argument, i.e., if 'the legal hurdles are clearly insurmountable', they should block their superior from reaching their policy objectives (Moss 2000: 1306). The drafter's primary duty is to the legislative process, which has crystallized into a body of law – not to individual political supervisors (Purdy 1987).

So as to prioritize legal requirements over incompatible political demands, the drafter has a menu of strategies at their disposal, ordered in terms of increasing severity (Purdy 1987: 83–5). First, and most benignly, they could try to advise the legislator on possible alternatives to their principal's proposal and advise on the implications and consequences of the various alternatives. This advice need not be limited to legal matters, but may comprise political, societal or other considerations (*ibid.*). Second, they could try to dissuade the principal of their desired course of action. Third, they could disassociate with the bill, by asking to withdraw from it, avoiding public endorsement, or avoiding 'signing off'. Fourth, much more sensitively, they could voice their concerns to others. Ultimately, they could decline to draw the bill altogether: 'If assisting the legislator would involve the drafter in clear wrongs … the drafter should refuse to so act' (Purdy 1987: 82). This is an extreme strategy, which according to Purdy (*ibid.*: 86), should only be used when no other means are available. In sum, according to this position, if national political demands are incompatible with legal injunctions, the drafter should prioritize the latter, a course of action for which a number of strategies are available.

Methods and data

Having sketched these alternative role conceptions, three questions present themselves: which of the role conceptions is dominant among Dutch legislative drafters; how do drafters with an integrated role conception try to connect EU legal requirements with national political demands; and which strategies do they use in case of irresolvable incompatibilities? These questions will be answered using data from a research project funded by the Dutch Ministry of Justice (Mastenbroek and Peeters Weem 2009), aimed at studying the extent, forms and depth of Europeanization of the work of Dutch legislative drafters. Part of this project concerned the role conceptions, dilemmas and coping strategies of drafters working on EU matters.

The research for this contribution consisted of two sets of interviews. First, 11 interviews were held with key persons in the field of legislative drafting in the Netherlands. These interviews served to explore the topic and important dimensions to the work of 'Europeanized' drafters. Second, 20 in-depth interviews were held with civil servants actually involved in legislative drafting. This contribution primarily focuses on the second series of interviews.

With an eye to case selection, the following considerations were central. Given the focus on EU-affected legislative drafting, the analysis was restricted to departments with both a sizeable law production and an important EU legal input. We thus excluded the Prime Minister's Office, the Ministry of Education, Culture & Science and the Defence Ministry. Second, we narrowed our scope to the work done in the central legislative divisions. At each of the departments studied, we interviewed both a legislative drafter and their manager in order to enhance representativeness of the findings. As the research was exploratory rather than theory-testing, we intended to maximize empirical heterogeneity by using a *most different systems design* (Przeworski and Teune 1970: 34), involving selection of respondents who differed on key background variables. The advantage of this design is that it maximizes the chances of identifying different ways of dealing with EU-related role conflict.

The background variables were seniority and role integration. *Seniority*, to begin with, is expected to affect the basic role orientation of civil servants, as civil servants with more years of tenure are expected to be more sensitive to political pressures (Christensen 1991: 309). In addition, as stressed by several respondents in the first interview round, a shift in role orientation has occurred over the last 15 years, resulting in a more pragmatic, i.e., more political, attitude towards EU-law. This is likely to affect the extent to which drafters experience EU law-induced role conflict and the ways in which they cope with role conflict in EU compliance. On the other hand, it could be argued that higher-level civil servants are more willing to speak up, given the fact that they already have an established reputation in the organization. A second background variable was *role integration*. The question here is whether drafters have a purely legislative role, or also operate as policy officials – primarily responsible for heeding policy demands.[8] The expectation is that legislative drafters who also have a policy responsibility are more attuned to political demands.

Christensen (1991: 305) distinguishes two types of questions concerning bureaucratic roles. The first type focuses on actual decision problems experienced by civil servants, and then serves to distil the political and professional elements in their role. The second type focuses on respondents' role perceptions and decision-making criteria in a more generalized fashion. Arguably, the advantage of the former strategy is that it is close to the world of meaning of the respondents. Tapping into real-life situations reduces the chances of socially desirable answers. At the same time, we can wonder to what extent these situations are representative of the full scope of activities these civil servants engaged in. Therefore, the interviews contained a mix of questions. The respondents were first asked to sketch their background: their training and career, as well as typical EU-related activities – either of themselves (drafters), or within their unit (managers). Next, follow-up questions were asked to gauge their EU-related role conceptions. Here, individuals would typically be asked which norms and values guide them when carrying out EU-related work or when they feel they have done a good job on their EU-related activities. Questions were phrased in such a way as to go beyond the specific dossier, in line with Christensen's (1991) second strategy. In addition, with an eye on the representativeness of the findings, managers were specifically asked to reflect on broader patterns in their unit and individual drafters were invited to sketch a general normative framework, not relevant to one 'dossier' only. The study thus mixed the two strategies suggested by Christensen (1991).

The role conceptions were established rather inductively, because the theory does not provide clear operationalization. Instead, potential 'codes' were derived from the theoretical descriptions of the three role conceptions. To be qualified as 'guardian of EU law' a respondent needed to mention policy objectives or policy wishes of their political superior as key norms and values. EU legal requirements could be mentioned, but in terms of risk assessment instead of intrinsic importance. The integrating role conceptions requires mention of policy objectives/wishes of their political superior as well as EU legal requirements as key norms and values underpinning one's work. Instead, mention of strategies to make the two available, and mention of the search for 'reasonable' arguments would lead to the qualification of an integrating role. Thirdly, in order to qualify as a 'guardian of EU law', a respondent would have to mention the importance of EU legal requirements as a key value, without mentioning the importance of policy objectives/policy wishes. Mention of the search for the 'best view of law' would also be an important indication. These codes were not regarded as fully exclusive, because respondents may use slightly different wording. Necessarily, therefore, the researcher needed to engage in some interpretation. To maximize transparency, the main empirical 'indications' for attaching a particular theoretical label to the role conception of a particular respondent are reported in the analysis (Table 1).

Next, those respondents who subscribed to an integrated position were questioned about their strategies for combining EU legal requirements with

Table 1. Role conception of respondents.

| | Position | Principle | | Role conception |
		Political demands	EU legality	
1	Drafter	/	Fine and timely implementation	Guardian of EU law
2	Manager	(Political) will formation	Legal aspects	Integrating professional
3	Drafter	Policy (objectives) / primary process	Limits of EU law	Integrating professional
4	Manager	Enable minister	/	Translator
5	Drafter	Make your minister happy	EU law	Integrating professional
6	Manager	Minister's choice	EU legal requirements	Integrating professional
7	Drafter	Rules, duties, and rights we want to enact in the NL	EU legal boundaries	Integrating professional
8	Manager	Policy wishes	(EU) legal boundaries	Integrating professional
9	Drafter	Policy objectives	(EU) legal boundaries	Integrating professional
10	Drafter	Political choices	Good legal implementation	Integrating professional
11	Manager	Think along with policy officials	(EU) legal requirements	Integrating professional
12	Drafter	Policy	(EU) law	Integrating professional
13	Drafter	*Not discussed*		
14	Manager	Policy wishes	(EU) legal boundaries	Integrating professional
15	Manager	Political wishes	EU law	Integrating professional
16	Drafter	National political wishes	EU requirements	Integrating professional
17	Manager	*Not discussed*		
18	Drafter	Material practice in the NL	EU law	Integrating professional
19	Manager	*Not discussed*		
20	Drafter	Minister's choice	EU legal requirements	Integrating professional

national political demands. With an eye on anonymity, though, specific examples are not reported. Furthermore, we invited them to provide information on the steps in case EU legal requirements proved incompatible with national political demands. Because such instances are rare, we asked the respondents whenever possible to provide information on specific instances of role conflict, rather than asking for generalized strategies. Finally, managers and drafters were interviewed separately where possible, to prevent socially desirable answers. To improve reliability, the interviews were analysed and coded by two coders. The first coder made a proposal for coding, which was later checked and, wherever necessary, amended by the second coder after joint deliberation.

Analysis

Role conceptions of Dutch legislative drafters

Most of the respondents were able and willing to reflect on their EU-related role conception.[9] As shown in Table 1, only one of these respondents – a drafter – explicitly fit our description of EU guardian role. He indicated that his primary objective is to ensure substantively 'fine' and timely implementation, without making any reference to the role of policy objectives.

At the other extreme, one respondent – a manager – explicitly subscribed to the role of translator. He explained he was driven by the principle of political loyalty. In his view, it is the drafter's duty to think along with his minister and to help him reach his objectives: 'you are an instrument maker rather than an inspector'. EU law, in his view, does not pose an insurmountable obstacle to policy objectives. As he explained, 'we have learnt that we don't need to treat directives as legislation … they are almost nothing more than a judicial decision or a parliamentary motion'. According to this respondent, this trend contrasts with the approach of the older generation of legislative drafters, who tended to implement directives somewhat fastidiously. 'Now we implement in the most attractive way possible. We try to get away with it.' In this respondent's view, it is the drafter's duty to enable the minister to make his or her own decision. If a minister's policy objectives run counter to EU law, the drafter has to advise him on the risks of the illegal course of action, which is in line with the translator position sketched above. 'I would point out the risks, by saying: "I wouldn't do it, but if you want to anyway, these are the risks. We are civil servants."

The great majority of the respondents, however, held an integrated role conception, trying to combine the demands of their political superior with EU legal requirements. To quote one of them, 'you have to make your minister happy, while ensuring correspondence with EU law.' More specifically, several respondents spoke about sensitivity to their ministers' policy wishes. As one of them explained: 'you think along about the rules, duties, and rights we want to enact in the Netherlands'. Such a position implies sensitivity to policy wishes, and hence cannot be resolved with the EU legal guardian role, which concerns developing the 'best view of law' in isolation from policy pressures. On the other hand, these respondents stressed that they try to stay within the boundaries of EU law.

Integrating EU law and national politics: the importance of interpretation

The interviews yielded interesting information about the ways in which legislative drafters try to integrate EU legal limits and political wishes. The strategy mentioned most often (eight drafters) was *interpretation* of the EU legal framework. As explained by one respondent:

> You have to be creative and flexible with the legal preconditions. ... The main challenge is to make possible what (the minister) wants – in one way or another.

Yet there are limits to this 'conceptual flexibility'. One respondent explained how he would explore the legal boundaries, while making sure that his interpretation remained justifiable. This remark may be connected to Moss's (2000) notion of 'reasonable argument'. As another respondent explained, interpretation in the end comes down to 'settling the boundaries of EU law'. This is not a straightforward task; it is a complicated balancing act involving creative puzzling, as one of them explained: 'When I shape it like this, it may be possible, but if I shape it differently, surely not.' Others seemed to be more flexible, as indicated by one manager: 'You shouldn't take EU law too literally, you have to treat it more flexibly.'

Limits of the integrating position: irresolvable compatibilities

Most respondents hence hold an integrated role conception, trying to connect national political demands with EU legal considerations. Yet, there are limits to this flexibility: incompatibilities may occur. Choosing to uphold EU law then means compromising one's loyalty to the minister, and vice versa. Most interviewees mentioned the occurrence of such incompatibilities. According to one of them: 'Politics and business don't want us to be the best pupil in the class. So you are under a lot of pressure to loosen the way you apply EU law.' Finally, it must be noted that most drafters argue that such incompatibilities are the exception rather than the rule.

Incompatibilities between political loyalty and EU legality were reported to occur at various stages of the EU policy process. First, tensions between legal quality and policy wishes may occur in the stage of transposition. According to one respondent, 'politicians have a hard time accepting a loss of policy freedom, when there is law coming from Brussels.' Another respondent mentioned the high costs of implementation, which may make suboptimal implementation attractive. Another dilemma relates to the actual application of the transposed EU law. Often, implementing agencies demand all kinds of exceptions to EU law. Policy officials are reported to then put pressure on legislative drafters to think of 'tricks'. According to a respondent, many dilemmas relating to EU law run along these lines. Incompatibilities may also occur during the *making of autonomous (domestic) legislation*, as explained by five respondents. One of them conveyed that his division often receives policy demands that go against EU law. Another interviewee gave the example of a vast deregulation scheme, proposed by a policy division, which entailed that half of all legislation in force was to be cut. The legislative division indicated that this was impossible, as some 90 per cent of this legislation originated from the EU. Another respondent added that these conflicts often concern EU law relating to procurement and state aid:

> In such a case I will tell them that this is against the rules. Yet in some cases they decide to go ahead anyway.

Dealing with incompatibilities

If interpretation runs against EU legal limits, the drafter is stuck between a rock and a hard place: he/she must prioritize either political loyalty or EU legality. According to the integrating role conception developed in legal ethics, law should ultimately prevail. Four of the 15 respondents with an integrated role conception – all of them drafters instead of managers – indeed indicated that they would ultimately prioritize EU law. There are limits to 'conceptual flexibility':

> In the end people have to accept the inevitable. ... If I'd have to exceed the limits of EU law, this simply would not happen.

Another respondent took a similar stance, stating that 'there is simply no room to help your own sector'. In such a case, a department's attitude towards the value of the EU works as a lubricant, as another respondent asserted: 'Everyone at the department understands that EU law takes primacy.' Similarly, at another highly Europeanized department, the policy divisions were reported to accept the EU's legal limitations on national policy.

One drafter explicitly stated that they would ultimately decline to draft the deficient measure, the most extreme strategy given by Purdy (1987). An alternative is to go along with the deficient draft, while avoiding signing it off – disassociation in Purdy's terms. Such steps are not taken lightly. Most drafters use various strategies before prioritizing EU law over political demands. Other strategies mentioned, much in line with Purdy's ladder, are trying to dissuade their policy counterpart and eventually the minister, and suggesting alternatives that are in line with EU law. Two respondents explained how they would focus on the EU level, by consulting the European Commission or seeking support from other member states for the Dutch policy objectives.

However, 11 of the 15 respondents (9 of which were managers) with an integrated role conception would ultimately prioritize political demands. Commonly, these respondents argued that their political principal has the final policy-making responsibility, and that the task of the drafter is to enable their minister to take sound decisions. 'As a civil servant,' one respondent explained, 'you have to be "as loyal as a puppy".' In someone else's words, this may mean having to work on something that is legally questionable. One manager was particularly outspoken about this possibility:

> A drafter is not a guardian of the law. … It is your job to serve your minister as well as possible. The minister is your boss. You have to inform the minister well, and … make sure that he knows what he does. But when push comes to shove, he is responsible. That is the core of a civil servant's existence.

According to these respondents, drafters should not slavishly follow policy demands, but instead make their minister well aware that he is violating EU law – and of the risks involved. Two respondents provided details on such risk assessments. Crucial considerations are the chances of a 'political mess', financial consequences – for instance resulting from possible ECJ cases – and the chances that stakeholders will file a lawsuit. On the basis of such an assessment, the minister must decide whether or not to maintain his plans; 'politics settle the dilemma in the end'. In other words:

> When (my minister) really wants something, we will think of a supporting argument.

Finally, one respondent disclosed a more covert way of serving their superior's political objectives, namely by *omitting* checks on EU legality. This strategy was also mentioned by the respondent who positioned himself as a translator. As one of them explained, drafters may decide *not* to inform their manager of inopportune EU legal requirements and risks involved if doing so would complicate the minister's position. By withholding information the minister 'may always claim ignorance.' Another manager conveyed that this is rather common practice, explaining how EU law 'used to be neglected out of ignorance, but now is neglected intentionally'.

Interestingly, the respondents also employ various strategies before prioritizing political demands over incompatible EU law: providing alternatives to their policy counterpart or minister; building rapport to increase the interest in drafters' arguments; and trying to dissuade their policy counterpart or minister. These are in line with the strategies listed by Purdy (1987). Accordingly, every step of the ladder provides the opportunity of yielding to politics. Other strategies mentioned were to find information about the limits of EU law, to negotiate with a policy division and surrender on less important points of contention. Finally, two additional respondents described that they would try to change EU law or seek support for the Dutch position from other member states or the European Commission. These strategies indicate that prioritization of politics over EU law is not a straightforward move for a legislative drafter, but an *ultimo remedio*.

Conclusion

This contribution has explored the role conceptions and strategies of Dutch legislative drafters with EU-related tasks. On the basis of the literature on legislative ethics, three distinct roles were constructed. *Translators*, working from a concern with political loyalty, are led by their ministers' policy demands. They may take EU legal limits into account, but only in a teleological sense, advising their ministers on the risk of an illegal course of action. Legality does not figure as an intrinsic concern. The *guardian of EU law* does not take into account policy demands during EU compliance, but strives for the best interpretation of EU law. The *integrating professional*, finally, seeks to connect policy demands with EU legal requirements, in case of clear incompatibilities prioritizing the latter.

Interviews with legislative drafters and their managers provided us with a wealth of information on their EU-related role perceptions. The majority of respondents recognized the dual roles shaping their work: they try to integrate EU legal requirements with national policy demands. This policy-sensitive attitude was alleged to be a recent development, also pertinent to law in general (cf. Van den Berg and Dijkstra 2015). The main strategy used by this group was to reinterpret EU law in such a way as to reconcile domestic political demands with EU legal requirements.

However, most respondents recognized that irresolvable incompatibilities may arise, either during implementation or national law-making. How do drafters go about settling such incompatibilities? A majority of respondents indicated that, ultimately, they prioritize political demands over EU legal requirements, even if this choice is not taken lightly and often is preceded by several strategies to guard EU law. A minority of respondents with an integrated position, all at the level of drafter, argued that they would not give in to policy pressure and, when push comes to shove, uphold EU law against incompatible national policy objectives. Managers seemed more attuned to the policy needs of their minister and more willing to compromise the 'best view of EU law'.

In sum, even Dutch legislative drafters, a group of civil servants very likely to prioritize EU legal requirements over incompatible national policy demands, may not do so if presented with irresolvable incompatibilities. Just like national civil servants engaged in EU decision-making, most legislative drafters ultimately prioritize political loyalty. Because Dutch legislative drafters may be seen as a rather crucial case for a normative correction on the politics of EU compliance, we should expect such pragmatic processes to operate in other member states as well – which strengthens the image of 'patchwork Europe' (Héritier 1996).

In the end, therefore, compliance indeed is driven by domestic preferences, as assumed by rationalist theories on EU compliance. Yet, this is not a matter of top–down adaptation. This study's findings are in line with the 'perform-ance' view of EU compliance charted in this collection (Thomann and Sager 2017). Compliance is often a creative process of wedding EU legal require-ments with domestic policy demands. Such interpretation may be seen as a key strategy leading to domestication (ibid.) of EU law at the domestic level.

Our analysis has three implications for the conceptual model used. First, whereas the integrated position sketched above prescribes an ultimate prior-itization of EU law, most drafters eventually prioritize political demands. Persons in an integrated position may thus shift to either of the two pure roles in case of persistent incompatibilities. Second, the strategies identified by Purdy (1987) may be used by both groups of drafters; each step of the ladder offers the possibility to proceed on the ladder of escalation, or to prior-itize either political demands or legal limits. Third, several strategies were identified in addition to those mentioned by Purdy (1987): omitting checks on legality; building rapport to strengthen one's position; finding additional information and negotiating with policy experts; trying to change EU law; or activating other actors.

This contribution offers various avenues for further research. First, the study was explicitly exploratory in nature. A logical next step would be a more deduc-tive approach, preferably using a large-N strategy, to obtain more representa-tive findings. The advantage of such an analysis would be to include other types of civil servants, and to incorporate background variables and theoreti-cally informed variables such as instrumental and normative considerations (Dörrenbächer 2017). Such a study would provide us with more representative insights into the prevalence of conflicting demands in the face of EU law and shed light on the variance and antecedents of EU-related attitudes. Second, this study raises the question of comparison. Initially, the Dutch administrative context seemed a rather likely case, given the rather strong EU rule of law (Gibson and Caldeira 1996). Yet, given the observation by both respondents and researchers (Van den Berg and Dijkstra 2015) that the rule of law among legislative drafters and other types of civils servants has declined more gener-ally, it would be interesting to repeat this study in other EU member states with a strong rule of law, such as Denmark and Sweden. Third, we could extend the analysis to a third group of national civil servants have been presented as an even more likely case to display pro-European loyalties: agency personnel. This group thus merits further empirical scrutiny to uncover normative checks on domestic non-compliance.

Notes

1. See http://academievoorwetgeving.nl/page/about-the-academy
2. Arguably, they are not a *most likely* case for the development of an independent EU loyalty, because they still form part of a ministry, if not positioned in the hierarchical line. This is different for agency personnel, which have been decoupled from the ministerial hierarchy, which may enhance the likeliness that they develop a sense of EU loyalty (Egeberg and Trondal 2009; Wockelberg 2014).
3. I thank one of the anonymous reviewers for the useful observation that the proposed distinction is somewhat of a simplification, as it neglects the fact that there is an additional dimension informing the role conceptions: EU- versus nationally informed. Combining this distinction with that made by Christensen (1991), we could conceive of two additional role conceptions: one prioritizing EU political demands; and one prioritizing national law. Yet, given this contribution's focus on the existence of a normative counterweight on political demands during processes of EU compliance, the choice is to focus on the role conceptions revolving around EU legal requirements and national political demands. See Dörrenbächer (2017) for an analysis of civil servants confronted with incompatibilities between EU and national law.
4. Technically, in line with the previous note, legislative drafters could also be loyal to an EU-level principal, for instance the European Commission. This option is not taken into account in the study, given its focus on the politics of compliance at the national level. The interviews also did not provide evidence for this possibility.
5. Confusingly, Purdy (1987) uses the term 'advocacy' to denote the drafter-as-translator role. Please note the difference with the advocacy model of Moss (2000), explained later in this section, which does recognize the existence of legal limitations to policy wishes.
6. The analysis by Wendel (2005) is not restricted to advising by governmental lawyers – it also encompasses lawyers more broadly.
7. It must be noted that there are many instances in which the EU's legal requirements are not clear, e.g., due to ambiguous or complicated phrasing or incompatibilities between pieces of EU law. In these cases, according to the normative position of the guardian of EU law, legislative drafters are to develop their best view of the law, using as many different sources as possible.
8. As explained in the introduction, in most Dutch ministries this function explicitly differs from that of the legislative drafter. The policy official or administrator is to realize the minister's policy demands, e.g., by developing policies and legislation (Tholen and Mastenbroek 2013: 490).
9. The three respondents who did not reflect on the role of a drafter in EU implementation/the making of autonomous legislation primarily talked about their role in EU negotiations, which is beyond the scope of this study.

Acknowledgments

The authors would like to thank the participants of the EGPA Permanent Study Group XIV meeting in Toulouse, France, 2015 for comments on an earlier version of this paper. Special thanks extend to the three anonymous reviewers of this contribution, for their extensive and helpful comments.

Disclosure statement

The authors reported no potential conflict of interest.

Funding

The article is based on a project funded by the Dutch Ministry of Justice (2008–2009). The results of this project have been reported in Mastenbroek and Peeters Weem, T. (2009).

References

Angelova, B., Dannwolf, T. and König, T. (2012) 'How robust are compliance findings? A research synthesis', *Journal of European Public Policy* 19(8): 1269–91.

Beyers, J. (2005) 'Multiple embeddedness and socialization in Europe: the case of Council officials', *International Organization* 59: 899–936.

Beyers, J. (2010) 'Conceptual and methodological challenges in the study of European socialization', *Journal of European Public Policy*, 17(6): 909–20.

Beyers, J. and Trondal, J. (2004) 'How nation states "hit" Europe: the case of Council officials', *West European Politics* 27(5): 919–42.

Bondarouk, E., and Mastenbroek, E. (forthcoming) 'Reconsidering EU compliance: implementation performance in the field of environmental policy', forthcoming in European Policy and Governance.

Burcu Bayram, A. (2017) 'Good Europeans? How European identity and costs interact to explain politician attitudes towards compliance with European Union Law', *Journal of European Public Policy* 24(1): 42–60.

Christensen, T. (1991) 'Bureaucratic roles: political loyalty and professional autonomy', *Scandinavian Political Studies* 14: 303–20.

Connaughton, B. (2015) 'Developing a hybrid identity? The Europeanisation of public servants at the continent's far West', in F. Sager and P. Overeem (eds.), *The European public servant: a shared administrative identity?* Colchester: ECPR Press, pp. 199–217.

Dimitrova, A. and Steunenberg, B. (2000) 'The search for convergence of national policies in the European Union: an impossible quest?' *European Union Politics* 1: 201–26.

Dörrenbächer, N. (2017) 'Europe at the frontline: Analyzing street-level motivations for the use of European Union migration law', *Journal of European Public Policy*, doi:10.1080/13501763.2017.1314535.

Driscoll, J.W. (1981) 'Coping with role conflict: an exploratory field study of union-management cooperation', *International Review of Applied Psychology* 30: 177–98.

Egeberg, M. (1999) 'Transcending intergovernmentalism? identity and role perceptions of national officals in EU decision-making', *Journal of European Public Policy* 6(3): 456–74.

Egeberg, M. and Trondal, J. (2009) 'National agencies in the European administrative space: government driven, Commission driven or networked?' *Public Administration* 87(4): 779–90.

Gibson, J.L. and Caldeira, G.A. (1996) 'The legal cultures of Europe', *Law & Society Review* 30(1): 55–86.

Hall, D.T. (1972) 'A model of coping with role conflict: the role behavior of college educated women', *Administrative Science Quarterly* 17(4): 471–86.

Héritier, A. (1996) 'The accomodation of diversity in European policy-making and its outcomes: regulatory policy as a patchwork', *Journal of European Policy* 3(2): 149-67.

Kaeding, M. (2008) 'Lost in translation or full steam ahead: the transposition of EU transport directives across member states', *European Union Politics* 9(1): 115–43.

Kapteyn, P.J.G. and VerLoren van Themaat, P. (1998). *Introduction to the law of the European Communities* [3rd edition]. Deventer: Kluwer International.

Luban, D. (2005) 'Selling indulgences: The unmistakable parallel between Lynne Stewart and the president's torture lawyers', Slate, available at http://www.slate. com/articles/news_and_politics/jurisprudence/2005/02/selling_indulgences.html (accessed 18 April 2017).

Luban, D. (2006) 'Liberalism, torture, and the ticking bomb', in K.J. Greenberg (ed.), *The Torture Debate in America*, Cambridge: Cambridge University Press, pp. 35–83.

MacNair, D. (2003) 'Legislative drafters: a discussion of ethical standards from a Canadian perspective', *Statute Law Review* 24(2): 125–56.

Maher, I. (1994) 'National courts as European Community courts', *Legal Studies* 14: 226–43.

Mastenbroek, E. (2005) 'EU compliance: still a black hole?' *Journal of European Public Policy* 12: 1103–20.

Mastenbroek, E. (2007) *The politics of compliance: explaining the transposition of EC directives in the Netherlands.* Leiden University. Accessed from https://openaccess. leidenuniv.nl/handle/1887/11861

Mastenbroek, E. and Kaeding, M. (2006) 'Europeanization beyond the goodness of fit: domestic politics in the forefront', *Comparative European Politics* 4: 331–54.

Mastenbroek, E., and Peeters Weem, T. (2009). *In Spagaat tussen Brussel en Den Haag: De Europeanisering van het Wetgevingsvak* [Balancing between Brussels and The Hague: The Europeanization of legal drafting]. Nijmegen: Radboud University.

Moss, R.D. (2000) 'Executive Branch Legal interpretation: a perspective from the Office of Legal Counsel', *Administrative Law Review* 52: 1303–30.

Page, E.C. (2003) 'The civil servant as legislator: law making in British administration', *Public Administration* 81(4): 651–79.

Przeworski, A. and Teune, H. (1970) *The Logic of Comparative Social Inquiry*, New York: Wiley.

Purdy, R. (1987) 'Professional responsibility for legislative drafters: suggested guidelines and discussion of ethics and role problems', *Seton Hall Legislative Journal* 11: 67–120.

Quaglia, L., De Francesco, F. and Radaelli, C. (2008) 'Committee governance and socialization in the European Union', *Journal of European Public Policy* 15(1): 155–66.

Rizzo, J.R., House, R.J. and Lirtzman, S.I. (1970) 'Role conflict and Ambiguity in Complex organizations', *Administrative Science Quarterly* 15(2): 150–63.

Steunenberg, B. (2006) 'Turning swift policymaking into deadlock and delay: national policy coordination and the transposition of EU directives', *European Union Politics* 7: 293–319.

Tholen, B., and Mastenbroek, E. (2013) 'Guardians of the law or loyal administrators? Towards a refined administrative ethos for legislative drafters', *Administrative Theory & Praxis* 35(4): 487–506.

Thomann, E. (2015) 'Customizing Europe: transposition as bottom-up implementation', *Journal of European Public Policy* 22(10): 1368–87. doi:10.1080/13501763.2015. 1008554

Thomann, E. and Sager, F. (2017) 'Moving beyond legal compliance: Innovative approaches to EU multi-level implementation', *Journal of European Public Policy*. doi:10.1080/13501763.2017.1314541

Toby, J. (1952) 'Some variables in role conflict analysis', *Social Forces* 30(3): 323–27. doi:10.2307/2571598

Treib, O. (2014) 'Implementing and complying with EU governance outputs', *Living Reviews in European Governance* 9(1), 1–47, available at http://www.europeangovernance-livingreviews.org/Articles/lreg-2014-1/ (accessed 1 September 2014).

Trondal, J. (2004) 'Re-socializing civil servants: The transformative powers of EU institutions', *Acta Politica* 39(4): 4–30. doi:10.1057/palgrave.ap.5500045

Van den Berg, C.F. and Dijkstra, G.S.A. (2015) 'Wetgevingsjuristen ten prooi aan New Political Governance? een inventarisatie [Legislative drafters: prey to New Political Governance? Taking stock]', *Regelmaat, tijdschrift voor wetgevingsvraagstukken* 2015(4): 247–66.

Veerman, G.J. (2007) *Over wetgeving. Principes, paradoxen en praktische beschouwingen.* [About legislation. Principles, paradoxes and practical reflections]. Den Haag: SDU Uitgevers.

Wahlke, J.C., Elau, H., Buchanan, W. and Ferguson, L.C. (1962) *The Legislative System: explorations in Legislative Behavior.* New York: John Wiley.

Wendel, W. B. (2005) 'Professionalism and Interpretation', *Northwestern University Law Review* 99 (Spring): 1167–233.

Wockelberg, H. (2014) 'Political servants or independent experts? A comparative study of bureaucratic role perceptions and the implementation of EU law in Denmark and Sweden', *Journal of European Integration* 36(7): 731–47. doi:10.1080/07036337.2014.942733

Policy implementation through multi-level governance: analysing practical implementation of EU air quality directives in Germany

Judith A.M. Gollata and Jens Newig

ABSTRACT

Eurpean Union (EU) environmental policy has increasingly advanced multi-level governance (MLG) to improve policy implementation. MLG approaches mandate (sub-) national planning and introduce functional governance layers to match the biophysical scale of environmental problems. Whereas the literature on policy implementation has focused on the *challenges* posed by multi-level systems, the described EU approach relies on MLG as a *strategy to better policy implementation*. This contribution studies the implementation of EU air quality directives, drawing on all 137 German air quality and action plans, to explore how requirements of multi-level implementation are delivered on the ground. Overall, we find the model of implementing air quality policy through MLG of limited success. In particular, sub-national policy-makers use their new planning competencies but struggle to implement functional governance layers. Mirroring experiences from neighbouring EU policy fields, our findings raise the broader issue of 'failed' implementation versus a still untapped potential for adaptation and governance learning.

1. Introduction

Policy implementation studies have, since the classic work of Pressman and Wildavsky (1973), dealt with systems of multiple levels of governance. Such multi-level systems, as found in federalist countries as well as in the European Union (EU), have typically been regarded as challenges or outright obstacles to effective policy implementation (e.g., Milio 2010). In contrast, the tradition of polycentric governance considers multiple levels of governance as conducive to effective policy-making and delivery. Famously advocated by the Ostrom Workshop (Ostrom 1999; Ostrom *et al.* 1961), polycentricity has informed modern thinking on multi-level governance (MLG) (Hooghe and Marks 2003).

Continuing the trend to 'new forms of governance' and proceduralization (Holzinger *et al.* 2009; Jordan *et al.* 2005), recent European Union environmental policies have increasingly advanced MLG approaches to improve policy implementation. Policies such as the Water Framework Directive (2000), the Floods Directive (2007) and the EU air quality directives (1996–2008) mandate (sub-) national planning – often involving the participation of non-state actors – and 'rescale' governance to match the biophysical level of environmental problems, thus adding to the existing complexity of the EU multi-level system (Newig and Koontz 2014). Rather than being an obstacle, MLG becomes an instrument to policy implementation.

But is this really the case? This contribution empirically investigates the problem-solving capacity of this 'implementation through MLG' model of policy-making by tracing on the ground implementation. Hitherto virtually non-researched, we study the implementation of recent EU air quality directives, which mandate the production of air quality and action plans on biophysical scales. Doing so, this contribution adds to current EU multi-level implementation research in a threefold way. First, it systematically studies the multi-level governance implications of policy implementation by considering newly introduced functional governance layers (*sensu* Hooghe and Marks 2003). Second, it investigates practical implementation on the subnational level which so far has been largely ignored by implementation research (Borghetto and Franchino 2010; Héritier 1999; Hupe and Hill 2016; Leventon 2015), although effective implementation of EU policies highly depends on sub-national authorities (Pridham 1996). Moving beyond the issue of legal compliance, this study sheds light on the widely recognized post-transposition implementation deficit on member state level in EU environmental policy, where compliance deficits may be created by mismatches between sub-national actors and the EU implementation approach (e.g., Leventon 2015; Thomann and Zhelyazkova 2017). Third, EU air quality policy and its implementation is a hugely under-researched policy field, in particular compared to other EU environmental directives, such as the Water Framework Directive. However, an estimated air pollution-related 46,000 premature deaths each year in Germany alone (Kallweit and Bünger 2015)[1] make it a relevant case.

Analysing all 137 German air quality and action plans, this contribution studies how the requirements of EU air quality directives are translated below member state level, and provides an overview of the implementation in 16 German federal states (*Länder*). Doing so, we investigate to what extent scale-adapted governance layers are in fact established by public administration. This involves studying the role of collaboration and co-ordination among municipalities, and the circumstances under which this happens. Moreover, we study how the different levels of government interact (municipal and states, in particular), and to what extent non-state actors participate in local planning.

The remainder of this contribution is organized as follows. The next section presents our analytical framework. In Section 3 key provisions of the directives to set out the broader policy context for the research are discussed. Section 4 operationalizes the directives' key provisions to assess implementation in Germany via the produced air quality and action plans. The presentation and discussion of key findings in relation to current debates in EU environmental policy implementation research is offered in Section 5, before drawing conclusions and suggesting avenues for further research in Section 6.

2. Conceptual lenses: enhancing policy implementation through multi-level governance

Environmental policy in Europe – and air quality policy is by no means an exception – has been suffering from a lack of effectiveness (EC 2015a; Jordan 1999; Knill and Liefferink 2007). In an attempt to improve environmental policy implementation and compliance, the EU is increasingly advancing multi-level governance approaches (Newig and Koontz 2014). The developments from the Mandelkern report on Better Regulation (Mandelkern Group 2001) up to the current attempts to drive 'smart regulation' (EC 2010) document how, more than ever, the EU is concerned about the effective delivery of its policies.

The policy implementation literature, however, has almost exclusively regarded multi-level structures as obstacles to implementation, rather than something conducive to it (Börzel 1998; Piattoni 2010). Pressman and Wildavsky (1973) conceptualized levels of government in the federal system of the United States (US) as clearance points which tend to water down policies and delay implementation. Milio (2010) found the EU multi-level governance system with the heterogeneity of member state polities to obstruct effective implementation of EU policies. That multi-level systems might also enhance the problem-solving capacity and be conducive to policy implementation has not been discussed in the policy implementation literature.

This is somewhat surprising because, in the governance literature, the problem-solving capacity of multi-level systems has been playing an important role (Thomann and Sager 2017). At the same time, implementation scholars increasingly recognize the many commonalities of governance and policy implementation (Hill and Hupe 2014). Policy implementation, after all, often entails more than simply carrying out policies or strictly complying with a rule. Rather, implementation typically involves a political process 'in the course of which policies are frequently re-shaped, re-defined or even completely overturned' (Pülzl and Treib 2007: 100). In that sense, 'implementation' can be seen as operational choice decisions (*sensu* Kiser and Ostrom 1982), whereas collective choice or constitutional decisions are reserved for 'policy-making'. Governance scholars acknowledge this complexity and the gradual differences between policy formulation and implementation.

Scholars of multi-level governance have put forward the following arguments why and how MLG could improve policy delivery:

(1) *Decentralization:* Part of the EU's rationale to draw on MLG in policy implementation is to devolve governance tasks to sub-national levels. It is argued that more local decisions can take into account local conditions more effectively and draw on local knowledge (see the argument on participation below) and thus arrive at more effective policy decisions (Larson and Ribot 2004; Newig and Fritsch 2009). As part of an MLG implementation system, local decision-making is embedded in the framework of higher-order regulation (which has been stressed by Ostrom [2010]).

(2) *Spatial fit:* Existing, territorially bound jurisdictions often do not match the phenomena to be governed. This is certainly the case with natural resources such as water and air. In order to enhance the 'spatial fit' (Kok and Veldkamp 2011; Moss 2012; Young 2002), spatially adapted governance scales – such as watersheds or airsheds – have been proposed to internalize spatial spillover effects across boundaries. Termed Type II MLG (Hooghe and Marks 2003), such governance levels are functionally specific and more flexible than territorial jurisdictions.

(3) *Participation:* Governance, as opposed to government, implies an opening up of decision-making to non-state actors – the state–society axis in Piattoni's (2010) model of MLG. Information, consultation and participation of non-state actors is expected to improve the quality of (local) decision-making through including (local) knowledge and achieving greater buy-in of participants (e.g., Brody *et al.* 2003; Newig and Fritsch 2009; Newig and Koontz 2014).

The present model of EU policy implementation through MLG couples these MLG-features (decentralization, spatially adapted governance scales, participation) with a central planning mandate and oversight. This has been described as an ideal-typical model of 'mandated participatory planning' (Newig and Koontz 2014).

In our empirical case presented below we will study the implementation of air quality directives in Germany, test it against the criteria presented here and thus assess the problem-solving capacity of the implementation through MLG approach.

3. EU air quality directives: key provisions and first assessments of their implementation in Germany

The term EU air quality directives refers to a series of European directives issued between 1996 and 2008[2] with the aim of lowering concentrations of certain pollutants, including particulate matter (PM_{10}) and nitrogen dioxide (NO_2), in ambient air.[3] They are currently among the strictest acts of legislation worldwide concerning PM_{10} air pollution (Wolff 2014).

EU air pollution policy is in transition (Lidskog and Sundqvist 2011: 2). While air pollution abatement is a well-established policy area within EU environmental regulation, air policy legislation has had limited successes since the late 1970s (EC 2015a). Levels of air pollution remain high throughout Europe, posing a high environmental risk factor for human health, vegetation and ecosystems. The World Health Organization (WHO) and the Organization for Economic Co-operation and Development (OECD) have shown the extent of the burden of disease and related economic cost in a recently published study (WHO/OECD 2015). In June 2015, the European Commission opened infringement proceedings against Germany for continuing non-compliance with annual and/or daily limit values for particulate matter (PM_{10}) and nitrogen dioxide (NO_2) (EC 2015b).

As part of the implementation process, member states must assess air quality, manage air quality where limit values are exceeded or might be exceeded, and ensure that information on ambient air quality is publicly available. The European Commission monitors implementation of the directives, yet no comprehensive implementation report has been published to date.

Germany's transpositions of EU air quality directives into national law has been late (2002) and not fully complete (Cancik 2011). After transposition, legal responsibility for implementation in Germany was handed down to the *Länder* level, leaving effective implementation to domestic actors, which provide the infrastructure for the practical application of the policy (process of analysing, developing and implementing measures) and for monitoring compliance. Figure 1 illustrates the German multi-level implementation structure.

The *Länder* in Germany have independent jurisdictional responsibilities. There is a high level of co-ordination between federal and regional governments, also termed 'co-operative federalism' (Schäffer 1992). The German constitution grants the *Länder* considerable leeway in the financing and execution of their duties. Each federal state has its individual form of organization of administrative entities, including different nested governance levels. Subnational implementation of air quality directives refers to this level as well as the stage of practical application and enforcement, which involves various actors on horizontal and vertical governance levels, as well as non-state actors to implement the complex and innovative provisions of the policy. The local level below the *Länder* level includes governmental regions (*Regierungsbezirke*), (rural) districts (*Landkreise*) and cities and municipalities.

To address the analytical aspects discussed so far, we focus our research on the following three provisions, related to MLG approaches indicated in the directives.

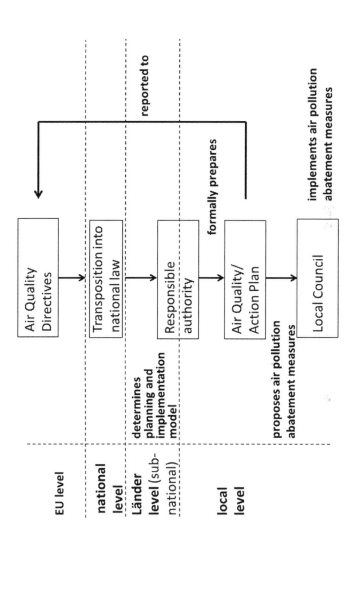

Figure 1. Air quality directive implementation process in Germany.

3.1. Mandated local planning – air quality and action plans

EU air quality directives follow a mandated planning approach. It requires the explicit formulation of certain plans or programmes (on local governance layers), which represent the essential vehicle for implementation (Durner and Ludwig 2008; Newig and Koontz 2014). Across the German *Länder*, this planning approach plays out differently, with regard to the choice of the responsible authority, the number of vertical governance levels and organizations involved, as well as the collaboration and co-operation with participating single actors and organizations.

Different from similar EU environmental directives, air quality legislation mandates planning only once zones or agglomerations exceed pollutant limit values. Authorities then have to establish air quality and action plans in order to meet limit values. Plans have to be updated if the abatement measures implemented still do not meet prescribed standards. Since the directives place particular importance on the local level, it is the local administration which shapes concrete policy measures. To do so, it can draw on environmentally relevant lay or local knowledge through participation mechanisms. Since measures transcend the functional division of municipal departments their implementation encourages cross-departmental co-operation and sharing of competences.

3.2. Scale-adapted governance – new functional layers

Air pollution problems typically do not fit within jurisdictional layers and therefore lack 'spatial fit' (Lidskog and Sundqvist 2011). Responding to calls for scale-adapted governance levels (e.g., Kok and Veldkamp 2011), air quality directives require EU member states to divide their territories into zones or agglomerations,[4] reflecting the purposes of air quality assessment and management as well as the population density. The responsibility for adapting this approach is left to the member states. Scales of air pollution depend on the localization of the problem. Air pollution problems can first be localized according to the spatial distribution of air pollutants. Second, larger geographical areas can also take into account the sources of air pollution (such as traffic or industry). Third, the indirect causes (such as commuter flows) could be considered for yet larger-scale spatial planning. In a general sense, EU legislation targets the local level as locus for implementation, assuming this to be the functionally most fitting level. Moreover, in introducing zones and agglomerations, it requires the creation of new, scale-adapted governance levels, thus drawing on an MLG approach. On an operational level, governance in zones and agglomerations involves vertical and horizontal co-operation and co-ordination of existing territorial jurisdictions, such as municipalities (Durner and Ludwig 2008; Haus and Zimmermann

2007). Possible forms of co-operation and co-ordination depend on individual localizations of air pollution problems and resulting spatial frames. So on one hand, local level planning is mandated; on the other hand a spatial fit between the problem issue and the governance scale is to be achieved. Our empirical study will assess in how far both can be realized.

3.3. Informing the public – participatory planning

Air quality directives stipulate the provision of information to the public in line with the Åarhus Convention on Access to Information, Public Participation in Decision-making and Access to Justice in Environmental Matters. Article 26 Directive 2008/50/EC expanded information rights and requires 'that the public as well as appropriate organizations such as environmental organizations, consumer organizations, organizations representing the interests of sensitive populations, other relevant health-care bodies and the relevant industrial federations are informed'. This wording leaves considerable room for interpretation as to the stage and the kind of involvement; for instance, whether the public would be included in the planning process. Contrary to similar environmental directives such as the Floods Directive or the Water Framework Directive (where participatory planning is mandated), such institutionalization of participation has not been emphasized much in the air quality directives. National legal discourses on the legitimacy of extended public participation have led to varying approaches among member states. In Germany a more comprehensive inclusion of the public was not deemed necessary by court ruling (Cancik 2011). Nevertheless, the EU air quality directives prescribe obligatory transparency by introducing new rights to standardized, easily accessible and free of charge information (Busch *et al.* 2012) and thus empower citizens to claim their right to clean air. If limit values are exceeded, German courts granted citizens the right to demand the establishment of an air quality and action plan, which has in fact been made use of (Cancik 2011).

In the following, we will explore how practical on-the-ground implementation of air quality directives plays out in Germany, considering in particular the aspects of mandated planning, decentralized and scale-adapted governance, and public participation.

4. Research design and methodology

The principal sources of data for this study are the German air quality and action plans. We assume that the essential information on how the key provisions of the directives were implemented is described in these publicly available plans. Plans follow an essentially predetermined structure and represent the process of plan-making over a period of time, allowing for comprehensive analysis. We study all 137 German air quality and action plans established since 2004, thus ensuring that individual approaches to sub-national implementation are not excluded and providing a complete picture of the variation and diversity in implementation approaches to EU air quality directives in Germany. The German Environment Agency (Umweltbundesamt) regularly collects plans and provides an overview on its website.[5]

To allow for a structured comparison of implementation across Germany we operationalized the key procedural provisions and a number of contextual factors in a set of variables. The first author read all plans and coded them according to the defined variables using a mix of quantitative and qualitative content analysis. In a first step we uncovered and compared general aspects of German plans and highlighted their similarities. To identify variation in sub-national implementation across *Länder* and individual plans, we identified the following variables, derived from the conceptual framework discussed above:

1. **Planning responsibility (GOV_LEVEL):** The governance level within the *Land* that has been assigned responsibility for implementation by a higher authority and oversees the process. In total four different levels can be distinguished: the federal state (*Land*), the governmental region (*Regierungsbezirk*), the (rural) district (*Landkreis*) and the municipalities. This is a measure of 'localness' of governance.
2. **Vertical governance levels (VERT_LEVEL):** The average number of different vertical governance levels involved in the planning process.
3. **Spatial planning reference (SPAT_REF):** Percentage of plans that identified a zone or agglomeration crossing municipal borders as spatial unit for the process of plan-making.
4. **Co-operation with other municipalities (COOP_MUN):** Percentage of plans that co-operated with neighbouring municipalities (also beyond spatial planning) in the process of plan-making.
5. **Organizations involved (NO_ORG):** The average number of organizations (governmental and non-governmental) involved in the process of plan-making.
6. **Collaboration with non-governmental organizations (COLL_NGO):** Percentage of plans that co-operated with non-state actors in the process of plan-making.
7. **Participatory involvement of citizens (PART_PROC):** Percentage of plans that incorporated participatory procedures in the process of plan-making.

5. Findings and discussion

5.1. Overall assessment of plans

Our analysis of all 137 German air quality and action plans reveals a variety of similarities and dissimilarities in approaches to sub-national implementation and compliance. If overall compliance is merely understood in terms of establishing and providing plans where required, there is no sufficient data available in Germany to evaluate how many affected municipalities or agglomerations did not produce a plan on time. Article 22 Directive 2008/50 concedes the right to apply for postponement of attainment deadlines and exemption from the obligation to apply certain limit values. Germany has indeed made use of this right, with 57 municipalities or agglomerations applying for postponement for compliance with limit values on NO_2 alone (UBA 2014).

Overall, German plans follow a very similar structure as prescribed in the corresponding national legislation, tying in with prior legislation on air quality reporting. Plans provide a detailed overview of the air quality situation in Germany. Comprising 88 pages on average, plans are rather comprehensive, with the majority of plans covering all thematic issues as requested by legislation. However, plans differ in a number of details owing to differences in size of municipality or agglomeration, responsible planning authority, methodological modelling and measuring techniques, emission source(s), chosen implementation process and proposed measures to improve the situation. Municipalities or agglomerations affected by ambient air pollution vary in size between 1.040 and 692.000 hectares, requiring varying inputs of resources (e.g., number of technical staff, cost of process, etc.) to tackle air pollution.

Regarding the sources of air pollution, urban traffic hotspots are the main contributor in overall emissions in regard to NO_2 and PM_{10}. This is followed by more generic background pollution, industrial emissions and domestic fuel use. Traffic hotspots are characterized by extensive traffic, often coupled with narrowly built road infrastructure, while background pollution can be caused by any source of dust emission, e.g., building sites or mining plants. Therefore, the majority of proposed pollution reduction measures focusses on traffic related abatement measures (71 per cent of overall measures included in plans), which are all of a non-technical nature. These can be classified in four categories (Wolff 2014):

1. expanding public transportation;
2. utilizing ring roads;
3. improving traffic flow;
4. implementing low-emission zones.

Our analysis shows that local authorities actually use the leeway they have for selecting appropriate measures. With an average of 14 measures proposed per plan, local authorities opt for a mixed-measures approach. The most popular choice has been the improvement of traffic flow, with 99 (72 per cent) plans following this approach. The problem here is that air pollutants are not reduced *per se* but just become more finely dispersed over a larger geographical area in order to keep with limit values, which does not effectively reduce air pollution. Fifty-nine plans (43 per cent) propose an expansion of public transport. Low emission zones (LEZ) have proven to be a drastic yet 'popular quick fix' for local governments in Germany to reduce traffic emissions (*ibid.*), applied by 56 (41 per cent) municipalities or agglomerations. LEZ represent a policy option that requires extensive efforts in terms of administration and surveillance, with far-reaching consequences and controversial benefits to the overall situation. There are problematic issues in this regard; for example, lower socioeconomic groups easily become excluded from restricted driving areas owing to associated costs (Cesaroni *et al.* 2012). Finally, the utilization of ring-roads is detected in 51 (37 per cent) of the plans considered, also leading to more finely distributed pollution.

Generally, local policy measures prove to be rather inefficient in pushing pollution below limit values (Diegmann *et al.* 2014). This result is supported by numerous statements in the concluding parts of the plans evaluated. For example, the city of Düsseldorf emphasized that even with the willingness to implement all available options on the local level, it deems it impossible to comply with the limit value for NO_2 without the support of national and/or European solutions (e.g., introduction of congestion charges, higher taxes for more polluting vehicles, ban of heavy goods traffic in inner cities, stricter emission standards for vehicles etc.) (Bezirksregierung Düsseldorf 2013). The fact that 57 plans were already in their updated version signals local authorities' inability to comply with limit values within short time frames. These findings are in line with empirical evidence from other policy fields such as water management (Koontz and Newig 2014; Liefferink *et al.* 2011). The local level in Germany is quite restricted in its administrative and political powers in the realm of air pollution abatement (Nagl *et al.* 2007) since measures available for implementation range within the four categories described above. This leads to the conclusion that the choice of the local level as sole locus for implementation is insufficient to effectively combat air pollution and comply with EU limit values. What we also observed are aspects of governance learning (*sensu* Newig *et al.* 2016) and capacity building, with municipal governments realizing that there is a strong need to integrate various cross-departmental and cross-municipal planning processes (air quality planning, environmental noise reduction planning, climate protection planning, traffic and urban planning) to achieve more effective and sustainable implementation (Blees 2011).

5.2. Patterns of multi-level governance and implementation

Table 1 provides an overview of the different aspects of sub-national implementation across the German *Länder*, which are legally responsible for air quality policy implementation. For a more comprehensive overview we subsumed the data collected on each plan under the corresponding *Land,*

Table 1. Variety in sub-national implementation ordered by problem pressure.

	POP_DEN	GOV_LEVEL	VERT_LEVEL	SPAT_REF	COOP_MUN	NO_ORG	COLL_NGO	PART_PROC
Overall means (n = 137)		0.76	2.23	10.9%	29.9%	4.4	45.3%	31.4%
Standard deviation (n = 137)		0.61	0.69	0.31	0.46	4.6	0.49	0.47
Baden-Wuerttemberg (n = 26)	971	1	2	8.0%	15%	3.0	35%	8.0%
Bavaria (n = 17)	1.129	1	3	12%	29%	5.4	24%	24%
Berlin (n = 1)	3.849	0	1	0	0	6.0	0	100%
Brandenburg (n = 6)	489	0	1	0	0	3.5	100%	33%
Bremen (n = 2)	1.603	0	1	0	0	2.5	50%	0
Hamburg (n = 1)	2.347	1	1	0	0	2.0	0	0
Hesse (n = 12)	1.330	0	2	33%	33%	4.0	0	0
Lower Saxony (n = 9)	1.104	2	1	0	0	2.4	56%	0
Mecklenburg-West Pomerania (n = 1)	1.122	0	2	0	0	7.0	0	0
North Rhine-Westphalia (n = 34)	1.452	1	3	12%	68%	12.3	100%	100%
Rhineland-Palatinate (n = 8)	1.184	0	2	0	13%	2.9	0	0
Saarland (n = 1)	1.061	2	2	100%	100%	5.0	100%	0
Saxony (n = 5)	1.175	2	2	0	0	2.8	0	0
Saxony-Anhalt (n = 4)	808	0	2	50%	50%	3.8	0	0
Schleswig-Holstein (n = 4)	1.227	0	2	0	25%	4.5	25%	0
Thuringia (n = 6)	635	0	2	0	0	3.2	17%	0

Notes: Variables relate to the individual plans, with the exception of GOV_LEVEL and VERT_LEVEL, which are defined on the level of the federal state and are thus constant for all plans in a given state. Percentages refer to relative number of plans; n = number of air quality and action plans; POP_DEN = average means of population density of affected munici-palities/agglomerations; GOV_LEVEL = level that has been assigned responsibility for implementation (0 = federal state level; 1 = governmental region level; 2 = rural district level); VERT_LEVEL = number of vertical governance levels involved; SPAT_REF = percentage of plans that identified a zone or agglomeration crossing municipal borders; COOP_MUN = percentage of plans produced in co-operation with neighbouring municipalities; NO_ORG = average number of governmental and non-governmental organizations involved; COLL_NGO = percentage of plans that co-operated with NGOs; PART_PROC = percentage of plans that incorporated participatory procedures.

based on our observation that approaches within a given *Land* do not differ hugely.

In the following, we describe and discuss the findings along the three conceptual lenses of decentralized planning, functional governance layers and participation.

5.2.1. Decentralized planning

Although the directives emphasize the local level as locus for implementation, most *Länder* established plans on the federal state level (9 out of 16 states) (variable GOV_LEVEL). Those *Länder* which have governmental regions used this level for implementation (Baden-Wurttemberg, Bavaria, Saxony until 2012), with the exception of Hesse. The remaining *Länder* implemented the directives on rural district level (Lower Saxony and Saarland). When looking at planning across vertical governance levels (variable VERT_LEVEL), we find that in most federal states (11 out of 16) at least two levels were involved in the process of plan-making, out of which three *Länder* co-operated across three levels. Including more than one level of governance presumably allows for more effective plan-making, since competences on different levels can be shared. Scholarly literature has remained scarce about the empirical effects of polycentric approaches in environmental policy implementation in Europe. However, first empirical research suggests that polycentric governance systems yield higher environmental outputs than rather monocentric governance systems (Newig and Fritsch 2009).

In reflection of the mandated planning approach, we observe that local administrations have generally been granted an expanded role in air quality governance. As responsible bodies they have gained significant influence in the implementation process through the planning and execution of pollution abatement measures, which in some cases were quite creative and innovative. On the other hand, they bear the responsibility of complying with ambitious limit values without support of higher governance levels. Following the trend of sub-national authorities as an increasingly important part of the implementation process of EU legislation, we find local level governments in a contradicting position when implementing EU air quality directives. On the one hand, local authorities are given more executive implementation power; on the other hand they lack substantial enforcement capabilities (e.g., legal and financial backing) and are unable to obligate higher levels. That being said, we find that sub-national administration effectively makes use of its leeway to choose among very different implementation structures.

5.2.2. Planning on functional governance layers

All together, only 15 plans (equalling 11 per cent) identified a zone or agglomeration that crossed municipal borders as spatial reference point for planning (variable SPAT_REF). Such cross-municipal planning was based in most cases on previously existing forms of co-operation and did not specifically address EU requirements. The city of Kassel in Hesse, for example, made use of a joint partnership agreement with neighbouring municipalities, established in 1974, and labelled this agglomeration as their spatial reference without reflecting on the situation of ambient air pollution. Only few municipalities co-operated based on a broader localization of air pollution problems. The city of Hambach in North Rhine-Westphalia, for instance, chose a particularly vast investigation area to account for all potential background pollution.

In the vast majority of plans, however, the geographical boundary was restricted to the municipality owing to the restrictedness of jurisdictional, administrative and financial powers of municipalities. In fact, this suggests a scalar mismatch because the above-mentioned spillovers (actual pollution, traffic flows, etc.) are not taken into account. In that sense, the flexibility of the spatial concept proposed by the EU's MLG approach to implementation has hardly been made use of in our sample.

However, spillovers can also be reduced by collaboration across boundaries. Of all the plans, 29.9 per cent displayed co-operation with other municipalities on a horizontal governance level (variable COOP_MUN). Co-operation can be observed in terms of joint plan-making or jointly implemented measures (such as regional low emission zones). The number of vertical governance levels involved (variable VERT_LEVEL) ranges between one and three. Next to the city states, only Lower Saxony and Brandenburg involved only one level. Most other states involved two levels, with Bavaria and North-Rhine Westphalia involving three levels. Overall, horizontal (variable COOP_MUN) and vertical (variable VERT_LEVEL) co-operation between different levels of government and administrative layers can be found in the *Länder* of North-Rhine Westphalia, Hesse, Schleswig-Holstein, Rhineland-Palatinate and Bavaria.

Taken together, high degrees of affectedness by air pollution seem to lead to more ambitious and motivated responses (for an analysis on affectedness as part of national policy adaptation to EU legislation, see Claes [2002]). In the cases listed, we see that MLG as an instrument to policy implementation, expressed by co-operation across vertical and horizontal governance levels and institutions, has been made use of and put into practice. However, the extension of planning boundaries to functional governance scales still only plays a marginal role.

5.2.3. Participatory planning
Participatory planning is indicated through the variables collaboration with non-governmental organizations (COLL_NGO) and participatory processes (PART_-PROC). For 62 plans (equalling 45 per cent) administrators chose to collaborate with non-governmental actors, which include private engineering consultancies to deal with the highly technical aspects of measuring and modelling, as well as civil society groups such as environmental non-governmental organizations

(NGOs) and climate activists. Participation commonly entailed planning work-shops during the process of plan-making or consultations on draft versions of plans. Along with that German *Länder* involved on average 4.4 governmental and non-governmental organizations in the plan-making (variable NO_ORG). The *Land* of North Rhine-Westphalia involved an average of 12.3 organizations across plans, opting for a very inclusive process design. The participatory plan-ning processes in almost half of considered plans, as well as the average number of organizations, indicate that many authorities have developed an understanding of the need to facilitate multi-organizational arrangements to solve problems that cannot be solved easily by single organizations, and engage in a purposive and official partnership involving stakeholders in a local area to address problems of local interest (Agranoff and McGuire 2003; Koontz and Newig 2014). Whether collaborative planning approaches in fact improve policy delivery needs to be subject to further research.

Regarding a broader involvement of citizens, 43 municipalities or agglom-erations (equalling 31.4 per cent) included participatory procedures in the overall plan-making, including open citizen councils, public meetings, discus-sion groups and the opportunity to comment on drafts. These involvement activities in the drafting of plans exceed the requirements of the directives, as outlined earlier, but are certainly in line with the Århus principles. Closer examination of one particular form of participation – the commenting on draft plans – showed that only a small number of all comments received were made by (lay) citizens. Mainly, citizens voiced their concerns to prevent driving restrictions. Thus, even where opportunities for citizen involvement were created, actual participation was rather low, which could be explained by the lack of understanding of personal consequences of air pollution as well as by the technical aspects of the topic as perceived by the wider public.

6. Conclusion

The policy implementation literature has regarded complex systems of multi-level governance chiefly as an obstacle to effective policy implementation. By contrast, current EU environmental policy builds on multi-level governance as a vehicle to delivery. This is in line with much of the governance literature, which propagates decentralized, spatially adapted and participatory MLG. In order to explore how the 'implementation through MLG' model plays out in practice, we have studied on-the-ground implementation of EU air quality directives in Germany. Drawing on the multi-level governance literature, we focused our research on the three arguments of decentralization, spatial fit and participation to assess how MLG could improve policy delivery rather than being conceptualized merely as an obstacle to effective implementation.

In the empirical case, the introduction of new functional governance layers and mandated planning has not led to more effective implementation of EU

environmental legislation overall, considering the continued struggle of municipalities to meet air quality targets. Our comparison of air quality and action
plans for implementing EU air quality directives in Germany has shown that
despite high levels of overall compliance in terms of legal transposition,
sub-national implementation deficits may be the result of the aforementioned
implementation approach coupled with a lack of support by national government in the German case. The contribution provides an illustration of how
MLG as a policy instrument has influenced sub-national authorities in the
interpretation and transfer of legislative requirements. The analysis shows
that significant variation exists between municipal implementation processes
across the *Länder*. By illustrating the variance in all 137 German municipalities
and agglomerations that have completed a plan, this study contributes to the
research on multi-level governance as implementation strategy, providing
insights into the problem-solving capacity of multi-level structures.

Devolving decision-making to the local level has in the case presented
proven to be ineffective in achieving target values. This is owing to local
administrations' ambiguous role in implementing EU air quality directives.
On the one hand, local authorities are given more executive implementation
power; on the other hand, they lack substantial enforcement capabilities (e.g.,
legal and financial backing) and are unable to obligate higher levels.

Considering planning on functional governance layers, we only found a
small number of plans which covered spatially adapted governance scales;
instead, planning remained largely tied to territorial jurisdictions. However,
cross-municipal co-operation as part of the mandated planning approach
did occur. A more thorough analysis of rationales and institutional prerequisites that drive the choice of governance approaches is necessary and expe-
dient. For example, one might suspect that diverging 'governance cultures'
might influence sub-national implementation designs in the implementation
of EU environmental policy in Germany.

Participatory planning practices were used to facilitate stakeholder
engagement in the process of plan-making. However, contrary to the
implementation of other environmental directives, where participatory planning is mandated, involving non-state actors in the process of air quality
and action plan-making remained voluntary and more arbitrary.

While overall the German local administration does comply with the requirement to establish air quality and action plans, we miss real ambitions to achieve
air quality objectives in the long term. For an actual rescaling of governance to
the spatial level a certain degree of legal and institutional adaptation was – or
would have been – necessary. Given the leeway conceded by the directives,
German administration has largely opted to keep with existing structures
and procedures and therefore chose a path of minimum compliance. On a
more positive side, we also observed aspects of governance learning activity
and capacity building as a result of repeated planning processes in this

particular reflexive governance approach. Here, the adaptation and flexibility of this decentralized layer shows its advantages. Municipalities are aware of the need to integrate environmental and traffic planning, and expand the scope of their efforts to successfully implement air quality legislation to neighbouring communities and municipalities in the future. We found that some municipalities take their implementation task more seriously than others.

Overall, our findings suggest that the sophisticated model of implementing air quality policy through multi-level governance bears limited success so far. This mirrors the experiences of other policy areas such as water management, which score only slightly better. Time will tell whether a more thorough adaptation of local administration to this model of policy implementation will lead to more effective policy delivery. More comparative research on the effect of the governance model versus that of contextual factors will be needed in order to assess the usefulness of policy implementation through multi-level governance.

Notes

1. The study relates to consequences of particulate matter (2007–2013).
2. The series comprises of Framework Directive 96/62/EC, 1-3 daughter Directives 1999/30/EC, 2000/69/EC, 2002/3/EC, Decision on Exchange of Information 97/101/EC and new Directive 2008/50/EC.
3. We focus our research on the two most problematic of the 13 pollutants regulated across Europe.
4. 'Zone' refers to part of the territory of a member state, as delimited by that member state for the purposes of air quality assessment and management (Preamble 16, Directive 2008/50/EC), while 'agglomeration' refers to a zone that is a conurbation with a population in excess of 250 000 inhabitants or, where the population is 250 000 inhabitants or less, with a given population density per km^2 to be established by the member states (Preamble 17, Directive 2008/50/EC).
5. http://gis.uba.de/website/umweltzonen/lrp.php (accessed May 2016).

Acknowledgements

We would like to thank two anonymous reviewers whose comments on an earlier version helped improve this manuscript.

Disclosure Statement

No potential conflict of interest was reported by the authors.

References

Agranoff, R. and McGuire, M. (2003) *Collaborative Public Management: New Strategies for Local Governments*, Washington, DC: Georgetown University Press.

Bezirksregierung Düsseldorf (ed.) (2013) *Luftreinhalteplan Düsseldorf 2013*, Düsseldorf: Bezirksregierung Düsseldorf.

Blees, V. (2011) 'Luftreinhaltung: Herausforderung für die kommunale Verkehrsentwicklungsplanung – Umwelt- und Verkehrsplanung am Beispiel der Region Frankfurt Rhein Main', *Kolloquium Luftqualität an Straßen 2011*, Bergisch-Gladbach: Bundesanstalt für Straßenwesen (BASt).

Borghetto, E. and Franchino, F. (2010) 'The role of subnational authorities in the implementation of EU directives', *Journal of European Public Policy* 17(6): 759–80.

Börzel, T. (1998) 'Shifting or sharing the burden? The implementation of EU environmental policy in Spain and Germany', *European Planning Studies* 6(5): 537–53.

Brody, S. D., Godschalk, D. R. and Burby, R. J. (2003) 'Mandating citizen participation in plan making. Six strategic planning choices', *Journal of the American Planning Association* 69(3): 245–64.

Busch, S., Lenschow, A. and Mehl, C. (2012) *'The Europeanisation of urban air quality policy. EU impact on patterns of politics'*, Paper presented at the UACES Conference 'Exchanging Ideas on Europe 2012. Old Borders – New Frontiers', Passau, Germany, 3–5 September.

Cancik, P. (2011) 'Europäische Luftreinhaltung - zur zweiten Phase der Implementation', *Zeitschrift für Umweltrecht* 2011(6): 283–96.

Cesaroni, G., Boogard, H., Jonkers, S., Porta, D., Badaloni, C., Cattani, G., Forastiere, F. and Hoek, G. (2012) 'Health benefits of traffic-related air pollution reduction in different socioeconomic groups: the effect of low-emission zoning in Rome', *Occupational & Environmental Medicine* 69: 133–39.

Claes, D. H. (2002) 'The process of Europeanization: Norway and the internal energy market', *Journal of Public Policy* 22(3): 299–323.

Diegmann, V., Pfäfflin, F. and Wursthorn, H. (eds) (2014) Bestandsaufnahme und Wirksamkeit von Maßnahmen der Luftreinhaltung, Dessau-Roßlau: Umweltbundesamt.

Durner, W. and Ludwig, R. (2008) 'Paradigmenwechsel in der europäischen Umweltrechtsetzung? Überlegungen zu Bedeutung und Grundstrukturen des Instruments der Maßnahmenplanung im neueren Umweltrecht der Gemeinschaft', *Natur und Recht* 30: 457–67.

European Commission (2010) 'Smart regulation in the European Union', *COM(2010) 543 final*, 8 October, Brussels.

European Commission (2015a) 'Environment report shows benefits of EU action', *Press Release IP/15/4534*

European Commission (2015b) 'Commission refers Belgium and Bulgaria to Court and gives Sweden a final warning over poor air quality', *Press Release IP/15/5197*

Haus, M. and Zimmermann, K. (2007) 'Die Feinstaubproblematik als Governance-Herausforderung für die lokale Umweltpolitik?' in K. Jacob et al. (eds.), Politik und Umwelt 39, Wiesbaden: VS Verlag für Sozialwissenschaften, pp. 243–61.

Héritier, A. (1999) *Policy-making and Diversity in Europe: Escaping Deadlock*, Cambridge: Cambridge University Press.

Hill, M. and Hupe, P. (2014) Implementing Public Policy. An Introduction to the Study of Operational Governance, London: SAGE Publications.

Holzinger, K., Knill, C. and Lenschow, A. (2009) 'Governance in EU environmental policy', in: I. Tömmel and A. Verdun (eds), Innovative Governance in the European Union, Lynne Rienner: Boulder, pp. 45–61.

Hooghe, L. and Marks, G. (2003) 'Unraveling the central state, but how? types of multi-level governance', American Political Science Review 97(2): 233–43.

Hupe, P. and Hill, M. (2016) 'And the rest is implementation'. comparing approaches to what happens in policy processes beyond great expectations', Public Policy and Administration 31(2): 103–21.

Jordan, A. (1999) 'The implementation of EU environmental policy; a policy problem without a political solution?' Environment and Planning C: Government and Policy 17: 69–90.

Jordan, A., Wurzel, R. K. W. and Zito, A. (2005) 'The rise of 'new' policy instruments in comparative perspective: has governance eclipsed government?' Political Studies 53: 477–96.

Kallweit, D. and Bünger, B. (2015) 'Feinstaub macht krank und kostet Leben – Berechnung jährlich entstehender Kosten durch die Feinstaubbelastung in Deutschland', in UMID: Umwelt und Mensch – Informationsdienst 2, pp. 96–72.

Kiser, L.L. and Ostrom, E. (1982) 'The three worlds of action: a metatheoretical synthesis of institutional approaches', in E. Ostrom (ed.), Strategies of Political Inquiry, Beverly Hills: Sage, pp. 179–222.

Knill, C. and Liefferink, D. (2007) Environmental Politics in the European Union: Policy-Making, Implementation and Patterns of Multi-Level Governance, Manchester: Manchester University Press.

Kok, K. and Veldkamp, T. (2011) 'Scale and governance: conceptual considerations and practical implications', Ecology and Society 16(2): 23, available at https://www.ecologyandsociety.org/vol16/iss2/art23/main.html.

Koontz, T. M. and Newig, J. (2014) 'From planning to implementation: top down and bottom up approaches for collaborative watershed management', Policy Studies Journal 42(3): 416–42.

Larson, A. M. and Ribot, J. C. (2004) 'Democratic decentralisation through a natural resource lens: an introduction', The European Journal of Development Research 16(1): 1–25.

Leventon, J. (2015) 'Explaining implementation deficits through multi-level governance in the EU's new member states: EU limits for arsenic in drinking water in Hungary', Journal of Environmental Planning and Management 58(7): 1137–53.

Lidskog, R. and Sundqvist, G. (2011) 'Transboundary air pollution policy in transition', in R. Lidskog and G. Sundqvist (eds.), Governing the Air: The Dynamics of Science, Policy, and Citizen Interaction, Cambridge, MA: MIT Press, pp. 1–38.

Liefferink, D., Wiering, M. and Uitenboogaart, Y. (2011) 'The EU water framework directive: a multi-dimensional analysis of implementation and domestic impact', Land Use Policy 28: 712–22.

Mandelkern Group (2001) 'Report on better regulation', Final report, 13 November.

Milio, S. (2010) From Policy to Implementation in the European Union. The Challenge of the Multi-Level Governance System, London, New York: I.B. Tauris Publishers.

Moss, T. (2012) 'Spatial fit, from panacea to practice: implementing the EU water framework directive', Ecology and Society 17: 1–12.

Nagl, C., Mossmann, L. and Schneider, J. (2007) Assessment of Plans and Programmes Reported Under 1996/62/EC – Final Report, Vienna: Umweltbundesamt.

Newig, J. and O. Fritsch (2009) 'Environmental governance: participatory, multi-level – and effective?' Environmental Policy and Governance 19(3): 197–214.

Newig, J. and Koontz, T.M. (2014) 'Multi-level governance, policy implementation and participation: the EU's mandated participatory planning approach to implementing environmental policy', Journal of European Public Policy 21(2): 248–67.

Newig, J., Kochskämper, E., Challies, E. and Jager, N.W. (2016) 'Exploring governance learning: how policymakers draw on evidence, experience and intuition in designing participatory flood risk planning', Environmental Science & Policy 55: 353–60.

Ostrom, E. (1999) 'Coping with tragedies of the commons', Annual Review of Political Science 2: 493–535.

Ostrom, E. (2010) 'Polycentric systems for coping with collective action and global environmental change', Global Environmental Change 20: 550–57.

Ostrom, V., Tiebout, C.M., and Warren, R. (1961) 'The organization of government in metropolitan areas: a theoretical inquiry', American Political Science Review 55 (4): 831–42.

Piattoni, S. (2010) The Theory of Multi-Level Governance. Conceptual, Empirical, and Normative Challenges, Oxford: Oxford University Press.

Pressman, J. L. and Wildavsky, A. (1984 [1973]) Implementation: How Great Expectations in Washington are Dashed in Oakland, Berkeley: University of California Press.

Pridham, G. (1996) 'Environmental policies and problems of european legislation in Southern Europe', South European Society and Politics, 1(1): 47–73.

Pülzl, H. and Treib, O. (2007) 'Policy implementation', in F. Fischer, G.J. Miller and M.S. Sidney (eds.), Handbook of Public Policy Analysis, New York: Dekker, pp. 89–108.

Schäffer, H. (1992) 'Bestandsaufnahme und weitere Wege der kooperativen Föderalismusreform (1963-1991)', in P. Pernthaler (ed.), Neue Wege der Föderalismusreform (Schriftenreihe des Instituts für Föderalismusforschung, Vol. 51), Vienna: Wilhelm Braumüller Universitäts-Verlagsbuchhandlung, pp. 13–87.

Thomann, E. and Sager, F. (2017). 'Toward a better understanding of implementation performance in the EU multilevel system', Journal of European Public Policy, doi:10. 1080/13501763.2017.1314542.

Thomann, E. and Zhelyazkova, A. (2017). 'Moving beyond (non-)compliance: the customization of European Union policies in 27 countries', Journal of European Public Policy, doi:10.1080/13501763.2017.1314536.

UBA (2014) 'Fristverlängerung NO_2 (Stand Oktober 2014)': http://www.umweltbundesamt.de/themen/luft/regelungen-strategien/luftreinhaltung-in-der-eu (last accessed 26 March 2016).

WHO/OECD (2015) Economic Cost of the Health Impact of Air Pollution in Europe: Clean Air, Health and Wealth, Copenhagen: WHO Regional Office for Europe.

Wolff, H. (2014) 'Keep your clunker in the suburb: low-emission zones and adoption of Green vehicles', The Economic Journal 124: F481–F512.

Young, O.R. (2002) The Institutional Dimensions of Environmental Change: Fit, Interplay, and Scale, Cambridge, MA: MIT Press.

ⓐ OPEN ACCESS

Europe at the frontline: analysing street-level motivations for the use of European Union migration law

Nora Dörrenbächer

ABSTRACT

This contribution investigates what motivates the use of European Union (EU) law at the street level of migration law implementation. The street level is a crucial venue for EU implementation because lower-level implementers critically influence the level of EU compliance eventually achieved. Employing a bottom–up approach towards implementation, the article combines insights from social psychology and the street-level literature to develop expectations about the relation between individuals' motivations and their use of EU law. The study investigates through qualitative interviews to what extent German migration administrators use EU law in three multilevel decision contexts. The main findings are that uses of EU law vary across contexts and individual implementers. Particularly when national regulatory frameworks are ambiguous, substantive moral norms and instrumental motivations trigger some implementers to rely on EU law. This reliance even has the potential to correct for problematic transposition.

Introduction

European Union (EU) law increasingly spreads into policy areas which used to be at the core of national law. A topical example is EU migration law which gradually shapes domestic legislation (Boswell and Geddes 2011; Zaun 2016). However, the Union lacks an implementation apparatus and relies on national administrations to apply its laws (Treib 2014: 6). This indirect implementation system leads to the question of whether individual national administrations turn into 'double-hatted' agents, serving a national and a European master (Egeberg and Trondal 2009), and to what extent they become 'guardians of EU law' (Mastenbroek 2017).

ⓑ Supplemental data for this article can be accessed https://doi.org/10.1080/13501763.2017.1314535.

This is an Open Access article distributed under the terms of the Creative Commons Attribution-NonCommercial-NoDerivatives License (http://creativecommons.org/licenses/by-nc-nd/4.0/), which permits non-commercial re-use, distribution, and reproduction in any medium, provided the original work is properly cited, and is not altered, transformed, or built upon in any way.

These questions have been analysed mainly for higher-level officials at the ministry level (e.g., Bach *et al.* 2015). Respectively, in EU implementation studies the practices of lower-level implementers remain largely unexplored (but see Gulbrandsen 2011). However, since Lipsky's (1980) seminal work, it is widely acknowledged that street-level implementers at the 'frontline', between the laws in the books and actual practice crucially influence the final outcome of policies.

EU law places street-level implementers at a second frontline, namely between domestic and EU regulatory frameworks. The second frontline can lead to new legal ambiguities because much EU law introduces fuzzy legal concepts (Treib 2014: 6), and national legislators frequently fail to transpose EU law in time, or do so in non-compliant ways (Angelova *et al.* 2012; Treib 2014). This can make EU law directly effective and raises the question: to what extent do street-level implementers use EU law to solve legal ambiguity and what motivates them when doing so?

By investigating this question, this study takes up the call by Woll and Jacquot (2010: 113) to explore variation in individuals' motivations for using EU law. So far, most compliance studies have adopted top–down perspectives that focus on the member state level to explain variation in EU implementation (Thomann and Sager 2017a). These studies have relied on rationalist or constructivist approaches (Dimitrova and Rhinard 2005; Mastenbroek and Kaeding 2006) assuming institutional logics of consequentiality or appropriateness (March and Olsen 1998).

Similarly, behavioural perspectives on frontline implementation (Maynard-Moody and Musheno 2012; Tummers *et al.* 2016) and social psychology studies (Tyler 2006) distinguish between *instrumental* and *normative motivations* to explain behaviour. Whereas actors driven by instrumental motivations evaluate risks connected to different applications of the law, actors driven by normative motivations take guidance from procedural or substantive norms. These conceptualizations overlap with institutional logics of consequentiality and appropriateness. While institutional actor logics are concerned with organizations and individuals, the social psychology literature has been proven to be particularly useful to investigate individual level motivations. Therefore, the latter perspective is used in this study.

Applied to the EU context, it is expected that instrumental motivations discourage use of EU law, but normative motivations can generate uses of EU law. By adding the behavioural perspective to EU implementation, this study contributes to clarify the role of and relationship between the institutional actor logics at the micro level of EU implementation. Additionally, the study adds to the emerging bottom–up approaches in EU implementation studies that go beyond legal compliance (Thomann 2015; Thomann and Zhelyazkova 2017; Thomann and Sager 2017a).

Furthermore, this study tackles the policy sector bias of many EU implementation studies (Treib 2014: 17; Gollata and Newig 2017) by exploring the use of EU law and implementation motivations in the topical context of EU migration law. EU migration law received most explicit attention in studies that focused on the Europeanization of the multilevel legal context (Boswell and Geddes 2011; Zaun 2016). The insights of these studies and the more general street-level migration literature, suggest that the field constitutes a crucial case for bottom–up investigations of motivations. First, migration law requires considerable street-level implementation (Ellermann 2006; Eule 2014). Second, the gradual addition of EU law adds a new liberal legal level to domestic regulations (Bonjour and Vink 2013). Member states are reluctant to adjust their regulatory frameworks to new EU pressure, leading to new ambiguity at the street level. Thus, when street-level implementers decide on residence permits, they not only affect the life chances of individual migrants, but they also determine to what extent EU migration laws become practice. Third, the normatively laden field of migration provides good conditions to observe variation in motivations because migration law implementers are often confronted with conflicting positions between their role as loyal implementers and their personal normative considerations (Düvell and Jordan 2003).

The study investigates decision-making of case workers of the foreign registration offices (*Ausländerbehörden*) of the German *Bundesland* of North Rhine-Westphalia. These case workers decide on residence permits while operating at a local level in decentralized administrative structure with much face-to-face interaction with their clients (Ellermann 2006; Eule 2014). Such working contexts are prone for variation in motivations.

Drawing on qualitative interviews with 21 implementers in ten *Ausländerbehörden*, the analysis reveals that street-level implementers use EU law to varying degrees. Generally, implementers do not use EU law by extending their discretion in nationally tightly regulated contexts, or by explicitly contradict national regulatory frameworks. However, when national regulations remain unclear, many implementers use EU law next to national law. In line with the expectations, implementers with pronounced substantive normative motivations use the legal levels creatively. In contrast to the expectations, also instrumental motivations trigger sometimes reliance on EU law. Procedural norms are limited in triggering uses of EU law.

Theorizing motivations for street-level use of EU law

During street-level implementation use of EU law can be conceptualized as reliance on the EU regulatory framework as a frame of reference during decision making. The availability of EU law as legal options depends on the multilevel legal context in which implementers operate. When EU and national laws are detailed and in line with each other, implementers will draw on the domestic regulatory framework established by the domestic principal to which they are directly accountable.

However, in at least three contexts EU law might play a role for street-level implementers. Firstly, EU law can demand margins of discretion beyond national law. Secondly, national law can provide frameworks that stand plainly in tension with EU law. Finally, when EU legislation is superficially incorporated, the national regulatory frameworks can be less explicit than EU rules. In these situations, implementers are confronted with ambiguity which they may resolve by relying on domestic regulations, EU law or by combining the frameworks.

In order to develop expectations about the use of EU law, a useful starting point is the social psychology literature (Tyler 2006). Combining the perspectives of this literature with insights of the street-level literature allows to group implementation motivations into instrumental and normative implementation motivations.

Instrumental motivations, to begin with, refer to the desire to avoid punishment and to evade risks (Winter and May 2001). In the street-level bureaucracy literature such motivations are prominently assumed by Lipsky (1980). He has argued that implementers are primarily driven by the desire to cope with limited resources, leading to routines, rationing services and other coping strategies. Thus, implementers focus on measurable indicators with low risks to be questioned by the outside world (*ibid.*, Hood 2011). Risks refer to punishments by political principals and courts, or personal consequences such as reputation loss and extra workload.

Applying this instrumental perspective to the multilevel legal context, one can assume that implementers are accountable to national principals. National principals will prefer implementers to rely closely on national goals (Huber and Shipan 2002). Judicial, legislative and executive checks will discourage implementers to bypass national law. Since there might be monetary and political costs if EU law is applied inconsistently, implementers will perceive it to be risky to stretch their competences by interpreting EU law. Moreover, mastering EU law constitutes extra work. Thus, implementers will continue to rely on national law and leave it to courts to challenge the national level for potentially non-compliant transposition.

This effect will be strengthened by the fact that there is no EU principal who directly scrutinizes street-level behaviour. Hence, there are no direct risks for implementers of being punished by EU principals for not relying on EU law. In sum, the instrumental perspective suggests that street-level implementers will consider it to be the safest choice to rely on national law, leading to the first expectation:

Expectation 1: Street-level implementers who are motivated by instrumental considerations do not use EU law to resolve ambiguities of the multilevel legal context.

In addition to instrumental motivations, research has shown that *normative motivations* play a crucial role in how people respond to the law (May 2005; Tyler 2006).

From a *procedural normative perspective*, individuals are loyal to the legal sources they consider legitimate (Tyler 2006). Loyalty as the primary bureaucratic motivation is seated deeply in Weberian views on bureaucracy. In street-level studies, loyalty is highlighted as a professional imperative according to which implementers see themselves as dutiful servants of the legitimated authority (Brodkin 1997).

Under multilevel legal ambiguity, implementers evaluate which legal source is most legitimate. If loyalties rest on the national level, implementers will continue to rely on domestic regulatory frameworks (see Mastenbroek 2017). Yet, implementers might have internalized that EU law is superior to national law and consider it as the legitimate legal source above national law. If implementers develop feelings of loyalty towards EU law, they rely on EU law, even if there are no direct benefits in taking it into account.

Higher administrators seem to develop only weak EU loyalties, even if they have direct contact with EU institutions (Egeberg and Trondal 2009; Mastenbroek 2017). At the street level, the distance to EU institutions and national policy making is wide. Thus, street-level implementers might have weaker attachments to national loyalties in the first place, leading to the second expectation:

> Expectation 2: Street-level implementers who are motivated by a sense of EU loyalty use EU law to resolve ambiguities of the multi-level legal context.

Finally, *substantive normative motivations*, which Tyler (2006) labels *morality considerations,* are found to be an important motivation for obeying laws. At the street-level, Hertogh (2009) has observed that regardless of whether or not it is the law, implementers are often committed to certain norms owing to personal feelings of justice (see also Tummers 2011). The close contact to real cases, make empathy and justice evaluations particularly likely to materialize (May 2005; Winter and May 2001). This can trigger street-level implementers to rely on moral judgments to make up for alleged limitations of national policies (Keiser and Soss 1998), using formal laws only as formal justification (Maynard-Moody and Musheno 2003).

Arguably, EU law offers implementers a new tool box to pick and choose within the web of national, local and EU laws those arguments that correspond best to their feeling of justice. More concretely, in case national law suggests a negative decision on a case, but an implementer has strong feelings of justice that point at a positive outcome, liberal EU law might provide for new legal arguments which the implementer can use to circumvent restrictive national laws. Vice versa, the domestic regulatory framework will be used if it fits implementers' justice evaluations. Thus, the following can be expected:

Expectation 3: Street-level implementers who are motivated by strong personal perceptions of justice pick and choose between national and EU law to resolve ambiguities of the multi-level legal context.

Method and data

A theory-driven explorative approach is adopted to investigate the expectations. This allows plausible connections of mechanisms that have previously not been explored or understood (Reiter 2013: 7). For explorative research, case selection should focus on cases for which the expected causal mechanism is likely to be most evident (*ibid.*).

Three scope conditions are necessary for the established expectations to apply. First, the policy field needs to have a multilevel legal character and frontline implementers are confronted with ambiguous domestic and EU regulatory frameworks. Second, street-level implementers have to have some discretion. Otherwise, instrumental motivations may dominate decision making. Finally, for normative motivations to play a role, the field needs to be normatively laden to challenge loyalties and to trigger feelings of justice.

Migration law fulfils these scope conditions particularly well and can be considered as a crucial case (Eckstein 1975). First, migration law is conducted at a multitude of levels, including the international, the European, the national, the regional and the local (Lahav and Guiraudon 2006). As a relatively young field of EU harmonization, it is highly dynamic and national implementers are constantly confronted with new multilevel legal frameworks and realities (Zaun 2016). Tension between the different levels are common because member states are reluctant to transpose liberal EU migration laws into their more restrictive national laws (Bonjour and Vink 2013). Additionally, many EU migration laws and the ensuing interpretations by the Court of Justice of the European Union (CJEU) established fuzzy legal concepts that are directly applicable for lower-level implementers.

Second, the policy field provides for considerable street-level discretion because it is very client intensive (Ellermann 2006; Eule 2014). Despite convergence of migration laws across the EU, decision-making in migration agencies has been highlighted as very diverse (Jordan *et al.* 2003). While migration laws appear to be clear on paper, they often lead to variation in practice, when implementers decide on individual migrants (*ibid.*).

Finally, the field is salient and normatively laden. Conflicting norms related to human rights, public welfare and security often clash with each other, and have to be resolved during implementation (Düvell and Jordan 2003; Eule 2014).

Overall, tension between national and EU migration regulations, wide discretion and the normatively laden context offer potential for competing street-level motivations. Thus, if we do not find street-level implementers who use EU law in this policy field, it is unlikely that implementers in more technical fields use EU law.

The expectations are investigated among German street-level implementers of the *Bundesland* of North Rhine-Westphalia (NRW). This administrative context constitutes again a crucial case. Germany has a decentralized migration implementation system and NRW established a particularly decentralized structure. Street-level implementation is organized and conducted in foreign registration offices (*Ausländerbehörden*) at county and city level. The federal level is the main legislator, and is responsible for transposition of EU norms. The *Länder* issue decrees that detail the federal law. There is no direct national oversight over the *Ausländerbehörden*, and only indirect oversight from five district governments. Thus, there is considerable street-level discretion.

Additionally, while there is a trend towards more e-service provision in many traditional street-level bureaucracies (Bovens and Zouridis 2002), the implementers in this study are typical street-level implementers. They have face-to-face contact with their clients and rely little on computer-assisted case assessment. Overall, the large margins of discretion and the personal contact provide particularly good conditions for normative motivations.

Important to note is that focusing on a single policy sector within a single member state limits the generalizability of the motivations found in this study. Motivations can derive from a variety of sources, such as national culture, organizational context and policy area (Jordan *et al.* 2003). However, the purpose of this study is to investigate how different motivations relate to the use of EU law. Thus, adding cross-country or sectoral variation would pose the danger of influencing both motivations and the use of EU law. This would make it difficult to disentangle the effects.

A qualitative data collection strategy was adopted. Qualitative methods allow uncovering the mechanisms behind decision-making and contributing to theory refinement (George and Bennett 2006). In-depth interviews with 21 implementers in 10 *Ausländerbehörden* were conducted in spring 2015. At each location a senior implementer (department leader) and in most locations one or two regular decision-makers were interviewed (see the Online Appendix). Interviews lasted 40–160 minutes; records were transcribed into English. Half the interviews were conducted individually, the other half in pairs or groups of three, permitting respondents to be interviewed in their daily working environment and to test whether responses differed when being observed by colleagues.

The interviews were semi-structured and left room for examples of difficult cases and personal evaluations of the respondents. This contributed to an in-depth image of the complex interplay between motivations, decision-making and the use of EU law. In order to measure the dependent variable – use of EU law – respondents were asked how they go about decision-making in three multilevel legal scenarios. The scenarios were tackled in open-ended questions in which the researcher sketched typical decision-making contexts (Table 1). Respondents were asked to specify their decision-making practices and detail their room for manoeuvre. Probing was used to investigate which legal tools respondents would use to take decisions and to what extent EU law would be used.

The first scenario concerned a situation where EU and national law were in line with each other, but EU law demands slightly more administrative discretion. The second scenario constituted a case in which EU law stands in tension with national guidelines. The third scenario captured a context of tension with vague national guidelines. The substances of the scenarios are described below.

Implementation motivations were investigated by encouraging respondents through open-ended questions to elaborate on what drives them when taking decisions, with what they struggle when taking decisions and what constitutes good decision-making. Based on examples and anecdotes told by the respondents, a list of motivational cues was established (see the Online Appendix). Motivational cues are arguments and justifications given explicitly or implicitly by the respondents to explain their practices. The cues were grouped under common themes. Motivations were instrumental, if respondents pointed at workload, risks of overstepping their competences, the importance that decisions have standing in court, or possible punishments. Risks creating precedent cases and risks to harm the national interest and/or the interests of the national legislator were inductively classified as intermediate motivations between instrumental and national loyalty motivations.

Motivations were placed under EU loyalty if respondents mentioned obligations and loyalty related to supremacy of EU law. Finally, motivations were grouped under the heading of substantive normative motivations when respondents invoked emotions or personal feelings of fairness to motivate their implementation practices. Respondents could be guided by complex combinations of motivations.

Analysis

The case studies are structured as follows. The first part outlines the substance of the three legal scenarios. The next part presents decision-making practices of the respondents and their use of EU law. The last part analyses the underlying implementation motivations in light of the established expectations.

Multilevel legal scenarios

Table 1 summarizes the substance of the EU and national legal framework of the three decision-making scenarios discussed with the respondents.

Table 1. Three legal scenarios.

Legal scenario	Main EU law	Main national law	Decision scenario
Scenario 1	**Income requirement for third country family reunification visa**		
Discretionary EU law	Member states may demand from sponsor of third country family reunification a minimum income as guiding criterion for granting the visa (Family Reunification Directive 2003/86 EC Art 7.1.) Guiding criterion may not be used as hard benchmark to limit right of family reunification (CJEU ruling *Chakroun*) Evaluations have to take individual circumstances and needs of family into account (CJEU ruling *Chakroun*)	Foreign registration offices required to use standard calculation to determine guiding benchmark (German Residence Act. Art. 27, Art. 5.1.1, Administrative Guidelines Art 2.3.4) Administrative decisions should be prognosis decision, evaluating if family can sustain itself in the future (national Administrative Guidelines Art 2.3.3) National interpretation of *Chakroun*: tax free amounts may no longer be used to the disadvantage of the applicants (BVerwG 1 C 20.09 and 1 C 21.09)	How does the case worker decide on the visa when the income of the sponsor remains 5-10 euro below the calculated monthly national benchmarks?
Scenario 2	**Language requirement for Turkish citizens for family reunification visa**		
Tension between EU and national law with explicit instructions	Member states may require third country nationals to comply with integration measures (Family Reunification Directive Art 6.2) German language requirements not compliant with the standstill clause of Turkey Association Agreement (CJEU ruling *Dogan*)	Language certificate is required for all visa for family reunification including Turkish citizens (Art 30. 1AufthG) National interpretation of *Dogan*: Implementation instruction from the Ministry of External Affairs: Implementers should not change their practices regarding Turkish citizens. Existing exceptions based on hardship cases are stressed.	How does the case work decide on the visa when the spouse of a Turkish citizen does not provide for the German language requirement?
Scenario 3	**Application of administrative fees for Turkish citizens and examples of transposition gaps**		
Tension between EU and national law with inexplicit national regulatory framework	a) Administrative fees for residence permits for Turkish citizens have to be in line with Turkey Association Agreement (see CJEU case *Sahin*)	a) Several years national legislators declared *Sahin* ruling not applicable to Germany. National ruling (BVerwG 1 C 12.12) eventually confirmed *Sahin* but it	a) How did the office handle the intermediate period between a national solution and the EU obligations?

(Continued)

Table 1. Continued.

Legal scenario	Main EU law	Main national law	Decision scenario
		took time until legislator formally clarified appropriate fees	b) How does the case worker handle situations in which EU directives and rulings are not fully transposed?
		b) late transposition and implicit EU principles in transposition laws	

The first scenario was taken from the field of family migration and related to the evaluation of the income requirement for visas for third country family reunification. The *Ausländerbehörden* decide on the visa together with the diplomatic missions abroad. One condition for the visa is a sufficient income of the sponsor. Both EU and national law demand an individual evaluation of the income condition. Yet EU law demands a slightly more discretionary approach to this condition than national law, by emphasizing an evaluation of the needs of each individual applicant (see CJEU ruling in *Chakroun*). Respondents were asked if, and under which conditions, they would agree to a visa application if applicants earn less than required by the national benchmarks.

The second scenario was also taken from the field of family migration and concerns the so-called language requirement for the visa of family reunification. The CJEU in *Dogan* has explicitly challenged the German obligations in light of the Turkey Association Agreement, suggesting that language requirements for Turkish citizens are not in line with EU law. However, the national legislator explicitly instructed its administrations not to change their practices. Respondents were asked if they would agree to a visa application of a Turkish applicant, provided the spouse had no language certificate.

For the third scenario, several situations were discussed. For example, several court rulings found that the administrative fees demanded for Turkish residence permits are too high under the Turkey Association Agreement. However, it took the legislator a considerable period of time to provide instructions of how to handle the fees. Here, the leaderships of the foreign registration offices were asked how they handled the intermediate period. In order to explore practices beyond the office leaders, respondents were asked to elaborate on their practices in the case that EU directives and CJEU rulings are not transposed into national law.

The three scenarios constitute everyday decision-making in a foreign registration office. The focus on family migration law was based on the fact that family migration constitutes a crucial source of migration and EU family migration law is relatively developed (Bonjour and Vink 2013). Moreover, the three scenarios do not directly touch upon aspects related to the current refugee crisis.

Scenario one: use of discretionary EU law

Starting with practices regarding the income requirement, all respondents stressed that they take the individual circumstances of applicants into account. However, respondents differed widely in interpreting their room for manoeuvre. At least seven respondents approached the criteria from a relatively discretionary perspective, while 10 took more restrictive approaches.

Respondents with discretionary approaches indicated that a discrepancy of around 5–8 euros per month below the national income benchmark constituts no problem. If they believed applicants can otherwise sustain themselves, they would still approve the visa application. With a positive prognosis, three respondents would even accept applicants up to 50–100 euros or 10 per cent below the calculated requirement. As one respondent commented:

> These margins are not explicitly codified … If there are 50 euros missing, we would decide that we take the risk that this family will not draw on social benefits for these 50 euros. We internally decided that you cannot take these requirements as hard benchmarks where one cent or euro less leads automatically to a rejection. (Resp._B1)

The more restrictive respondents would normally not agree to a visa if the sponsor's income was below the calculated benchmark. As one respondent explained:

> When someone has 10 euro less, we no longer have the option to decide positively. … We strictly rely on the legal demands. I cannot paint a nice picture if the requirements are not fulfilled. (Resp._I1)

Coming to the use of EU law, it became clear that even though respondents differed considerably in how lenient they were with the income requirement, discretion was not informed by EU law but by federal court rulings. Even if respondents argued closely in line with the *Chakroun* ruling (Resp._B1), the ruling was mostly not explicitly mentioned.

Two respondents mentioned national rulings that referred to *Chakroun*, but they considered *Chakroun* as a restriction to their scope of action that no longer allowed them to include tax-free amounts in the income benchmark. One respondent claimed that this liberalization would trigger him to consider the calculated benchmark now more restrictively (Resp._E1). Only one respondent referred explicitly to *Chakroun*. However, even he did not use the ruling to extent his room for manoeuvre beyond national law (Resp.-_C1). Overall, EU law was not used explicitly in case of discretionary EU law.

Scenario two: use of EU law under tension with explicit national instructions

Practices regarding the language requirements differed only slightly among respondents. Whereas some argued that the embassies are responsible for the language requirement, other respondents saw their role in checking this condition more actively. Overall, respondents referred more often to EU law than in the previous scenario. The *Dogan* ruling was mentioned by most respondents. However, eventually all but one respondent gave priority to the national interpretation of the judgment. Some respondents pointed to the wording of the CJEU ruling to justify the national interpretation (Resp._F1, I1). Other respondents agreed that there is a conflict between the legal levels, but as one respondent explained:

> If the national legislator eventually issues instructions for us, I try to orientate myself on that and not explicitly contradict the national interpretation. (Resp._J1)

Thus, while some respondents questioned the national interpretations in light of EU law (Resp._A1), they still pointed at the national regulatory framework as the ultimate decision tool. Only one respondent did not mention the national interpretations and only referred to the CJEU ruling (Resp._C1). Overall, under legal conflict between EU law and explicit national regulatory frameworks, respondents were surprisingly aware of EU law, but eventually they relied on the national regulatory framework or pointed to the diplomatic missions as ultimate decision-makers.

Scenario three: use of EU law with inexplicit national regulatory framework

Concerning situations in which national regulatory frameworks remain inexplicit, respondents indicated highly diverse practices. Regarding the fees for Turkish applicants, the leadership of some of the foreign registration offices decided to waive the fees before there were explicit national instructions (Location_C). Other office leaders decided to keep demanding the fees awaiting an official adjustment of national regulations (Location_I, E). More generally, when EU legislation or CJEU rulings are not explicitly transposed, six respondents indicated that for them EU law is not relevant. As these respondents put it, 'we are mainly implementers of national law' (Resp._A2) or 'CJEU rulings confront us sometimes with the situation that national law is no longer applicable, but for us legally binding are of course only the national laws' (Resp._D1).

However, in situations in which national regulations are missing or not clear, the majority of respondents described that they would use EU law next to national law. As one respondent explained:

> The EU has established some general legal principles which somehow are implied in our national law, but you cannot read them anywhere. In these cases we more or less use our discretion to read the national law in light of the principles which derive out of EU law or CJEU rulings. (Resp._F1)

Two respondents even pointed out how they themselves or their colleagues sometimes use EU directives which are not yet transposed (Resp._J1; Resp._A1). As Respondent A1 claimed:

> The problem in Germany is that almost all EU requirements are transposed in the last minute or even with delay. I feel this is a mentality issue of the German legislator, to hope that nobody will notice. So, if a new ruling or directive emerges, we try to take this into account even it is not yet part of the German law or administrative guidelines. Even if the EU law conflicts with the national law we take the EU rules into account.

In sum, when national law does not explicitly define implementation guidelines, implementers were surprisingly open to EU law as an additional source of decision-making. Table 2 summarizes the use of EU law across the scenarios.

Implementation motivations and the use of EU law

In the following, the established expectations are explored. Starting with *instrumental motivations*, the interviews showed that the most important guidance for respondents was that their decisions have standing in front of national courts. Regarding the income requirement, several respondents argued that national courts demand a restrictive approach. Therefore, they could not apply the condition in a discretionary way (Resp._D1). Additionally, several respondents argued that they are afraid that it would backfire on them, and that social welfare offices would ask them critical questions if applicants eventually relied on social welfare (Resp._F1; Resp._F2; Resp._E1; Resp._J2). In line with the expectation, these respondents did not see it as an option to extend their room for manoeuvre by using EU law.

Instrumental motivations were articulated even more explicitly when respondents reflected on their practices for the second scenario. Many respondents argued that they consider it risky to apply original EU jurisprudence when the national legislator provided explicit instructions. For example, six respondents highlighted that interpreting EU law goes beyond

Table 2. Use of EU law across scenarios.

Legal context	Legal scenario	Use of EU law
Discretionary EU law	Income criterion for third country family reunification	Little use
Tension between EU and national law with explicit national instructions	Language requirement for Turkish family reunification	Active reference but eventual reliance on national instructions
Tension between EU and national law with inexplicit national regulatory framework	Administrative fees for Turkish citizens and gaps in transposition law	Some very actively use EU law by correcting problematic transposition, most respondents combine national and EU instructions

their competences as implementers (Resp._I1; Resp._I2; Resp._J1; Resp._J2; Resp._H1; Resp._H2). Overall, risk, staying within the assigned competences and securing standing in front of the court were considerations which triggered reluctant approaches towards EU law and were dominant among leading and regular decision-makers.

However, contrary to the first expectation, instrumental motivations were also articulated by respondents in leadership positions who used EU law in the third scenario. As one respondent argued:

> In terms of the direct results it can be a safe choice for us to follow the (national and local) rules. However, it does not always go well in the long run. Sometimes it leads eventually to a change in the rules if there are too many (EU) rulings. That leaves us with a mess if we took a lot of decisions based on old rules … We are always in between and eventually we have to take responsibilities for messy decisions which we did not cause. … So we evaluate the consequences of the different legal options and then decide. (Resp._C1)

Hence, in contrast to expectation one, in the face of tension between the different levels of law, combined with unclear domestic guidelines, leading implementers consider it to be risky not to rely on EU law. Following the respondents, national courts might eventually rely on EU law even if the national legislator did not adjust the law. Therefore, inconsistent decision-making can harm the reputation of the *Ausländerbehörde* and it constitutes extra workload when decisions need to be corrected. Consequently, the first expectation that instrumental implementation motivations trigger inactive use of EU law only holds in the context of explicit national guidelines. Without clear national guidelines, instrumental motivations exist that can trigger use of EU law.

Coming to normative motivations, the analysis showed that both procedural and substantive norms played a role for respondents. Around half the respondents pointed towards their professional norms as implementers. Often, these norms were connected to instrumental motivations. For example, respondents pointed at their responsibilities as a good implementer to balance the interests of national society and tax payers, to stay within national legal bounds and their assigned national duty (Resp._A1; Resp._B1; Resp._C2; Resp._D1; Resp._F1; Resp._H1). Professional norms were mainly related to national loyalties. Loyalty towards EU law was articulated to a much lesser extent. If it was articulated, it was mentioned implicitly and in combination with other obligations. As one respondent argued:

> It is in many ways a balancing act because particularly our local government always says we should only do what is written in the (national) law … but we observe all the new developments, we also get the relevant journals that include EU judgments. On the working floor, we are confronted with these new developments and we want to take them on board. Yet, when we meet with politicians, they always ask in which national laws we find these things. (Resp._H2)

This respondent finds it challenging not to do justice to EU law and general new rulings, but he also receives steering signals from local policy-makers not to rely on the new developments. Eventually, this motivates reluctant uses of EU law. Similarly, another respondent argued:

> Of course we are aware that EU law comes before national law and national law is superior to Länder law … But I think I would get a punishment if I would start transposing EU law myself … For such activities my competences are clearly too limited … However, if CJEU judgments with direct effect challenge national law, than I take it into account and we define a common practice for our office, similar as with the Turkey cases. (Resp._I1)

Overall, EU loyalties are subordinated to instrumental motivations and professional norms of not overstepping one's competences. Thus, expectation two receives no support: because EU loyalties were generally weak.

The last expectation held that personal justice evaluations trigger implementers to pick and choose between national and EU norms. Almost all respondents mentioned their struggle between emotions, morality and legal demands. However, respondents differed on the emphasis they put on such personal considerations. Some implementers explained that they are not first of all implementers of the law, but rather 'client advisors' (Resp._A1). In light of the income requirement these respondents explained how they try to help clients to meet the critical benchmarks (Resp._F2; Resp._G1; Resp._G2; Resp._I2; Resp._J1). Several implementers called this 'an informal practice', because national law does not oblige them to advice clients (Resp._A1). These, respondents relied creatively on different levels of law, but rarely used the EU jurisprudence to justify discretion.

The expectation that substantive morality norms trigger use of EU law is most clearly met in the case of legal conflict and ambiguity of national law. For example, one respondent pointed out that he encourages his colleagues to:

> use the law in line with the principle of the IKEA slogan: 'discover the possibilities'. You always have to stay within the law but if the law offers you possibilities no one should hinder us to use them … European law provides us especially regarding Turkish citizens more possibilities than the German law and it is interesting for us to discover these new opportunities within the law. (Resp._B1)

This respondent referred to EU law as a source that offers new opportunities to become creative. While he stressed that this is only possible within the limits of national law, another respondent explicitly argued that he would even interpret EU law on his own when the national level failed to do so because 'in this way we maybe harm the German state, but at least we do not harm the individual migrant' (Resp._A1).

Overall, few respondents would rely on EU law at the expense of national law this openly. Risk and national loyalty motivations trigger mostly reluctant approaches towards EU law. Respondents are particularly afraid to be responsible for precedent cases. However, if national law fails to provide clear guidelines, most implementers use EU law parallel to national law. In line with the expectations, a group of respondents uses EU law to bring the law closer to their personal justice evaluations. Contrary to expectation, one also instrumental motivations can trigger use of EU law.

Conclusion

This contribution explored the extent to which street-level implementers use EU law and what motivates them when doing so. Three decision contexts in which EU law might play a role were identified. The scenarios differed in the level of legal ambiguity between national and EU regulatory frameworks.

In order to analyse the use of EU law, the study adopted a bottom–up approach (Thomann and Sager 2017a). By relying on the insights of social psychology (Tyler 2006) and the behavioural street-level bureaucracy literature (Lipsky 1980; Maynard-Moody and Musheno 2012), two perspectives on implementation motivations were identified. First, from an instrumental perspective, one could expect that there are few incentives for street-level implementers to use EU law. Second, procedural and substantive normative motivations were expected to trigger use of EU law. The study explored the expectations empirically in the context of EU migration law implementation in Germany.

Four main insights can be drawn from this analysis. First, the study demonstrated that EU implementation at the micro-level fruitfully complements the rational and constructivist institutional actor logics (March and Olsen 1998) that have been used to explain EU implementation at the member state level.

Second, in line with the street-level literature (Lipsky 1980; Maynard-Moody and Musheno 2012) and studies on migration management (Ellermann 2006; Eule 2014; Jordan *et al.* 2003), the implementers investigated in this study were creative and flexible in their use of legal tools. While the limited literature on practical EU implementation has treated administrations as yet another source for non-compliance (Versluis 2007) or ignored the street-level of EU implementation (Treib 2014), this study has shown that lower level implementers are surprisingly aware of the multilevel legal context in which they operate. Most implementers eventually give priority to national guidance in their decisions (see also Mastenbroek 2017). However, a considerable group of implementers sometimes uses EU law, particularly when the national level provides superficial guidelines. Some implementers even correct for missing EU transposition. Consequently, the study highlighted the importance of adding bottom–up approaches towards EU compliance.

Third, the study showed that implementers draw on EU law for varying purposes, leading to variation in implementation practices. This suggests that Europeanization does not necessarily harmonize domestic decision-making.

Often, active approaches towards EU law are contingent on normative implementation motivations. This is in line with the theoretical expectations. However, contrary to the established expectations, loyalty towards EU law has its limits in promoting uses of EU law. Instead, use of EU law can be motivated by substantive morality norms. In light of Egeberg and Trondal's (2009) 'double-hatted' agents who promote the interests of their national and European master owing to loyalty to the two masters, 'double-hatted' street-level implementers sometime use the different levels of law to bring about policy outcomes they personally consider as just.

Finally, this study showed that instrumental motivations trigger mostly no use of EU law. Particularly when national regulatory frameworks are explicit, implementers consider it risky to draw on EU law and focus, in line with Lipsky's (1980) expectations, on decision-making with low risks of being questioned by the outside world. However, in case of conflict between national and EU norms, combined with lacking national guidance, some implementers considered it risky not to rely on EU law. This indicates that even though there are no direct personal consequences for implementers, there are implicit instrumental motivations for relying on EU law.

Importantly, this study was limited to a very specific administrative context, namely the highly decentralized German administrative setting of North Rhine-Westphalia. As a result, motivational patterns observed in this study might be specific to several scope conditions, such as the presence of a multi-level legal context with ambiguity between national and EU obligations, the high level of discretion in the German administrative setting and the normatively laden policy field that requires considerable client interactions at the frontline. Yet, from the street-level bureaucracy literature, we can expect that other client-intensive and normatively laden fields comparable to migration, such as social policies, might reveal similar motivational mechanisms as found in this study (Maynard-Moody and Musheno 2012). The study might be less representative for more technical fields of EU law which may trigger less normative motivations. Nevertheless, as this study has shown, even instrumental motivations can trigger use of EU law, which suggests that street-level use of EU law might not be limited to normatively laden policy fields.

Follow-up studies should add external validity by bringing in a cross-country or cross-sectoral comparative perspective (Thomann and Sager 2017b). That is to say, what role does EU law play for implementers who operate under less discretion? Additionally, this study with its explorative elements calls for a more generalizable explanatory test of the relationship between motivations and use of EU law. For example, a quantitative survey among implementers across policy sectors that differ in normative sensitivity could provide such a test to further enhance our understating of the role of motivations for EU implementation.

Acknowledgements

Besides the constructive anonymous reviewers and editors of the collection, I would like to thank Ellen Mastenbroek and Lars Tummers for their helpful comments on previous versions of this contribution. Additionally, I thank the discussants and participants of the EGPA conference 2015 who commented on an earlier version. Special thanks also to all respondents who took the time to talk to me.

Disclosure statement

No potential conflict of interest was reported by the author.

References

Angelova, M., Dannwolf, T. and König, T. (2012) 'How robust are compliance findings? A research synthesis', *Journal of European Public Policy* 19(8): 1269–91.

Bach, T., Ruffing, E. and Yesilkagit, K. (2015) 'The differential empowering effects of Europeanization on the autonomy of national agencies', *Governance* 28(3): 285–304.

Bonjour, S. and Vink, M. (2013) 'When Europeanization backfires: the normalization of European migration politics', *Acta Politica* 48(4): 389–407.

Boswell, C. and Geddes, A. (2011) *Migration and Mobility in the European Union*, Houndmills, Basingstoke: Palgrave Macmillan.

Bovens, M. and Zouridis, S. (2002) 'From street-level to system-level bureaucracies: how information and communication technology is transforming administrative discretion and constitutional Control', *Public Administration Review* 62(2): 174–84.

Brodkin, E.Z. (1997) 'Inside the welfare contract: discretion and accountability in state welfare administration', *Social Service Review* 71(1): 1–33.

Dimitrova, A. and Rhinard, M. (2005) 'The power of norms in the transposition of EU directives', *European Integration Online Papers* 9(16): 1–18.

Düvell, F. and Jordan, B. (2003) 'Immigration control and the management of economic migration in the United Kingdom: organisational culture, implementation, enforcement and identity processes in public services', *Journal of Ethnic and Migration Studies* 29(2): 299–336.

Eckstein, H. (1975) 'Case studies and theory in political science', in F. Greenstein and N. Polsby (eds), *Handbook of Political Science*, Reading: Addison-Wesley, pp. 79–138.

Egeberg, M. and Trondal, J. (2009) 'National agencies in the European administrative space: government driven, commission driven or networked?', *Public Administration* 87(4): 779–90.

Ellermann, A. (2006) 'Street-level democracy: how immigration bureaucrats manage public opposition', *West European Politics* 29(2): 293–309.

Eule, T. (2014) *Inside Immigration Law. Migration Management and Policy Application in Germany*, Farnham: Ashgate.

George, A.L. and Bennett, A. (2006) *Case Studies and Theory Development in the Social Sciences*, Cambridge: MIT Press.

Gollata, J.A.M. and Newig, J. (2017) 'Policy implementation through multi-level governance: analysing practical implementation of EU air quality directives in Germany',
Journal of European Public Policy, doi:10.1080/13501763.2017.1314539

Gulbrandsen, C. (2011) 'The EU and the implementation of international law: the case
of 'sea-level bureaucrats'', *Journal of European Public Policy* 18(7): 1034–51.

Hertogh, M. (2009) 'Through the eyes of bureaucrats: how front-line officials understand administrative Justice', in M. Adler (ed.), *Administrative Justice in Context*,
Oxford: Oxford Hart Publishing Ltd, pp. 203–25.

Hood, C. (2011) *The Blame Game: Spin, Bureaucracy and Self-Preservation in Government.*
Princeton, NJ: Princeton University Press.

Huber, J. and Shipan, C. (2002) *Deliberate Discretion? The Institutional Foundations of
Bureaucratic Autonomy*, Cambridge: Cambridge University Press.

Jordan, B., Stråth, B. and Triandafyllidou, A. (2003) 'Comparing cultures of discretion',
Journal of Ethnic and Migration Studies 29(2): 373–95.

Keiser, L.R. and Soss, J. (1998) 'With good cause: bureaucratic discretion and the politics
of child support Enforcement', *American Journal of Political Science* 42(4): 1133–56.

Lahav, G. and Guiraudon, V. (2006) 'Actors and venues in immigration control: closing
the gap between political demands and policy outcomes', *West European Politics* 29
(2): 201–23.

Lipsky, M. (1980) *Street-level Bureaucracy*, New York: Russel Sage Foundation.

March, J.G. and Olsen, J.P. (1998) 'The institutional dynamics of international political
orders', *International Organization* 52(4): 943–69.

Mastenbroek, E. (2017) 'Guardians of EU law? Analysing roles and behavior of Dutch
legislative drafters involved in EU compliance', *Journal of European Public Policy*,
doi:10.1080/13501763.2017.1314537

Mastenbroek, E. and Kaeding, M. (2006) 'Europeanization beyond the goodness of Fit:
domestic politics in the Forefront', *Comparative European Politics* 4(4): 331–54.

May, P. (2005) 'Compliance motivations: perspectives of farmers, homebuilders, and
marine Facilities', *Law & Policy* 27(2): 317–47.

Maynard-Moody, S. and Musheno, M. (2003) *Cops, Teachers, Counselors: Stories from the
Front Lines of Public Service*, Ann Arbor: Michigan University of Michigan Press.

Maynard-Moody, S. and Musheno, M. (2012) 'Social equities and inequities in practice:
street-level workers as agents and Pragmatists', *Public Administration Review* 72(S1):
S16–23.

Reiter, B. (2013) *The Dialectics of Citizenship: Exploring Privilege, Exclusion, and
Racialization*, Michigan: Michigan State University Press.

Thomann, E. (2015) 'Customizing Europe: transposition as bottom-up implementation',
Journal of European Public Policy 22(10): 1368–87.

Thomann, E. and Sager, F. (2017a) 'Moving beyond legal compliance: Innovative
approaches to EU multilevel implementation', *Journal of European Public Policy*,
doi:10.1080/13501763.2017.1314541

Thomann, E. and Sager, F. (2017b) 'Toward a better understanding of implementation
performance in the EU multilevel system', *Journal of European Public Policy*, doi:10.
1080/13501763.2017.1314542

Thomann, E. and Zhelyazkova, A. (2017) 'Moving beyond (non-)compliance: the customization of European Union policies in 27 countries', *Journal of European Public
Policy*, doi:10.1080/13501763.2017.1314536

Treib, O. (2014) 'Implementing and complying with EU governance Outputs', *Living
Reviews in European Governance* 9(1): 1–47.

Tummers, L.G. (2011) 'Explaining the willingness of public professionals to implement new policies: a policy alienation framework', *International Review of Administrative Sciences* 77(3): 555–81.

Tummers, L.G., Olsen, A.L., Jilke, S. and Grimmelikhuijsen, S.G. (2016) 'Introduction to the virtual issue on behavioral public Administration', *Journal of Public Administration Research And Theory* 1–3, doi:10.1093/jopart/muv039

Tyler, T.R. (2006) 'Psychological perspectives on legitimacy and legitimation', *Annual Review of Psychology* 57: 375–400.

Versluis, E. (2007) 'Even rules, uneven practices: opening the "black box" of EU law in action', *West European Politics* 30(1): 50–67.

Winter, S.C. and May, P.J. (2001) 'Motivation for compliance with environmental Regulations', *Journal of Policy Analysis and Management* 20: 675–98.

Woll, C. and Jacquot, S. (2010) 'Using Europe: strategic action in multi-level politics', *Comparative European Politics* 8(1): 110–26.

Zaun, N. (2016) 'Why EU asylum standards exceed the lowest common denominator: the role of regulatory expertise in EU decision-making', *Journal of European Public Policy* 23(1): 136–54.

ð OPEN ACCESS

Mind the trend! Enforcement of EU law has been moving to 'Brussels'

Miroslava Scholten

ABSTRACT
The EU has become increasingly involved in enforcing European Union (EU) law, including directly *vis-à-vis* private actors. (Multilevel implementation) research has so far neglected the question of what role it is necessary for the EU to play in this direct enforcement of EU law in order to promote the implementation of EU policies. Given the purpose of this collection of works to discuss innovative approaches in multilevel implementation, this contribution unravels three of the EU's direct enforcement strategies. It provides original data in relation to proliferating EU entities with direct enforcement powers and to EU enforcement networks, as well as discussing the EU's growing influence over national direct enforcement via EU hard, soft and case law. It outlines the problem-solving potential of such enforcement strategies and signals the challenges that they bring along. The aim is to urge and facilitate further research on the EU's (direct) enforcement strategies, their legitimacy, effectiveness and operation.

Introduction

The enforcement of European Union (EU) law is a crucial element in the implementation of policies (Falkner *et al.* 2005; Knill and Tosun 2012). How does the European Aviation Safety Agency (EASA), for instance, know whether air companies fly airplanes which comply with EU airworthiness and environmental requirements if they are not being checked? Enforcement, i.e., monitoring compliance, investigating an alleged violation and the sanctioning of a violation, can rectify non-compliance and promote the attainment of policy goals. (Multilevel implementation) research on the enforcement of EU law has been scarce and has focused largely on domestic compliance with EU law, mostly at the transposition stage (but see Thomann

This is an Open Access article distributed under the terms of the Creative Commons Attribution-NonCommercial-NoDerivatives License (http://creativecommons.org/licenses/by-nc-nd/4.0/), which permits non-commercial re-use, distribution, and reproduction in any medium, provided the original work is properly cited, and is not altered, transformed, or built upon in any way.

2015), the enforcement of EU law by national authorities, especially in the field of environmental law (Faure 2004; Martens 2006; Tosun 2012; Treib 2014; Versluis 2003; Versluis and Tarr 2013; Vervaele 1999a; Wenneras 2007) and the area of financial fraud (Pujas 2003; Quirke 2010; Vervaele and Luchtman 2015; Vervaele 2013), and the traditional area of EU direct enforcement in competition law (Articles 101 and 102 Treaty on the Functioning of the European Union [TFEU]; Cseres 2016; Jones and Sufrin 2014; Monti 2007). The traditional division between regulatory and enforcement stages of the policy cycle belonging to the EU and national levels respectively can explain the existing focus. This division has, however, changed drastically in recent years.

In approximately the last 15 years, the number of EU enforcement authorities (EEAs) has grown from one to seven. EEAs enforce EU law directly *vis-à-vis* private actors like banks and air companies. Some EEAs trace their roots back to EU *enforcement* (not necessarily regulatory) networks, the number of which has been growing considerably and today includes at least 20 entities. Also, enforcement standards deriving from EU hard, soft and case law have been increasingly regulating domestic enforcement. The EU thus seems to have employed three enforcement strategies in promoting the implementation of its policies. Little is known, however, on whether and upon what circumstances these strategies can be and have been effective. In this light, the trend of 'enforcement moving to "Brussels"' adds a so far neglected perspective in EU (multilevel implementation) research, namely the question of what role is there for the EU to play in the traditionally national enforcement of EU law.

This contribution is only a first step in exploring this perspective. Based on an analysis of relevant legal sources, official documents and multi-disciplinary literature, it addresses three questions. First, what enforcement strategies does the EU have? In light of the three developments in EU law and governance, part 1 identifies three enforcement strategies, demonstrates and explains the trend of 'enforcement moving to Brussels'. Second, which non-implementation problems can these strategies potentially address? Part 2 connects the non-implementation problems identified in the literature with the enforcement strategies to determine what strategies could be used and when. Third, what challenges do the EU's enforcement competences bring? Part 3 signals the costs of possible solutions to non-implementation problems (the identified EU enforcement strategies). The contribution aims to lay down a fundament on proliferating EU (direct) enforcement powers, their possibilities, limits and challenges to urge and facilitate further (comparative) research into the appropriate role of the EU in promoting the implementation of its policies.

EU enforcement strategies: what, how and why

Direct and indirect enforcement

Enforcement aims at 'preventing or responding to the violation of a norm' in order to promote the implementation of the set laws and policies (Röben 2009: 821). Direct enforcement implies monitoring, investigating and sanctioning *vis-à-vis* those subjects that are subject to substantive norms, e.g., companies and citizens (Duk 1999; Rowe 2009; Vervaele 1999b). As a matter of national sovereignty, the direct enforcement of EU law has been traditionally kept at the national level, except for the field of EU competition law. The EU has had indirect enforcement powers, i.e., involvement in 'the supervision of the application of the law by public authorities – and foremost of the Member States – but not directly over whether citizens as such obey it' (Rowe [2009]: 189). The EU Commission (e.g., the Food and Veterinary Office) and later also EU agencies such as the European Maritime Safety Agency (EMSA) and the Court of Auditors have been among the key actors in checking EU member states. The Commission monitors the transposition and application of EU laws at the national level and, where necessary, it can initiate infringement procedures against member states (Articles 258, 259 and 260 TFEU).

In recent years, the EU's competences in direct enforcement have expanded along with the proliferation of EEAs with direct enforcement powers. The EU has been increasingly regulating matters of national direct enforcement via a rapid growth in the number of EU enforcement networks and hard, soft and case law-based enforcement standards. All in all, the EU seems to have become increasingly involved in the direct enforcement of EU law in the three ways or enforcement strategies on which this contribution focuses.

The trend

(1) Concerning the EU's own direct enforcement power, since 2008 the number of EEAs has doubled – from three (during 1962–2004) to seven (during 2008–2013). This list is exhaustive; it is the result of a scan of all EU policy areas and actors in the ongoing RENFORCE project.[1] Functionally, these EEAs can be divided into two groups:

- the Commission's Directorate General on Competition (DG COMP), the European Securities and Markets Authority (ESMA) and the European Central Bank (ECB) enjoy powers to exercise all enforcement stages: monitoring specific sectors e.g., by requesting reports from industry; investigating suspicious cases e.g., via searching offices; and sanctioning violations e.g., via imposing a fine.

- The Anti-Fraud Office (OLAF), the European Medicines Agency (EMA), EASA and the European Fisheries Control Agency (EFCA) have only some enforcement powers, most of which are investigative. Some of them may impose fines but only via the Commission or national authorities.

Table 1 provides an overview of the currently existing EEAs and their powers in relation to the enforcement stages based on a legal analysis of the mentioned regulations governing these entities' enforcement powers. It shows that each EEA can have a different type of relationship with its national counterpart. Yet, three types of such a relationship can be identified: parallel; hierarchical; and supportive (Scholten *et al.* 2017). The area of competition law is an example of parallel enforcement. The Commission and national competition authorities divide the cases based on relevant legal criteria (Regulation 1/2003 on a 'one-stop shop' system) and in the 'grey area of competence division' within the European Competition Network. What is shared is the responsibility to enforce EU law, not necessarily the powers/process of enforcement. EEAs are the primary enforcement authorities in the hierarchical relationship. For instance, ESMA monitors, investigates and sanctions violations of relevant EU law by itself. The only sharing of enforcement power can be when ESMA asks (which is at ESMA's discretion) its national counterpart to, for instance, inspect the premises of a credit rating agency or trade repository on its behalf. Finally, EEAs and their national counterparts can share the enforcement process as a whole; EEAs have then limited enforcement power and the powers of national authorities are essential to complete the enforcement process (e.g., EMA or EFCA).

Table 1. EEAs and their (shared) enforcement powers (with national authorities).

EEA	Monitoring	Investigating	Sanctioning
1 Commission (DG COMP ; Artt. 101-102 TFEU, Regulation 1/2003)	(+)	(+)	(+)
2 OLAF (Commission Decision 1999/352; Regulation 883/2013)	−	(+)	Indirectly via the Commission or national authorities
3 EFCA (Regulation 1224/2009)	(+)	(+)	− (national authorities)
4 EMA (Regulation 726/2004, Commission Regulation 658/2007)	(+)	−	Indirectly via the Commission
5 EASA (Regulation 216/2008)	(+)	(+)	+/via the Commission
6 ESMA (Regulations 1060/2009, 513/2011 and 648/2012)	+	(+)	+
7 ECB (Regulation 1024/2013)	(+)	(+)	+

The trend of expanding the EU's direct enforcement power is ongoing. Article 86 TFEU provides a possibility to establish a European Public Prosecutor's Office (EPPO) to investigate, prosecute and adjudicate crimes affecting the financial interest of the EU (Luchtman and Vervaele 2014). The European Banking Authority (EBA) and the European Railway Agency (ERA) may also be given some direct enforcement powers.[2] In July 2016, the proposal for establishing the European Border and Coast Guard, replacing the European Agency for the Management of Operational Co-operation at the External Borders of the Member States of the European Union (Frontex) but with stronger enforcement competences, has been adopted (Press release from the Commission 2015).

(2) Some EEAs started as EU networks of national enforcement authorities, the number of which has also recently increased. The scope of the proliferation of EU networks of national *enforcement* authorities depends on the definition of the term 'network'. In interpreting it narrowly, i.e., limiting it to the institutional form of organization, approximately 20 enforcement networks exist;[3] five networks were created in the 1990s and 15 in 2000–2014. The Consumer Protection Cooperation (CPC) Network, for instance, brings together relevant national authorities responsible for the enforcement of EU consumer protection laws. These national authorities are obliged to provide mutual assistance to each other. This may involve an exchange of information and taking enforcement measures (Articles 6–8, Regulation 2006/2004). While such networks do not have direct enforcement powers on their own, the Commission, being part of these networks, can influence national enforcement through co-ordination and data, which they receive from the member states and collect on their own initiative (Coen and Thatcher 2008; Cseres 2016; Kekelekis 2009; Levi-Faur 2011; Wilks 2005). It is important to note that connecting national relevant authorities within a network may be seen as a first step towards moving enforcement to the EU level in the shape of an EU agency with possibly more enhanced enforcement authority (Levi-Faur 2011), e.g., the case of ESMA (Scholten and Ottow 2014).

Taking a functional approach, some EU agencies which assist the Commission and/or the member states in the implementation of EU law and policies can also be considered as EU enforcement networks. Ten such EU agencies have been identified (Kaeding and Versluis 2014): the earlier mentioned EASA, ESMA, EFCA, and the Agency for the Co-operation of Energy Regulators, the Body of European Regulators for Electronic Communications, EBA, the European Chemicals Agency, the European Insurance and Occupational Pensions Authority, EMSA and ERA, all of which have been created since 2002 (Scholten 2014).

(3) Since approximately the mid-1980s, the EU has been regulating matters of national enforcement by setting up enforcement standards in EU hard, soft and case law (de Moor-van Vugt and Widdershoven 2015). These norms can

prescribe procedural and substantive requirements for direct national enforcement and influence the methods of national enforcement (Bastings *et al.* 2016; Kelemen 2011 (the 'Eurolegalism' argument)). Regulation 2729/2000, for instance, prescribes the powers for the national authorities in the wine sector; they must have access to vineyards, wine-making and storage installations. 'The most extensive Community influence is to be found in the olive oil and tobacco sectors' (Jans *et al.* 2007: 222). Relevant EU legislation has required specialized national enforcement agencies to be established, whose duties and organization are determined by the EU, which also partly finances their operation. Furthermore, the Court of Justice of the European Union (CJEU) has been playing an important role in fostering EU integration in general (Stone Sweet 2010; Tallberg 2000) and in influencing the enforcement of EU law in particular starting with such landmark cases as *Meroni* (Case 9/56) on the delegation to agencies, and *Amsterdam Bulb* (Case 50/76) and *Greek Maize* (Case 68/88)) influencing national sanctions. Finally, the EU has been guiding national direct enforcement by its soft law guidelines and instructions (Falkner *et al.* 2005; Maggetti and Gilardi 2014).

While many norms regulate direct national enforcement (de Moor-van Vugt and Widdershoven 2015), further quantitative research is necessary to establish the exact scope thereof. The qualitative expansion can be demonstrated by the development in prescribing the type of sanctions, which has gone from reparatory to administrative punitive to criminal sanctions (Case C-176/03 Commission v. Council; Communication from the Commission 2011; Jans *et al.* 2007; Vervaele 2007).

Understanding the trend

The EU's increasing involvement in the enforcement of EU law can be explained by the desire to ensure the implementation of EU policies, compliance with EU law and, to a certain degree, uniform enforcement and the limits of the 'traditional tool' of indirect enforcement (de Moor-van Vugt and Widdershoven 2015). Non-compliance by the member states has had different reasons, from the complexity of EU law to a lack of resources and political will, especially if other countries (also) fail to comply or if compliance may affect the economic competitiveness of member states (de Moor-van Vugt and Widdershoven 2015; but see also Mastenbroek 2005). The indirect enforcement mechanism has its limits when member states repeatedly violate EU law, even after a successful action brought by the Commission before the CJEU. For instance, France had not complied with EU fishing quotas since 1988, resulting in two actions by the Commission before the CJEU (Wenneras 2006, see also Slepcevic 2009). In any case, it is an *ex post* mechanism, a tool of last resort, a stick rather than a carrot. Additional enforcement strategies appear to be essential to prevent violations and non-compliance and to ensure implementation in the complex multilevel governance system, which the EU is.

Scholten and Scholten (2016) explain the expansion of the EU's competences from one (regulatory) step in the policy cycle to another (enforcement) from a functional spillover perspective; if the implementation of EU law is failing at the national level, enforcement at the EU level is likely to follow. However, how could the member states allow the EU to gain additional powers in the traditionally national remit of enforcement? The problematic enforcement and non-implementation of EU policies affect the member states; 'British and Spanish fishermen' are damaged when the French have not respected fishing quotas for more than 15 years. The delegation of power to the EU level has been explained, in part, by the desire to ensure the observance of commitments by the member states at the EU level (Thatcher and Stone Sweet 2003). Furthermore, creating an EU institutional framework for (co-operation on) enforcement can resolve problems of transnational enforcement; it gives the advantages of what is called 'European territoriality' (Ryngaert and Vervaele 2015). Whereas the enforcement jurisdiction of national authorities is restricted by national borders, the territorial competences of EU authorities include the joint territories of all the participating member states. Depending on their specific institutional designs, these advantages gain even greater weight when time-consuming schemes for mutual legal (administrative or criminal law) assistance are removed from their legal design. In the latter case, EU authorities can have the legal power to gather information anywhere in the EU.

While the EU's (direct) enforcement competences have expanded, the member states retain control over enforcement thanks to the (institutional) choices made. The existing literature on the proliferation of EU networks and agencies explains the institutional choice upon delegation by functional needs, political motives and social logics (Eberlein and Newman 2008; Groenleer *et al*. 2010; Kelemen 2002; Martens 2006; Wilks 2005). EU agencies, an institutional form for nearly all the EEAs, represent a more acceptable solution for the member states to transfer some powers to the EU level and yet retain control over these powers. This is in contrast to allowing the Commission to gain more powers. A network can enhance co-ordination, co-operation, the exchange of best practices and sometimes centralize certain enforcement tasks while keeping the power at the national level.

'Problem-solving' potential

What strategy should be employed – creating an EEA or a network or regulating domestic enforcement via EU norms – to ensure the effective enforcement of EU law and policies and when? Table 2 gives a succinct overview of the problem-solving potential of the three enforcement strategies. It shows that

Table 2. EU's competences in direct EU/national enforcement-resolving problems of non-implementation

	Direct enforcement by EEA	EU networks of national enforcers	EU norms for national direct enforcement
Late transposition	+	+/−	−
Incorrect transposition	+	+/−	−
Lack of resources to apply and enforce	+	+/−	+/−
Unwillingness to apply and enforce	+	+/−	−
Differences in national laws and practices	+	+/−	+

Notes:
+ potential is high;
+/− potential is present;
− potential is unlikely.

directly enforcing EU law by an EU entity has the greatest problem-solving potential. EU influence on national enforcement via networks is possible and EU influence via norm-setting has the lowest potential.

Non-implementation can occur for procedural and/or substantive reasons (Commission's annual reports on the Application of EU law; Groenleer *et al.* 2010; de Moor-van Vugt and Widdershoven 2015; Versluis 2003, 2007). Procedurally, the member states could be late in transposing EU legislation at home and could lack financial and human resources to apply and enforce EU law properly. Substantively, an incorrect transposition (whether or not this is on purpose) and (political) unwillingness could lead to non-implementation (see also Thomann and Zhelyazkova (2017) on the differences between *de jure* and *de facto* implementation). In addition, differences in national laws and procedures could result in disparities in the uniform application of EU law and the ineffectiveness of EU policies (Scholten and Ottow 2014).

Creating *strong* EEAs with direct enforcement powers, like ESMA, could potentially address all problems related to non-compliance by the member states. In this case, EU law is directly applied and enforced by EEAs *vis-à-vis* private parties. The member states can be involved in enforcement procedures , for instance, when they provide specific data on specific entities and make investigations regularly and upon the request of EEAs, but their role (if any) becomes more of an assistant than of the main enforcer or can be bypassed. In addition, since EEAs enforce EU law directly, the problem of the late and incorrect transposition of substantive rules on the enforcement of a specific policy does not arise; national rules do not need to be adapted, with the possible exception of the rules on the work and responsibilities of relevant national authorities *vis-a-vis* EEAs. A lack of national resources to enforce EU law effectively could be mitigated by the fact that work is now done (also or only) by the EU and possibly national staff from other member states. The EASA is the primary example of how this EEA and some national authorities assist other understaffed authorities in order to enforce EU law. Only 10 member states have relevant industry and hence expertise and resources to do this.[4] The problem of an unwillingness to apply and enforce EU law by national authorities can be addressed by empowering an EU authority with its own direct enforcement power and/or emergency powers to act if national enforcement fails. The uniform laws and practices of EEAs could diminish the negative implications from differences in national laws and practices. ESMA, for instance, would apply the same EU rules and practices in enforcing relevant EU policies irrespective of the member states where a credit rating agency is situated (but see van Rijsbergen and Scholten [2016] on how differences in national judicial control could affect accountability). It is important to note that EEAs vary greatly with regard to their powers and the degree of power sharing with the Commission and national counterparts. This can influence the discussed potential and result in different models of EU direct enforcement (Heidbreder 2015; Scholten and Ottow 2014). Since this field is understudied, it is unclear how far EEAs are exposed to the problems faced by national enforcement authorities (such as a lack of resources) or whether they could face additional challenges, e.g., an impossibility to oversee the extensive EU territory or less trust by the supervised in arguably less legitimate and trusted EU entities.

Networks of enforcement authorities bring together national counterparts and the Commission, and could be used as a venue for promoting convergence and 'naming and shaming' when it comes to late and incorrect transposition, non-application and problematic enforcement in terms of an unwillingness to co-operate and enforce and a lack of resources (Ottow 2012). Since these structures have predominately co-ordinating rather than strong direct enforcement powers, their enforcement capacity can be limited (e.g., the case of three financial networks in the EU [Scholten and Ottow 2014]). However, they could promote the implementation of EU policies by enhancing mutual learning and co-operation by relevant authorities (Groenleer *et al.* 2010).

Regulating national enforcement via prescribing specific institutional characteristics and sanctions for national enforcement authorities could promote convergence in enforcement laws and practices, at least *de jure*. In addition, EU norms may oblige the enhancement of possibly lacking resources for the application and enforcement of EU law. However, just as any piece of EU legislation, they can still be transposed late or incorrectly and may not be applied or enforced properly (Thomann and Zhelyazkova (2017)).

How does one choose between different (competing) strategies? The key principles governing the division of competences in the EU (subsidiarity and proportionality) would dictate the EU's involvement only when necessary and in the least intrusive manner in order to respect the national diversity of (legal) cultures. In this light, one could order the discussed strategies according to the increase in impact that the EU may have on national enforcement – from regulating domestic enforcement through norms and via networks to creating EEAs and enhancing their (and hence the EU's) powers. In light of Table 2, the problem-solving potential seems to be increasing as the impact grows. In fact, the EU regulation of national enforcement preceded the establishment of six out of the seven EEAs, with the exception of DG COMP (Scholten and Scholten 2016). The EU legislator seemed to have tried to regulate first problematic domestic enforcement via norms and/or networks. Once that strategy did not bring the desired results, it adopted another one, i.e., creating an EEA. Further research is essential in order to determine the realization of the discussed potential and the effectiveness of these strategies.

Challenges

The identified strategies that the EU has been using in enforcing EU law indicate an expansion of the EU's enforcement competences. This gives rise, in turn, to the question of whether the growth in and, to a certain extent, the shift of power from the national to the EU level is legitimate. Once this is established, shared enforcement gives rise to the question of how to arrange controls and organize it.

Legitimacy

The EU's democratic legitimacy and accountability have been debated for a long time (Majone 2014; Moravcsik 2002; Scharpf 1999). In short, the debate is centred around the following issues: (1) weakly legitimated principal decision-makers, including the absence of the collective accountability of the Council and of the 'EU citizen' and low turnouts in elections to the European Parliament (Corbett *et al.* 2011); and (2) an undemocratic decision-making process, i.e., an 'integration by stealth' mode of integration. The latter implies integration 'as an exercise of technocratic problem-solving in closed diplomatic, administrative and judicial elite arenas', instead of in the arena of mass politics (Genschel and Jachtenfuchs 2014: 11).

The expansion of the EU's enforcement competences takes place largely by acts of the principal decision-makers and 'by stealth'. The Treaties have not explicitly provided EU institutions and agencies with all the enforcement authority, which EEAs enjoy. The expansion has taken place via inserting bits and pieces of institutional centralization and substantive harmonization here and there in hard, soft and case law. Be it the example of the criminalization of EU law or of the creation of EU agencies, legitimacy has often been gained implicitly. The CJEU has played a decisive role on these occasions. However, these individual (legal) pieces brought together have a far-reaching cumulative effect of establishing and expanding the EU's enforcement competences, which the existing Treaties largely establishing a 'rule-making EU' have not foreseen. While some prominent authors on the EU's democratic legitimacy have pointed to a close link between input and output legitimacy (Scharpf 1999) and a possibility for the latter to compensate for the former (Majone 2014), the effectiveness of different types of EU's enforcement competences is yet to be assessed. This is not that easy to do, however, owing to the difficulties in establishing a reference level to assess against (Majone 2014).[5] Let me illustrate this point.

The example concerns the introduction of criminal sanctions in the area of environmental law (Directive 2008/99/EC on the protection of the environment through criminal law). In its proposal (2007), the Commission saw the differences in sanctioning regimes as a major problem in the proper protection of the environment. The solution it proposed was to oblige all member states to use criminal sanctions for specific offences. It referred to studies which, according to the Commission, demonstrated the need for criminal sanctions because existing sanctions were not always sufficient for effective policy implementation. A closer look at the studies, however, shows that they focused largely on mapping out the differences between the sanctioning regimes of the member states.[6] One study explicitly stated that it did not include 'a thorough analysis of the effectiveness of each sanction' (Huglo Lepage and Partners 2007: 6). Furthermore, the Commission reasoned that action by the Union was a necessity, as violators could easily circumvent certain member states and operate from places having more lenient legislation (Commission 2007). However, the Commission did not provide any evidence to prove that perpetrators had been easily circumventing those member states that had stricter sanctions in place.

Has the Directive addressed the problem that it wished to address? At first glance, it surely has. It requires all member states to use criminal sanctions for certain environmental offences; the diversity of sanctions now seems to have been eliminated. At the same time, the idea behind the reform was to enhance the protection of the environment; is it now better protected by having uniform criminal sanctions? The effectiveness of the action may be difficult to establish because the scope of the problem, i.e., how far the diversity of sanctioning regimes has negatively affected the protection of the environment, which could have been the reference level for an *ex post* assessment, was not properly identified in the first place. A diversity in sanctions is not necessarily a problem, unless it leads to negative implications for enforcement. The discussed example raises the question of to what extent the establishment of the EU's enforcement competences have been justified; weak or non-existing justifications will clearly undermine legitimacy. Justification is crucial for accepting the authority of an EU rule or an EEA. The risk of not having identified the actual problem when it comes to problematic enforcement amounts to trouble-shooting without any problems being in place and creating (additional) unnecessary challenges in such areas as accountability and the organization of shared enforcement.

Accountability

Legitimacy can be enhanced by accountability (Bovens 2007). The question of accountability is intriguing, however, in relation to EU institutions and agencies, which enjoy direct enforcement powers. This is because the seven EEAs have gained far-reaching enforcement powers *vis-à-vis* private actors, but they do not completely replace national enforcement authorities. Rather, enforcement powers have become increasingly shared between EU and national authorities (Della Cananea 2004; Hofmann 2009; Ottow 2012; Prechal *et al.* 2015). However, EU and national systems of democratic and judicial control over EU law enforcement remain strictly separated: national parliaments and courts for national authorities, the EU parliament and courts for EEAs. This challenges the system of controls (e.g., Court of Auditors 2014; Craig 2009; Eliantonio 2014; Hofmann 2009; Papadopoulos 2010; Türk 2009).

The most recent example concerns the European Central Bank (ECB). As of November 2014, it is 'exclusively competent' (Article 4, Regulation 1024/2013) to supervise significant credit institutions, representing almost 85 per cent of total banking assets in the euro area (Scholten and Ottow 2014). Is it also exclusively accountable for financial supervision? No, even though national relevant authorities 'shall follow the instructions given by the ECB' (Articles 6, 20 and 21) when they, among other things, monitor the sector and register banks. When rendering account before the EU or a national parliament respectively, the EU and national enforcement authorities can point the finger at each other and escape accountability ('the problem of many hands' [Bovens 1998: 45]). From a judicial perspective, the new system can result in gaps in legal protection for private actors, such as banks. For example, EU law assumes a national judicial check of the arbitrariness of an inspection from the ECB before the inspection of bank premises (Article 13). However, some jurisdictions, like the Netherlands, allow this check only after the imposition of a fine. The fines are imposed, however, by the ECB and are hence challenged before an EU court. The ECB will escape a check on the arbitrariness of its inspection action (Prechal *et al.* 2015). In addition, if the ECB objects to the draft authorization of a bank issued by a national supervisor according to national rules, the question is then whether the bank can challenge this decision before the EU court, which in this situation will have to apply national law, which does not fall within the CJEU's remit.

Which parliament or court (national or EU?) is competent to check what in the shared enforcement process? If a part of (preparatory) acts or 'competent' actors are beyond their remit, can they be held to account? To avoid control gaps and undesired voids, merging enforcement tasks raises the question of the necessity to connect other accountability forums in one way or another, e.g., via such new tools as the recently created joint parliamentary scrutiny committee for Europol (Europol Regulation 2016). The distinguished types of relationships between EEAs and national authorities are likely to have different accountability needs.

Organization of shared enforcement

Another important question is how to organize shared enforcement institutionally, procedurally, and substantively. The comprehensive analysis by Luchtman and Vervaele (2014) of the legislative proposals to create the European Public Prosecutor's Office shows various challenges when building a system of shared enforcement in the field of criminal justice. Creating such a system may negatively affect established requirements in every criminal justice system (accessibility and foreseeability), but may also give rise other questions. For instance, given the different rules on the use of evidence in a fair trial among the member states, can a written statement taken by a judge in France be accepted in the United Kingdom (UK) where, according to the hearsay rule, the witness needs to give evidence orally? The existing legislative proposals have been silent on the limits of procedural harmonization. Furthermore, such a system entails risks for the judicial protection of citizens, which requires further integration introducing common terminology, procedures and enforcement strategies, at a minimum. This is a challenging exercise when we consider the role of legal cultures which contribute to effective enforcement strategies in different member states (Versluis 2003). Therefore, we should ensure that 'moving' direct enforcement competences to 'Brussels' is legitimate before we open a Pandora's box of constructing shared enforcement in the EU, and we should also ensure that such a complex system actually works (see Heidbreder [2017]).

The way forward

This contribution invites both academics and policy-makers at the EU and national levels to take a closer look at and to adopt a critical stance concerning the (to date) under-investigated trend of enforcement moving to 'Brussels'. This trend indicates an expansion of the EU's competences in direct enforcement, which arguably takes place 'underground' according to three strategies – the proliferation of EEAs and regulating national enforcement via EU networks and norms. This contribution has provided a comprehensive overview and original data on the EU's enforcement strategies, their problem-solving potential in relation to promoting the implementation of EU policies, as well as their limits and challenges, so as to facilitate research in the following direction.

The primary question is what role is there for the EU to play in enforcing EU law to promote the implementation of its policies? This contribution recommends further (comparative) case studies on the extent to which the EU's enforcement competences (direct and indirect) have been effective in promoting the implementation of EU law and policies. Which enforcement strategies have been able to address which non-implementation problems and subject to which conditions? Why do they create EEAs in some areas and not in others, and why do they give some EEAs more enforcement powers than others? Such studies could contribute to building a model, which would also be useful for policy-makers, to determine what type of EU's enforcement competences should be desirable in specific circumstances: EEA or a network (and with what powers) or a (legislative) norm. The findings on effectiveness could also inform researchers investigating the legitimacy of the EU and the 'underground' method of expanding power.

The existing research has focused largely on the enforcement of EU law by national authorities and indirect enforcement against non-complying member states. The expanding power of (direct) enforcement by EU institutions and agencies adds new questions in this respect. How far is it possible to control the implementation of EU laws and policies by EU joint teams of enforcers? At this point in time, enforcement powers have been merged, but the system of controls remains separated by the governance levels. The separated controls for shared tasks run the risk of blame avoidance. Ironically, for the issue of judicial accountability, the traditional question of *national compliance* with *EU law* is reversed. In light of the discussed example concerning the ECB, how can *EEAs' compliance* with *national laws* be checked and at what level? The puzzle is that national courts cannot annul the decisions of EU entities, whereas the CJEU is not empowered to apply national law. All in all, the topic stresses the need to investigate whether and what type of EU enforcement competences can and have effectively addressed certain non-implementation problems of EU law and policies. Given the challenges that this possible 'solution' brings in terms of legitimacy, accountability and the organization of shared enforcement, future studies also need to consider whether, in light of these challenges, this 'solution' is indeed worthy.

Notes

1. http://renforce.rebo.uu.nl/bouwsteenprojecten/verticalisering-en-toezichthouders/ (accessed December 2016).
2. See the proposal concerning the European Railway Agency at http://ec.europa.eu/archives/commission_2010-2014/kallas/headlines/news/2013/01/doc/com

(2013)-27_en.pdf (accessed March 2016). Concerning the EBA, the European Court of Auditors recommended expanding its mandate to enforcement competences (http://www.eca.europa.eu/Lists/ECADocuments/SR14_05/SR14_05_EN. pdf (accessed March 2016)).
3. This information is taken from an ongoing RENFORCE research project by Prof. M. Luchtman.
4. Information obtained from an official from the EASA in the course of an ongoing research project (September 2016).
5. Majone argues that the output legitimacy of the EU has so far been measured in procedural terms; he notes the difficulties in measuring effectiveness substantively.
6. The studies can be found at the official webpage of the European Commission: http://ec.europa.eu/environment/legal/crime/studies_en.htm (accessed March 2016).

Acknowledgements

I gratefully acknowledge funding by RENFORCE (the 'verticalisation and supervisors' project) and by the Netherlands Organization for Scientific Research (NWO, the 'veni' grant), which made this contribution possible. My special thanks are extended to the (guest) editors for the organization of this collection and review process, to all the anonymous referees for their useful comments and to Prof. Dr Michiel Luchtman for his valuable suggestions on the very first draft.

Disclosure statement

No potential conflict of interest was reported by the author.

Funding

This work was supported by the Nederlandse Organisatie voor Wetenschappelijk Onderzoek [grant number Veni award].

References

Bastings, L., Mastenbroek, E., and Versluis, E. (2016) The other face of Eurolegalism: the multifaceted convergence of national enforcement styles. *Regulation & Governance*, doi: 10.1111/rego.12126.

Bovens, M. (1998) *The Quest for Responsibility - Accountability and Citizenship in Complex Organisations*, Cambridge: Cambridge University Press.

Bovens, M. (2007) 'Analysing and assessing public accountability: a conceptual framework', *European Law Journal*, 13(4): 447–68.

Coen, D. and Thatcher, M. (2008) 'Network governance and multi-level delegation: European networks of regulatory agencies', *Journal of Public Policy* 28: 49–71.

Commission's annual reports on Application of EU law. Available at: http://ec.europa.eu/atwork/applying-eu-law/infringements-proceedings/annual-reports/index_en.htm (last visited March 2016).

Commission proposal. (2007) 'Proposal for a Directive of the European Parliament and of the Council on the protection of the environment through criminal law', February. Available at: http://register.consilium.europa.eu/doc/srv?l=EN&f=ST%206297%202007%20INIT (last visited March 2016).

Communication from the Commission (2011) 'Towards an EU Criminal Policy: Ensuring the effective implementation of EU policies through criminal law', COM (2011) 573 final. Available at: http://ec.europa.eu/justice/criminal/files/act_en.pdf (last visited March 2016).

Corbett, R., Jacobs, F., and Shackleton, M. (2011) *The European Parliament*, 8th ed., London: John Harper Publishing.

Court of Auditors (2014) 'European banking supervision taking shape — EBA and its changing context', Report 5. Available at: http://www.eca.europa.eu/Lists/ECADocuments/SR14_05/SR14_05_EN.pdf (last visited March 2016).

Craig, P. (2009) 'Shared administration, disbursement of community funds and the regulatory state in legal challenges', in H. Hofmann and A. Türk (eds.), *EU Administrative Law: Towards an Integrated Administration*, Cheltenham: Edward Elgar Publishing, pp. 34–62.

Cseres, K. (2016) 'Competition law enforcement beyond the nation-State: a model for transnational enforcement mechanisms?' in H. Micklitz and A. Wechsler (eds.), *The Transformation of enforcement: European Economic Law in a Global Perspective*, Oxford: Hart Publishing, pp. 319–40.

Della Cananea, G. (2004) 'The European Union's mixed administrative proceedings', *Law and Contemporary Problems* 68: 197–217.

Duk, W. (1999) *Recht en Slecht: Beginselen van Algemene Rechtsleer*, Nijmegen: Ars Aequi Libri.

Eberlein, B., and Newman, A. (2008) 'Escaping the international governance dilemma? Incorporated transgovernmental networks in the European Union', *Governance* 21 (1): 25–52.

Eliantonio, M. (2014) 'Judicial review in an integrated administration: the case of 'composite procedures", *Review of European Administrative Law* 7(2): 65–102.

Europol Regulation 2016, before publication in the Official Journal available as Report of the European Parliament of 7 February 2014 on the proposal for a regulation of the European Parliament and of the Council on the European Union Agency for Law Enforcement Cooperation and Training (Europol): http://www.europarl.europa.eu/sides/getDoc.do?type = REPORT&reference = A7-2014-0096&language = EN (last visited August 2016).

Falkner, G., Treib, O., Hartlapp, M., and Leiber, S. (2005) *Complying with Europe: EU Harmonisation and Soft Law in the Member States*, Cambridge: Cambridge University Press.

Faure, M. (2004) 'European environmental criminal law: do we really need it?' *European Environmental Law Review* January: 18–29.

Genschel, P., and Jachtenfuchs, M., (2014) 'Introduction: beyond market. Analysing the European Integration of core state powers', in P. Genschel and M. Jachtenfuchs (eds.), *Beyond the Regulatory Polity?* Oxford: Oxford University Press, pp. 1–23.

Groenleer, M., Kaeding, M., and Versluis, E. (2010) 'Regulatory governance through agencies of the European Union? The role of the European agencies for maritime and aviation safety in the implementation of European transport legislation', *Journal of European Public Policy* 17(8): 1212–30.

Heidbreder, E. (2015) 'Multilevel policy enforcement: innovations in how to administer liberalized 21 global markets', *Public Administration* 93(4): 940–55.

Heidbreder, E. G. (2017) 'Strategies in multilevel policy implementation: moving beyond the limited focus on compliance', *Journal of European Public Policy*, doi:10.1080/13501763.2017.1314540.

Hofmann, H. (2009) 'Composite decision making procedures in EU administrative law', in H. Hofmann and A. Türk (eds.), *Legal Challenges in EU Administrative Law: Towards an Integrated Administration*, Cheltenham: Edward Elgar Publishing, pp. 136–67.

Huglo Lepage & Partners. (2007) 'Study on environmental crime in the 27 Member States', 5 April 2007. Available at: http://ec.europa.eu/environment/legal/crime/pdf/report_environmental_crime.pdf (last visited March 2016).

Jans, J., de Lange, R., Prechal, S., and Widdershoven, R. (2007) *Europeanisation of Public Law*, 1st ed., Groningen: Europa Law Publishing.

Jones, A., and Sufrin, B. (2014) *EU Competition Law*, 5th ed., Oxford: Oxford University Press.

Kaeding, M., and Versluis, E. (2014) 'EU agencies as a solution to Pan-European implementation problems', in: M. Everson, C. Monda and E. Vos, *European Agencies in Between Institutions and Member States*, Alphen aan de Rijn: Kluwer.

Kekelekis, M. (2009) 'The European Competition Network (ECN): It Does Actually Work Well', *EIPAscope* 1. Available at: http://aei.pitt.edu/12378/1/20090709111900_Study_Eipascoop2009_01.pdf (last visited March 2016).

Kelemen, D. R. (2002) 'The Politics of 'Eurocratic' structure and the New European agencies', *West European Politics* 25(4): 93–118.

Kelemen, D. (2011) *Eurolegalism: The Transformation of Law and Regulation in the European Union*, Cambridge, MA: Harvard University Press.

Knill, C., and Tosun, J. (2012) *Public Policy: A New Introduction*, Hampshire, NY: Palgrave Macmillan.

Levi-Faur, D. (2011) 'Regulatory networks and regulatory agencification: towards a Single European Regulatory Space', *Journal of European Public Policy* 18(6): 810–29.

Luchtman, M., and Vervaele, J. (2014) 'European agencies for criminal Justice and shared enforcement (Eurojust and the European Public Prosecutor's Office)', *Utrecht Law Review* 10(5): 132–50.

Maggetti, M., and Gilardi, F. (2014) 'Network governance and the domestic adoption of soft rules', *Journal of European Public Policy*, 21(9): 1293–310.

Majone, G. (2014) *Rethinking the Union of Europe Post-Crisis, Has Integration Gone Too Far?*, Cambridge: Cambridge University Press.

Martens, M. (2006) 'National regulators between union and fovernments: a study of the EU's environmental policy network IMPEL', in M. Egeberg (ed.), *Multilevel Union Administration. The Transformation of Executive Politics in Europe*, Basingstoke: Palgrave Macmillan, pp. 124–42.

Mastenbroek, E. (2005) 'EU compliance: still a 'black hole'? *Journal of European Public Policy* 12(6): 1103–20.

Monti, A. (2007) *EU Competition Law*, Cambridge: Cambridge University Press.

de Moor-van Vugt, A., and Widdershoven, R. (2015) 'Administrative enforcement', in J. Jans, S. Prechal and R. Widdershoven (eds.), *Europeanisation of Public Law*, 2nd ed. Groningen: European Law Publishing, pp. 263–330.

Moravcsik, A. (2002) 'Reassessing legitimacy in the European Union', *JCMS: Journal of Common Market Studies* 40(4): 603–24.

Ottow, A. (2012) 'Europeanization of the supervision of competitive markets', *European Public Law* 18(1): 191–221.

Papadopoulos, Y. (2010) 'Accountability and multi-level governance: more accountability, less democracy?' *West European Politics* 33(5): 1030–49.

Prechal, S., Widdershoven, R., and Jans, J. (2015) 'Chapter 1. Introduction', in J. Jans, S. Prechal and R. Widdershoven (eds.), *Europeanisation of Public Law*, 2nd ed. Groningen: European Law Publishing, pp. 3–36.

Press Release from the Commission. (2015) 'A European Border and Coast Guard to protect Europe's External Borders', 15 December. Available at: http://europa.eu/rapid/press-release_IP-15-6327_en.htm (last visited March 2016).

Pujas, V. (2003) 'The European Anti-Fraud Office (OLAF): a European policy to fight against economic and financial fraud?' *Journal of European Public Policy* 10(5): 778–97.

Quirke, B. (2010) 'OLAF's role in the fight against fraud in the European Union: do too many cooks spoil the broth?' *Crime, Law and Social Change* 53: 97–108.

van Rijsbergen, M., and Scholten, M. (2016) 'ESMA inspecting: the implications for judicial control under shared enforcement', *European Journal of Risk Regulation* 7(3): 569–79.

Röben, V. (2009) 'The enforcement authority of international institutions' in: A. von Bogdandy *et al.* (eds.), *The Exercise of Public Authority by International Institutions: Advancing International Institutional Law*, Heidelberg: Springer, pp. 819–42.

Rowe, G. (2009) 'Administrative supervision of administrative action in the European Union' in H. Hofmann and A. Türk (eds.), *Legal Challenges in EU Administrative Law: Towards an Integrated Administration*, Cheltenham: Edward Elgar Publishing, pp. 136–67.

Ryngaert, C., and Vervaele, J. (2015) 'Core values beyond territories and borders: the internal and external dimension of EU regulation and enforcement', in T. van den Brink, M. Luchtman, and M. Scholten, *Sovereignty in the Shared Legal Order of the EU: Core Values of Regulation and Enforcement*, Antwerp: Intersentia, pp. 299–324.

Scharpf, F. (1999) *Governing in Europe: Effective and Democratic?* Oxford: Oxford University Press.

Scholten, M. (2014) *The Political Accountability of EU and US Independent Regulatory Agencies*, Leiden: Brill.

Scholten, M., and Ottow, A. (2014) 'Institutional design of enforcement in the EU: the case of financial markets', *Utrecht Law Review* 10(5): 80–91.

Scholten, M., and Scholten, D. (2016) 'From regulation to enforcement in the EU policy cycle: A new type of functional spillover?' Paper presented at the Sixth Biennial Conference, ECPR Standing Group on Regulatory Governance, July 6, 2016 (forthcoming in *JCMS*).

Scholten, M., Maggetti, M., and Versluis, E. (2017) 'Political and judicial accountability in shared enforcement in the EU', in M. Luchtman and M. Scholten, *Law Enforcement by EU Authorities*, Cheltenham: Edward Elgar, *forthcoming*.

Slepcevic, R. (2009) 'The judicial enforcement of EU law through national courts: possibilities and limits', *Journal of European Public Policy* 16(3): 378–94.

Stone Sweet, A. (2010) 'The European Court of Justice and the judicialization of EU governance'. *Living Reviews in European Governance* 5(2). Available at http://www.livingreviews.org/lreg-2010-2 (last visited January 2016).

Tallberg, J. (2000) 'Supranational influence in EU enforcement: the ECJ and the principle of state liability', *Journal of European Public Policy* 7(1): 104–21.

Thatcher, M., and Stone Sweet, A. (2003) 'Theory and practice of delegation to Non-Majoritarian institutions', in M. Thatcher and A. Stone Sweet (eds.), *The Politics of Delegation*, London: Routledge, pp. 1–22.

Thomann, E. (2015) 'Customizing Europe: transposition as bottom-up implementation', *Journal of European Public Policy* 22(10): 1368–87.

Thomann, E. and Zhelyazkova, A. (2017) 'Moving beyond (non-)compliance: the customization of European Union policies in 27 countries', *Journal of European Public Policy*, doi:10.1080/13501763.2017.1314536.

Tosun, J. (2012) 'Environmental monitoring and enforcement in Europe: a review of empirical research', *Environmental Policy and Governance* 22: 437–48.

Treib, O. (2014) 'Implementing and complying with EU governance outputs', *Living Reviews in European Governance* 9(1): 1–47.

Türk, A. (2009) 'Judicial review of integrated administration in the EU', in H. Hofmann and A. Türk (eds.), *Legal Challenges in EU Administrative Law: Towards an Integrated Administration*, Cheltenham: Edward Elgar Publishing, pp. 218–56.

Versluis, E. (2003) *Enforcement matters. Enforcement and Compliance of European Directives in Four Member States*, Delft: Eburon.

Versluis, E. (2007) 'Even rules, uneven practices: opening the 'black box' of EU law in action', *West European Politics* 30(1): 50–67.

Versluis, E., and Tarr, E. (2013) 'Improving compliance with European Union Law via agencies: the case of the European railway agency', *Journal of Common Market Studies* 51(2): 316–33.

Vervaele, J. (1999a) *Compliance and Enforcement of European Community Law*, Alphen aan den Rijn: Kluwer.

Vervaele, J. (1999b) 'Shared governance and enforcement of European Law: from comitology to a multi-level agency structure?' in C. Joerges and E. Vos, *EU Committees: Social Regulation, Law and Politics*, Oxford: Hart Publishing, pp. 129–50.

Vervaele, J. (2007) 'The European community and harmonization of the criminal law enforcement of community policy. A Cessio Bonorum from the Third to the First Pillar?', in K. Nuotio (ed.), *Festschrift in honour of R. Lahti*, Helsinki: University of Helsinki, pp. 119–42.

Vervaele, J. (2013) 'European territoriality and jurisdiction: the protection of the EU's financial interests in its Horizontal and Vertical (EPPO) dimension' in M. Luchtman (eds.), *Choice of Forum in Cooperation against EU Financial Crime*, The Hague-Portland: Eleven international publishing, pp. 167–84.

Vervaele, J., and Luchtman, M. (2015) 'Criminal law enforcement of EU Harmonised financial policies - The need for a shared criminal policy' in F. de Jong, J. Vervaele, M. Boone, C. Kelk, F. Koenraadt, F. Kristen, D. Rozenblit and E. Sikkema (Eds.), *Overarching views of Crime and Deviancy - Rethinking the Legacy of the Utrecht School*, Pompe reeks: Eleven International Publishers, pp. 335–65.

Wenneras, P. (2007) *The Enforcement of EC Environmental Law*, Oxford: Oxford University Press.

Wenneras, P. (2006) 'A new dawn for Commission enforcement under Articles 226 and 228 EC: General and persistent (gap) infringements, lump sums and penalty payments', *Common Market Law Review* 43(1): 31–62.

Wilks, S. (2005) 'Agency Escape: Decentralization or Dominance of the European Commission in the Modernization of Competition Policy?' *Governance* 18(3): 431–52.

Strategies in multilevel policy implementation: moving beyond the limited focus on compliance

Eva G. Heidbreder

ABSTRACT

Policy implementation in the European Union is most prominently analysed taking compliance as a conceptual starting point. However, compliance has an inherent top–down and state-centred bias. To overcome this limitation, a conceptual framework that links dimensions based on top–down/bottom–up implementation and vertical/horizontal multilevel governance is proposed. The thus derived four ideal-types of implementation in multilevel settings – centralization, agencification, convergence and networking – are complemented by functional expectations about policy-makers' strategic choices over these types. A screening of existing research completes the contribution. The results show that the suggested conceptualization offers indeed a comprehensive framework to describe the implementation strategies to propose avenues for future explanatory studies on strategic choices over implementation types.

1. Implementation beyond compliance in a multilevel polity

To 'go beyond compliance', this contribution takes issue with two shortcomings the editors of this collection highlight in their introductory piece: the top–down and the state-centred biases of the compliance perspective (Thomann and Sager 2017). The starting assumption is that compliance is only one of many implementation logics in European Union (EU) policy-making. Noticeably, multilevel polities such as the EU are precisely marked by limited top–down and state-like competences. The underpinning implementation logic of compliance stands, therefore, even in contrast to defining features of multilevel policy-making. The aim of this contribution is to offer a conceptualization that differentiates theoretically between distinct implementation types multilevel policy-making and the strategies to select a specific implantation type. Characteristic of multilevel implementation is that policies are formulated on the supranational level but are implemented and enforced at the lower levels (spelling out the conceptual *problematique*; see Joosen and Brandsma [2017]). This implies also that the concern with multilevel policy implementation is primarily with the interaction between the various levels. As the typology developed below indicates, different implementation types rely on distinct mechanisms instead of the delegation logic of compliance alone, and it is possible to discern conditions under which one particular type is more likely applied than another.

To realize this aim, the first objective is to offer a descriptive typology of the various implementation logics applied in the EU. The thus-defined four implementation types are subsequently linked to strategic choices by policy-makers. A strategy is here not a mere rational choice but a function of interest congruence and ambiguity amongst policy-makers. The second objective is consequently an explanatory one whose value-added is illustrated by existing research and by promising future puzzles. Empirically, the contribution builds hence on derived findings, but offers nonetheless relevant new insights because it links streams of literature that exist by-and-large unconnected.

The contribution proceeds as follows. Section 2 introduces the typology of multilevel implementation, summarized in a single typology. The value-added of this typology is primarily descriptive; its purpose is to discern theoretically deduced implementation types that solve the multilevel problem of realizing a policy on a lower level based on distinct mechanisms. The following section moves a step further by asking why policy-makers should opt for one or other type. From this theoretical step, one can draw causal expectations. Section 2 serves both an illustrative and a reflective purpose. Linked to the first objective, by-and-large separated literatures are reviewed applying the typology. Furthermore, where existing, research findings that support the causal expectations about implementation type choices are added, or avenues for future research are pointed out. The contribution concludes that in order to understand multilevel policy implementation, we need to consider how the different implementation types interact in order to be able to analyse more accurately and to improve policy implementation in multilevel policy-making.

2. The theoretical framework: implementation types in multilevel governance

This section first develops a framework of multilevel implementation types, to then add causal expectations about the strategic selection between these types. To derive implementation types in multilevel settings, two dimensions are applied that respond to the above-cited critique of the compliance approach. To overcome the top–down bias, the first dimension distinguishes between top–down and bottom–up implementation. Even though the dichotomy underlying this conceptualization has been widely criticized (e.g., Sabatier 1986), it serves well to escape the top–down bias which focuses mostly on the delegation from higher to lower levels. As Hupe (2014), illustrates, it remains one of the major challenges of implementation research to disentangle analytically the effects of implementation that involves multiple layers, not least because in the real-life implementation environment '[t]he single lonely organization may be dead, but it has not been replaced by any single model of implementing structure' (Peters 2014: 131–44). In the EU, these features are particularly significant (Knill 2015), because:

> even if legislation has been adopted by the EU and even if some common rules for implementation of these rules have been adopted at the EU level, final decisions vis-à-vis individuals implementing EU policies are taken by the Member State bodies. (Hofmann 2014: 198)

Given that member state implementers remain formally independent, implementation is not merely an execution of delegated tasks but involves independent decision-making or other processes. The distinction helps identifying different implementation logics that are at work side-by-side,[1] and helps to understand how top–down and bottom–up elements are intertwined in the EU policy implementation at large. On the second dimension, the state-centred bias is remedied by drawing on multilevel governance research that focuses on interactions between actors beyond the hierarchical steering mode (Benz 2009). Hooghe and Marks's two types of multilevel governance (2003) offer an alternative view to overcome the limitation of state-centeredness. Type one rests on vertical relationships in which different levels of the institutional architecture are attributed exclusive authority over specific fields. Type two connects task-specific jurisdictions horizontally, which means that authority can be shifted if the context changes. Moreover, the different units can be members of various jurisdictional entities that co-exist. Notably, the EU applies both logics: type one in areas where the EU holds exclusive competence to vertically regulate and implement, type two where logics such as mutual recognition between member states apply, based on horizontal peer-to-peer implementation. This second dimension thus widens our perspective to the various forms of actor relations in multilevel polities that lack basic hierarchical and centralized state-powers. Together, the top–down/bottom–up implementation and vertical/horizontal multilevel governance dimensions cover the space of possible implementation solutions conceivable in a multilevel system.

In the second analytical step, expectations about implementation strategies are formulated adopting the concepts of ambiguity and conflict from Matland (1995). Having defined distinct implementation types, an obvious question is, under which conditions which type will be strategically selected to produce effective implementation. The starting assumption here is that policy-makers have to act frequently in contexts troubled with uncertainties about available policy options and unintended consequences. In addition to factual uncertainties about instrument selection, policy-makers have to act in a political context of competing interests and demands. In EU policy-making (Heidbreder and Brandsma 2017), these challenges are particularly pronounced. Owing to limited supranational resources and high heterogeneity across its territory, the EU often faces challenges to produce adequate policy expertise for dissimilar national contexts (Gornitzka and Sverdrup 2008). In addition, the particularly high number of institutionalized veto players increases the probability of interest competition (Tsebelis and Hahm 2014). These two dominant features of EU decision-making are suitably captured by Matland's (1995) notions of ambiguity and conflict, which the next section will introduce to develop a causal argument about implementation type selection.

2.1. Theorizing implementation types in multilevel complexity

Relating the top–down/bottom–up implementation and vertical/horizontal multilevel governance dimensions to each other, I identify four theoretically distinct implementation types: centralization; convergence; agencification; and networking (Figure 1). These types offer different strategies available in multilevel policy implementation. On the implementation dimension, top–down approaches suggest that policies are formulated on a higher level

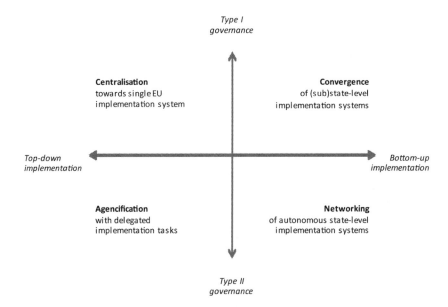

Figure 1. Implementation ideal types in multilevel policy-making. Source: Author's own graph.

and imposed by lower-level implementing bodies. In a multilevel system this means *harmonization through joint higher-level policy formulation*. The bottom–up notion is based on mechanisms of horizontal co-ordination, i.e., non-delegated implementation linkages between formally autonomous national jurisdictions that lead to *horizontal approximation of task-specific capacities*. On the multilevel governance dimension, type one governance operates by unifying structures within a single general-purpose jurisdiction with non-intersecting membership. This means an implementation strategy that reduces the number of competent levels in a single system-wide architecture. Implementation is aligned with *harmonization inside an integrated administrative structure*. The more flexible alternative strategy is to limit the specific tasks with which a jurisdiction deals. Thus, implementation is realized by *pooling task-specific capacities*.

The intersections of the two dimensions define four implementation types. *Centralization* is the most encompassing mechanism of multilevel policy implementation.[2] It combines the type one and top–down dimensions. *Agencification* also pools authority on the supranational level, yet delegation is limited to specific tasks and the institutional actors created are clearly restricted in their authority, while the delegating authorities retain formal control functions over the agencies. The agencies are steered top–down through delegation. At the same time, type two governance applies because new intersecting judicial units with horizontal co-operation are created instead of a single integrated administrative entity. Implementation based on increasing *convergence* between national systems shares the notion of assimilation with the centralization concept, but is not based on delegation. Convergence is not designed in a top–down manner that would entail harmonization, but evolves in bottom–up mechanisms (policy diffusion: functional; emulation; learning; etc.). The logic of networks is equally based on a bottom–up mechanism, but does not involve the creation of similar structures across states. *Networking* is understood as increasing horizontal linkages and connectedness of autonomous national bodies that focus on similar tasks or are co-operating in joint cross-jurisdictional procedures, without any further claims on joint supranational institution-building or approximation of national administrative systems. It matches thus the bottom–up and type two governance type. Networking in this sense is the least encompassing implementation strategy because it does not imply any transfer of authority to higher levels of the system. Agencification and convergence offer different – top–down and bottom–up – intermediate solutions compared to the least binding networking and most-binding centralization. In sum, the two dimensions define four ideal-types for policy implementation that have a heuristic value. On this basis, the next section will establish functional arguments about the implementation type selection.

2.2. Causal expectations about implementation type selection

To develop causal expectations about which implementation type is selected under which conditions, I will adapt Matland's conceptualization that defines implementation strategies according to their level of ambiguity and conflict. On the one hand, ambiguity 'can be characterized broadly as falling into two categories: ambiguity of goals and ambiguity of means' (Matland 1995: 157). Ambiguity about implementation objectives (goals), and implementation tools (means) are multiplied in EU multilevel policy implementation owing to the large variety of policy-making and implementation systems across the member states. On the other hand, for Matland '[p]olicy conflict will exist when more than one organization sees a policy as directly relevant to its inter-ests and when the organizations have incongruous views' (Matland 1995: 156). Applied to the EU, this is basically always the case, given that decisions over which implementation type to choose pend on the legislative act itself, i.e., agreement among member states, the European Parliament and indirectly the Commission – or on member states' decisions to pre-empt legislation altogether. During the implementation phase, conflict may emerge between the implementing member states and the Commission's oversight, or horizon-tally interdependent implementers. Cross-tabling these two dimensions (high/low conflict and ambiguity), Matland defines different implementation pro-cesses.[3] Applying the conflict and ambiguity values to the above-developed implementation types instead offers a fruitful way to move towards some causal inference about multilevel implementation type selection.

To start with, '[t]raditional top-down models, based on the public adminis-tration tradition, present an accurate description of the implementation process when policy is clear and conflict is low. ... Because there is a clear policy, macroimplementation planners wield considerable influence' (Matland 1995: 171). Applied to the above-developed framework, this corre-sponds with *centralized* implementation under which member state auth-orities confer full implementing powers to the supranational level, which can then instruct the lower levels with detailed implementation plans. The implementation strategy is a vertically structured hierarchical command-and-control system. The most prominent EU example is monetary policy whose implementation is fully controlled by the European Central Bank (ECB). Notably, the ECB's powers go far beyond those of a delegated agent, because powers have been so fully conferred that member states can hardly exercise the role of principals (Majone 2001b). Such centralization of implementing competences in the EU is only possible if the member states agree to confer sovereignty, which presupposes low levels of conflict and ambiguity. Hence, if actors share interests and the level of ambiguity is low, centralized implementation that confers implementation powers to the EU level can be functionally expected.

If, instead, high ambiguity is matched with strong, shared interests, delegation to an *agency* should be the most likely outcome. Following standard principal–agent theory, the delegation of responsibilities to an agent serves precisely the purpose of reducing ambiguity, given generally shared interests. In this case, the delegation of selected tasks to an agent with discretion over limited goal and instrument selection is the best matching strategy. A vivid illustration is the extended delegation to the new European Border and Coast Guard Agency, founded as part of Frontex in 2016. Given strong, shared interests to secure EU borders but low agreement about which instruments could achieve this objective, EU policy-makers were willing to delegate certain powers under the condition to widen the scope to revise decisions – in other words, delegate implementation to an EU agency.

If, in contrast, interests are not shared and ambiguity is low, we should expect neither a conferral nor a delegation of implementing powers because of a general lack of agreement, most obviously visible in passing no EU legislation of policy programmes at all. Yet, given little ambiguity on goals and means, solutions developed on the authority-maintaining (sub-)national level should lead to convergence. A striking case in point is the introduction of Bachelor and Master degrees across Europe, which was a voluntary, bottom–up initiative by governments who agreed on the means to increase scholarly mobility – without any shared view of how university systems should look like and without any EU decision-making involved at all. In short, if multiple actors have diverging interests they will refrain from conferring powers to the supranational level and the most likely outcome should be the (voluntary) adaptation of the national implementation approaches leading to convergence.

Finally, if shared interests are absent and ambiguity is high, policy-specific networking that creates intersections between independent organizations is the most likely strategic choice to increase implementation effectiveness. Various networks of national regulators and implementers, such as the LEADER (Liaison Entre Actions de Développement de l'Économie Rurale) approach for rural development, serve as examples. Assuming strongly diverging interests to delegate powers combined with high ambiguity about goals and means should lead us to expect networking, which represents the least autonomy-constraining and most flexible strategy to multilevel policy implementation.

Table 1 summarizes the implementation types, their defining characteristics, creation mechanisms, implementation logic and the functional link to conflicts of interest and ambiguity. In order to render the typology and implementation type selection more comprehensible, I will now turn to the empirical illustration derived from different streams in EU research.

Table 1. Multilevel implementing strategies.

	Characteristic	Creation mechanism	Implementation logic	Policy decision traits
Centralization	State-building (harmonization organizational, systemic)	Conferral *of implementing powers from MS to EU level*	Command-and-control, vertical hierarchy	Shared interests/ low level of ambiguity
Agencification	Sub-delegation (harmonization functional, task-specific)	Delegation *of singled-out tasks to (semi-)autonomous agent*	Delegation and de-politicization of ambiguous goal / tool selection	Shared interests/ high level of ambiguity
Convergence	Assimilation (approximation organizational, systemic)	Diffusion *implementing models across MS*	Incremental horizontal assimilation (fusion)	Diverging interests/low level of ambiguity
Networking	Co-ordination (approximation function, task-specific)	Intersecting *of formally independent bodies*	Interface management between administrative units	Diverging interests/high level of ambiguity

Source: Author's own table, *cf.* Matland (1995) for selected categories.

3. Illustration: policy implementation in the EU

The question of how to cope with the pitfalls of multilevel policy implementation is anything but new on the EU research agenda. As actual implementation practices developed in a rather *ad hoc* and contingent manner in the EU, research on these practices emerged from different and largely unconnected academic angles. This section serves two purposes. First, it illustrates the descriptive value added of the typology as it systematically structures the different implementation logics operating in multilevel policy implementation. Second, drawing on the theoretical expectations about the strategic implementation type choice, explanations in existing research can be embedded into the larger implementation perspective and research gaps can be identified. The following therefore discusses selected contributions of the dominant research streams on EU policy implementation and how the above-developed causal expectations should advance the field.

3.1. Centralization

The core of the EU, the single market, is predominantly implemented by harmonized EU law, which makes centralization the most prominent implementation type. Most expressly, Trondal (2010) has interpreted such centralization as an emerging executive order in its own right. Essentially, the Commission is empowered with implementing authority and oversees the application of EU law. Even though national administrations remain formally independent, they are bound by a set of general administrative law principles and at times detailed implementation rules (Heidbreder 2011). Two important streams in EU literature deal with centralized implementation. The first, *comitology*, tackles the need for co-ordination to effectively implement EU law (for an overview, see Vos [2009]). Under comitology, national implementers and the Commission meet on the EU level to decide on common rules and procedures. Research on the rather complex comitology proceedings has concentrated mainly on the balance of authority between the Commission and the member states and, more recently, the European Parliament (EP) (Bergström *et al.* 2007; Egeberg *et al.* 2003; Franchino 2000). A connected topic deals with how far changes in comitology rules adapt the inter-institutional balance (Moury and Héritier 2012), and thus the actual degree of centralization (Héritier *et al.* 2013). In addition, scholars have studied how comitology has been increasingly 'constitutionalized' (Joerges and Neyer 1997), especially in terms of inter-institutional control and accountability (Brandsma 2013), how informal and formal rules interact (Christiansen and Dobbels 2013), and how inter-institutional agreement is achieved even if interests do not coincide (Blom-Hansen 2013). The Treaty of Lisbon altered the comitology system by introducing the distinction between delegated and implementing acts, limiting comitology to implementing acts, while delegated acts give the Commission limited discretion to adopt non-legislative acts of general application (Brandsma 2016; Brandsma and Blom-Hansen 2012).

The second large body of literature, *compliance*, tackles the core of centralized implementation (for an overview, see Treib [2014]). Compliance research investigates under which conditions (sub-)national actors rightfully implement EU law. The ultimate central issue behind studies on compliance is why states comply at all (Börzel and Heidbreder 2017; Haas 1998). The main aim is to explain variance in compliance performances between member states (Falkner *et al.* 2005; Falkner *et al.* 2008). The field covers a large number of case studies, but has nonetheless produced more general findings, featuring a few reoccurring plus 'a myriad of other variables' (Toshkov 2011: 12). Additionally, a reoccurring challenge for compliance scholars is to go beyond the top–down transposition of EU law (Thomann 2015), and to observe actual enforcement (Mastenbroek 2005; Versluis 1997).

Both comitology and compliance research offer some insights on the expectations summarized in Figure 1. First, the expectation about policy conflict is supported, for instance, by results that show how lowering political agreement between the Council and the Parliament reduces the legislators' willingness to opt for delegated acts that grant more centralized implementing powers to the Commission (Brandsma and Blom-Hansen 2015). Second, studying compliance, König and Mäder show that member state positions are a crucial explanatory factor for the conferral of centralized powers. Since the Commission as centralized EU agency knows the member states' interest and power distribution, 'it can easily anticipate the probability of enforcement success and the potential sanctioning costs … [Thus it] is prevented from taking action … in less favorable situations where the enforcement success is low respectively and sanctioning costs are very high' (König and Mäder 2014: 260). Thus, even if powers are centralized, diverging interests and high ambiguity can undermine their effectiveness. This finding invites further research on centralized implementation as independent variable and how it is affected by the interplay of ambiguity and interests. Stressing not only the relevance of conflict but also ambiguity, the here-introduced conceptualization offers further starting points to scrutinize the conditions for centralization to produce effective implementation.

3.2. Agencification

Delegation to agencies has been a major research topic in recent years (Jordana et al. 2011). In practice, the EU has well over 40 agencies that match the above-described type. Research on agencies focuses to a great part on discretion and agency independence (Bauer 2002), which has been shown to increase for national and EU agencies with the rising status they have in EU policy-making (Wonka and Rittberger 2010). The increase in the number and task-range of EU agencies is in line with the claim that the non-redistributive regulatory mode of policy-making in the EU makes agency rule a particularly well-suited governance mode (Majone 2001a, 2002). In addition, this stream of research analyses the differentiation between EU and national agencies (Barbieri and Ongaro 2008) and the EU agencies' role in policy-making and polity development more generally (Egeberg and Trondal 2009). It highlights that delegation of supranational tasks to national agencies leads to a decoupling of national agencies from national control chains. However, it could also be shown that the 'increasingly common involvement of national agencies in European policy-making processes thereby increases these agencies' policy-development autonomy, but does not change their role in policy implementation' (Bach et al. 2015: 285). The core tenet of the research on EU agencies is that there is a clear trend of increasing agencification, often normatively interpreted as essential part and parcel of a larger transformation of executive governance in the EU (Trondal and Jeppesen 2008).

The findings offered by agency research correspond with the expectation about low conflict and high ambiguity. The agency literature considers the role of ambiguity to a larger extent than the other streams. In particular for areas in which ambiguity has led to policy failure – prominently in some food-scandal cases – agencies have been founded or strengthened precisely to reduce ambiguity (Krapohl 2003). The expectation about the interaction between interest convergence and high technical and/or normative ambiguity could offer a valuable starting point to go beyond the principal–agent delegation logic the agencification literature focuses on. This would promote a better understanding of the conditions under which agencification is selected as well as, if treating agencification as independent variable, conditions for an effective performance.

3.3. Convergence

Convergence features both as a political and a theoretical expectation in the literature. In EU research, it lingers as hidden assumption in most writings on *Europeanization* (for overviews, see Featherstone and Radaelli [2003]; Graziano and Vink [2006]; Green Cowles *et al.* [2001]). The two standard definitions of Europeanization are the impact of EU policy-making on the national policy, politics and policies (top–down Europeanization) and the inverse impact of the national input on the EU-level policy-making (bottom–up Europeaniza-tion) (Börzel 2002; Héritier 2005; Knill *et al.* 2009). Europeanization research has brought forth different causal explanations based both on rational choice and more sociological theory (Dimitrova and Steunenberg 2000; Hol-zinger and Knill 2005). In relation to our conceptual framework it is important to stress that Europeanization literature often only implicitly raises the expec-tation that domestic change in the EU member states will lead to convergence (Holzinger and Knill 2005; Olsen 2003; Plümper and Schneider 2009). In studies focusing explicitly on Europeanization of public administrations, certain empirical findings challenge that convergence is indeed increasing (Goetz 2006; Pollitt 2001, 2002), while others highlight convergence on selected dimensions (Kassim 2003; Knill 2001). However, theoretically, Eur-opeanization depends at least on an implicit convergence logic – even if dis-confirmed – because otherwise no overreaching EU effect can be conceptualized (Heidbreder 2013; Olsen 2003).

Another strand that builds more explicitly on bottom–up convergence relates to tools that promote mutual learning and policy diffusion. The most relevant application in EU policy implementation is the open method of co-ordination (OMC), and more generally 'experimental governance' (Sabel and Zeitlin 2012). The first generation of OMC research raised high expectations about the potential effect of voluntary co-ordination (Borrás and Jacobsson 2004; Radaelli 2008; Trubek and Trubek 2005). Similar to the disputable empirical evidence for convergence in Europeanization research, the actual effect of the OMC has been vigorously challenged theoretically (Benz 2007; Büchs 2008; Hatzopoulos 2007; Idema and Kelemen 2006) and empirically (De la Porte and Pochet 2012; de Ruiter 2012; Heidbreder 2015a).

Despite the ambiguous findings on convergence, the literature offers good backing for the expected strategic choices for this implementation type. Theor-etical and empirical work on Europeanization and the OMC show that diver-ging interests of central actors match with a low level of ambiguity are functionally linked to convergence, either theoretically or as a hands-on desired political outcome. Notably, the OMC was first introduced in 2001 for areas in which co-ordination pressure was high but member states lacked agreement to confer substantive competences to the EU level. The theoretical expectations about low ambiguity as pre-condition for convergence may be fruitfully used in future research to better understand implementation short-comings or failure in Europeanization and OMC research.

3.4. Networking

As loosely coupled implementation systems networks are widely spread across the EU and in this regard the specific 'patchworked' and 'networked' character of EU policy-making has been noted early on (Héritier 1996; Richardson 1996). The literature that speaks directly to the proposed network type of implemen-tation defines networks narrowly as informal or formal loosely coupled actor linkages that lack a centralized organizational core (as agencies provide to net-works) but create still stable relationships (in contrast to convergence or policy diffusion processes). Interestingly, the European Commission has in more recent years increased its efforts to improve implementation through such net-works. It does so by facilitating direct horizontal co-operation between national administrative bodies (Heidbreder 2015b), without making any claims to cen-tralize authority or adapt national implementation. The distinguishing feature of such co-operation is that the member states or private actors oblige themselves to co-operate, most relevantly regarding the exchange of information. Practically, the Services Directive (2009) has been a crucial mile-stone in developing this co-ordination approach (Schmidt 2007). In addition, the development of Informations and Communications Technology (ICT) tools that enables immediate information exchange has been crucial for enabling such direct networking (Heidbreder 2013).

As expected, in areas where member states reject harmonization and ambi-guity is high, various forms of network building have been observed. One example are bottom–up voluntary networks of labour inspectorates that started to independently tackle implementation failures that occurred as side-effects of EU market integration (Hartlapp and Heidbreder 2017). A rel-evant insight for all four implementation types can be derived, if conceptua-lizing them as independent variables. More than other implementation types, networking has been shown as a more effective response to particular implementation failures linked to information exchange or interface manage-ment. In contrast, problems linked to substantive legal mismatch cannot be resolved by networking but networked implementation may even invoke new problems (Heidbreder 2015c: 952). The presented typology and causal links can hence offer valuable starting points both as dependent and indepen-dent variables that raise further questions about the strategic choice of implementation styles in multilevel policy-making and changes from one implementation type to another (Mavrot and Sager 2016).

4. Conclusion: the choice over implementation types

In order to move 'beyond compliance', this contribution started off from the two crucial limitations that mark compliance research: its top–down and state-centred biases. Drawing from conceptualizations of policy implementation and multilevel policy-making, two dimensions were theoretically identified that describe the space for multilevel policy implementation. Intersecting the top–down/bottom–up implementation with the vertically/horizontally structured multilevel governance dimension four distinct types of policy implementation in a multilevel setting were defined. Confronting this conceptualization with existing literature on the EU fleshed out the descriptive value-added of this contribution. Instead of perceiving the EU policy implementation as either or, the typology allows to see the full picture consisting of four distinct implementation types that are applied in parallel but are by-and-large discussed in insulated streams of research: literature on comitology and compliance focus on centralized implementation; the literature on agencies offers insights on agencification; research focusing on networks informs us about networked implementation; convergence underpins the literatures on Europeanization, policy learning and assimilation, extensively studied for the Open Method of Co-ordination. Considering the parallel application of the different implementation logics emphasizes not only the different mechanisms to implement policies in multilevel policy-making. It also raises the eminent question, when which type is selected and best suited to achieve effective implementation. Taking up the former question, the contribution theorized as strategies of implementation type selection. Assuming a functional link between conflicts of interest as well as functional and normative ambiguity leads to expectations about the conditions under which policy-makers choose a particular implementation type. In essence, the less conflict and ambiguity, the more constraining the implementation type, whereas the more conflict and ambiguity, the least constraining implementation strategies should be selected. The limited literature overview does not offer a fully satisfying answer to these expectations. However, it can offer theoretical guidance for possible future research, which includes the treatment of implementation types as independent variables to study conditions for effectiveness of specific implementation types. Theoretically, the expectations compete with some hypotheses about instrument selection and policy effectiveness and may hence offer alternative explanations. For example, the mere focus on interest convergence to establish centralization tends to oversee that with high levels of ambiguity, centralized implementation may still fail. Especially, a more systematic analysis of factual and normative ambiguity as explanatory variables promise interesting findings about implementation type selection. The main explanatory value added can thus eventually be found in the interaction between different implementation types. Such insights should be equally valuable for analysts and practitioners in multilevel polities, as they suggest that only under certain conditions a particular strategy will lead to effective implementation. Hence, at times it may be more effective to opt for a less constraining implementation strategy that matches the actual level of complexity because this promises more effective implementation than a more constraining strategy that will eventually be annihilated by conflicts over interests and ambiguity.

Notes

1. The distinction serves accordingly a purely descriptive and not a normative purpose. Barrett points further out that the top–down/bottom–up can be further linked to notions of conformance and performance (Barrett 2004: 255). Whilst this view is shared, for the current purpose it suffices to apply the older distinction because it sufficiently captures the actors/levels involved – rather than the intended objective of the conformance/performance distinction. Nonetheless, the extension is worthwhile to consider also for EU policy implementation.
2. Full centralization actually implies the subordination of the lower levels, and eventually the move from a multilevel to an integrated single system of governance.
3. Synthesizing implementation literature, the four combinations on the conflict and ambiguity dimensions lead Matland (1995: 160) to expect administrative (low/low), experimental (low/high), political (high/low), and symbolic (high/high) implementation. For the purpose of this contribution, we are not interested in these implementation processes but in the interaction between the multilevel elements as developed in Section 2.1.

Disclosure statement

No potential conflict of interest was reported by the author.

References

Bach, Tobias, Ruffing, Eva and Yesilkagit, Kustal. (2015) 'The differential empowering effects of Europeanization on the autonomy of national agencies', *Governance* 28 (3): 285–304.

Barbieri, Dario and Ongaro, Edoardo. (2008) 'EU agencies: what is common and what is distinctive compared with national-level public agencies', *International Review of Administrative Sciences* 74(3): 395–420.

Barrett, Susan M. (2004) 'Implementation studies: time for a revival? Personal reflections on 20 years of implementation studies', *Public Administration* 82(2): 249–62.

Bauer, Michael W. (2002) 'The commission and the poverty programmes', *JCMS: Journal of Common Market Studies* 40(3): 381–400.

Benz, Arthur. (2007) 'Accountable multilevel governance by the open method of coordination?', *European Law Journal* 13(4): 505–22.

Benz, Arthur. (2009) 'Combined modes of governance in EU policymaking,' in Ingeborg Tömmel and Amy Verdun (eds.), *Innovative Governance in the European Union*, Boulder: Lynne Rienner, pp. 27–44.

Bergström, Carl-Fredrik, Farrell, Henry and Héritier, Adrienne. (2007) 'Legislate or delegate? Bargaining over implementation and legislative authority in the EU', *West European Politics* 30(2): 338–66.

Blom-Hansen, Jens. (2013) 'Comitology choices in the EU legislative process: contested or consensual decisions?', *Public Administration* 92(1): 55–70.

Borrás, Susana and Jacobsson, Kerstin. (2004) 'The open method of coordination and new governance patterns in the EU', *Journal of European Public Policy* 11(2): 185–208.

Börzel, Tanja A. (2002) *States and Regions in the European Union: Institutional Adaptation in Germany and Spain*, Cambridge: Cambridge University Press.

Börzel, Tanja and Heidbreder, Eva G. (2017) 'Enforcement and compliance', in Carol Harlow, Pävi Leino-Sandberg and Giacinto della Cananea (eds.), *Research Handbook on EU Administrative Law*, Cheltenham: Edward Elgar.

Brandsma, Gijs Jan. (2013) *Controlling Comitology: Accountability in a Multi-Level System*, Houndmills: Palgrave MacMillan.

Brandsma, Gijs Jan. (2016) 'Holding the European commission to account: the promise of delegated acts', *International Review of Administrative Sciences* 82(4): 656–73.

Brandsma, Gijs Jan and Blom-Hansen, Jens. (2012) 'Negotiating the post-Lisbon comitology system: institutional battles over delegated decision-making', *JCMS: Journal of Common Market Studies* 50: 939–57.

Brandsma, Gijs Jan and Blom-Hansen, Jens. (2015) 'Controlling delegated powers in the post-Lisbon European Union', *Journal of European Public Policy* 23(4): 531–49.

Büchs, Melina. (2008) 'How legitimate is the open method of co-ordination?', *JCMS: Journal of Common Market Studies* 46(4): 765–86.

Christiansen, Thomas and Dobbels, Mathias. (2013) 'Non-legislative rule making after the Lisbon treaty: implementing the new system of comitology and delegated Acts', *European Law Journal* 19: 42–56.

De la Porte, Caroline and Pochet, Philippe. (2012) 'Why and how (still) study the open method of co-ordination (OMC)?', *Journal of European Social Policy* 22(3): 336–49.

Dimitrova, Antoneta L. and Steunenberg, Bernard. (2000) 'The search for convergence of national policies in the European Union: an impossible quest?', *European Union Politics* 1(2): 201–26.

Egeberg, Morten and Trondal, Jarle. (2009) 'National agencies in the European administrative space: government driven, commission driven or networked?', *Public Administration* 87(4): 779–90.

Egeberg, Morten, Schaefer Günther and Trondal, Jarle. (2003) 'The many faces of EU committee governance', *West European Politics* 26(3): 19–40.

Falkner, Gerda, Treib, Oliver, Miriam, Hartlapp and Leiber, Simone. (2005) *Complying with Europe: EU Harmonisation and Soft Law in the Member States*, Cambridge: Cambridge University Press.

Falkner, Gerda, Treib, Oliver and Holzleitner, Elisabeth. (2008) *Compliance in the European Union. Living Rights or Dead Letters?*, Aldershot: Ashgate.

Featherstone, Kevin and Radaelli, Claudio M. (eds.). (2003) *The Politics of Europeanization*, Oxford: Oxford University Press.

Franchino, Fabio. (2000) 'The commission's executive discretion, information and comitology', *Journal of Theoretical Politics* 12(2): 155–81.

Goetz, Klaus H. (2006) 'Europäisierung der öffentlichen Verwaltung – oder europäische Verwaltung?', in Jörg Bogumil, Werner Jann and Frank Nullmeier (eds.), *PVS-Sonderheft 37: Politik und Verwaltung*, pp. 472–90.

Gornitzka, Ase and Sverdrup, Ulf. (2008) 'Who consults? The configuration of expert groups in the European Union', *West European Politics* 31(4): 725–50.

Graziano, Paolo and Vink, Maarten P. (eds.). (2006) *Europeanization: New Research Agendas*, Basingstoke: Palgrave.

Green Cowles, Maria, Caporaso, James and Risse, Thomas (eds.). (2001) *Transforming Europe: Europeanisation and Domestic Change*, Ithaca: Cornell University Press.

Haas, Peter M. (1998) 'Compliance with EU directives: insights from International relations and comparative politics', *Journal of European Public Policy* 5(1): 17–37.

Hartlapp, Miriam and Heidbreder, Eva G. (2017) 'Mending the hole in multilevel implementation: administrative cooperation related to worker mobility', *Governance* 00: 1–17.

Hatzopoulos, Vassilis. (2007) 'Why the open method of coordination is bad for you: a letter to the EU', *European Law Journal* 13(3): 309–342.

Heidbreder, Eva G. (2011) 'Structuring the European administrative space: policy instruments of multi-level administration', *Journal of European Public Policy* 18(5): 709–727.

Heidbreder, Eva G. (2013) 'Regulating capacity building by stealth: pattern and extent of EU involvement in public administration', in Philipp Genschel and Markus Jachtenfuchs (eds.), *Beyond the Regulatory Polity*, Oxford: Oxford University Press, pp. 145–65.

Heidbreder, Eva G. (2015a) 'Governance in the European Union: a policy analysis of the attempts to raise legitimacy through civil society participation', *Journal of Comparative Policy Analysis: Research and Practice* 17(4): 359–77.

Heidbreder, Eva G. (2015b) 'Horizontal capacity pooling: direct, decentralised, joint policy execution', in Michael W. Bauer and Jarle Trondal (eds.), *The Palgrave Handbook of the European Administratve System*, Houndmills: Palgrave, pp. 369–82.

Heidbreder, Eva G. (2015c) 'Multilevel policy enforcement: innovations in how to administer liberalized global markets', *Public Administration* 93(4): 940–55.

Heidbreder, Eva G. and Brandsma, Gijs Jan. (2017) 'The EU policy process', in Edoardo Ongaro and Sandra van Thiel (eds.), *The Palgrave Handbook of Public Administration and Management in Europe*, London: Palgrave.

Héritier, Adrienne. (1996) 'The accommodation of diversity in European policy-making and its outcomes: regulatory policy as a patchwork', *Journal of European Public Policy* 3(2): 149–67.

Héritier, Adrienne. (2005) 'Europeanization research East and West: a comparative assessment', in Frank Schimmelfennig and Ulrich Sedelmeier (eds.), *The Europeanization of Central and Eastern Europe*, Ithaca, NY: Cornell University Press, pp. 199–209.

Héritier, Adrienne, Moury, Catherine, Bischoff, Carina and Bergström, Carl Fredrik (eds.). (2013) *Changing Rules of Delegation: A Contest for Power in Comitology*, Oxford: OUP.

Hofmann, Herwig. (2014) 'General principles of EU law and EU administrative law', in Catherine Bernard and Steve Peers (eds.), *European Union Law*, Oxford: OUP, pp. 196–225.

Holzinger, Katharina and Knill, Christoph. (2005) 'Causes and conditions of cross-national policy convergence', *Journal of European Public Policy* 12(5): 775–96.

Hooghe, Liesbet and Marks, Gary. (2003) 'Unraveling the central state, but how? Types of multi-level governance', *American Political Science Review* 97(2): 233–43.

Hupe, Peter. (2014) 'What happens on the ground: persistent issues in implementation research', *Public Policy and Administration* 29(2): 164–82.

Idema, Timo and Kelemen, Daniel R. (2006) 'New modes of governance, the open method of co-ordination and other fashionable red herring', *Perspectives on European Politics and Society* 7(1): 108–23.

Joerges, Christian and Neyer, Jürgen. (1997) 'From intergovernmental bargaining to deliberative political processes: the constitutionalisation of comitology', *European Law Journal* 3(4): 273–99.

Joosen, Rik and Brandsma, Gijs Jan. (2017) 'Transnational executive bodies: EU policy implementation between the EU and member State level', *Public Administration* early view: 1–14.

Jordana, Jacint, Levi-Faur, David and Fernández i Marín, Xavier. (2011) 'The global diffusion of regulatory agencies: channels of transfer and stages of diffusion', *Comparative Political Studies* 20(5): 1–27.

Kassim, Hussein. (2003) 'The european administration: between Europeanization and domestication', in Jack Hayward and Anand Menon (eds.), *Governing Europe*, Oxford: Oxford University Press, pp. 139–61.

Knill, Christoph. (2001) *The Europeanisation of National Administrations: Patterns of Institutional Change and Persistence*, Cambridge: Cambridge University Press.

Knill, Christoph. (2015) 'Implementation', in Jeremy Richardson and Sonia Mazey (eds.), *European Union: Power and Policy-making*, London: Routledge, pp. 371–96.

Knill, Christoph, Tosun, Jale and Bauer, Michael W. (2009) 'Neglected faces of Europeanization: the differential impact of the EU on the dismantling and expansion of domestic policies', *Public Administration* 87(3): 519–37.

König, Thomas and Mäder, Lars. (2014) 'The strategic nature of compliance: an empirical evaluation of law implementation in the central monitoring system of the European Union', *American Journal of Political Science* 58(1): 246–63.

Krapohl, Sebastian. (2003) 'Risk regulation in the EU between interests and expertise: the case of BSE', *Journal of European Public Policy* 10(2): 189–207.

Majone, Giandomenico. (2001a) 'Nonmajoritarian institutions and the limits of democratic governance: a political transaction-cost approach', *Journal of Institutional and Theoretical Economics JITE* 157(3): 57–78.

Majone, Giandomenico. (2001b) 'Two logics of delegation: agency and fiduciary relations in EU governance', *European Union Politics* 2(1): 103–22.

Majone, Giandomenico. (2002) 'Delegation of regulatory powers in a mixed polity', *European Law Journal* 8(3): 319–39.

Mastenbroek, Ellen. (2005) 'EU compliance: still a "black hole"?', *Journal of European Public Policy* 12(6): 1103–120.

Matland, Richard E. (1995) 'Synthesizing the implementation literature: the ambiguity-conflict model of policy implementation', *Journal of Public Administration Research & Theory* 5(2): 145–74.

Mavrot, Céline and Sager, Fritz. (2016) 'Vertical epistemic communities in multilevel governance', *Policy & Politics* early view(11 November).

Moury, Catherine and Héritier, Adrienne. (2012) 'Shifting competences and changing preferences: the case of delegation to comitology', *Journal of European Public Policy* 19(9): 1316–35.

Olsen, Johan (2003) 'Towards a European administrative space?', *Journal of European Public Policy* 10(4): 506–31.

Peters, B. Guy. (2014) 'Implementation structures as institutions', *Public Policy and Administration* 29(2): 131–44.

Plümper, Thomas and Schneider, Christina J. (2009) 'The analysis of policy convergence, or: how to chase a black cat in a dark room', *Journal of European Public Policy* 16(7): 990–1011.

Pollitt, Christopher. (2001) 'Convergence: the useful Myth?', *Public Administration* 79(4): 933–47.

Pollitt, Christopher. (2002) 'Clarifying convergence: striking similarities and durable differences in public management reform', *Public Management Review* 4(1): 471–92.

Radaelli, Claudio M. (2008) 'Europeanization, policy learning, and new modes of governance', *Journal of Comparative Policy Analysis: Research and Practice* 10(3): 239–54.

Richardson, Jeremy. (1996) 'Policy-making in the EU', in Jeremy Richardson (ed.), *European Union: Power and Policy-Making*, London: Routledge, pp. 3–23.

de Ruiter, Rik. (2012) 'Full disclosure? The open method of coordination, parliamentary debates and media coverage', *European Union Politics* October(online first): 1–20.

Sabatier, Paul. (1986) 'Top-down and bottom-up approaches to implementation research: a critical analysis and suggested synthesis', *Journal of Public Policy* 6(1): 21–48.

Sabel, Charles F. and Jonathan Zeitlin. (2012) 'Experimentalism in the EU: common ground and persistent differences', *Regulation & Governance* 6(3): 410–26.

Schmidt, Susanne K. (2007) 'Mutual recognition as a new mode of governance', *Journal of European Public Policy* 14(5): 667–81.

Thomann, E. and Sager F. (2017) 'Moving beyond legal compliance: Innovative approaches to EU multi-level implementation', *Journal of European Public Policy*, doi:10.1080/13501763.2017.1314541.

Thomann, Eva. (2015) 'Customizing Europe: transposition as bottom-up implementation', *Journal of European Public Policy* 22(10): 1368–87.

Toshkov, Dimiter. (2011) 'The quest for relevance: research on compliance with EU law'. in.

Treib, Oliver. (2014) 'Implementing and complying with EU governance outputs', in *Living Reviews in European Govovernance*.

Trondal, Jarle. (2010) *An Emergent European Executive Order*, Oxford: Oxford University Press.

Trondal, Jarle and Jeppesen, Lene. (2008) 'Images of agency governance in the European Union', *West European Politics* 31(3): 417–41.

Trubek, David M. and Trubek, Louise G. (2005) 'Hard and soft law in the construction of social Europe: the role of the open method of Co-ORDINATION', *European Law Journal* 11(3): 343–64.

Tsebelis, George and Hahm, Hyeonho. (2014) 'Suspending vetoes: how the Euro countries achieved unanimity in the fiscal compact', *Journal of European Public Policy* 21(10): 1388–411.

Versluis, E. (1997) 'Even rules, uneven practices: opening the 'black box' of EU law in action', *West European Politics* 30(1): 50–67.

Vos, Ellen. (2009) '50 years of European integration, 45 years of Comitology', *Maastricht Faculty of Law Working Paper* 3.

Wonka, Arndt and Rittberger, Berthold. (2010) 'Credibility, complexity and uncertainty: explaining the institutional independence of 29 EU agencies', *West European Politics* 33(4): 730–52.

Toward a better understanding of implementation performance in the EU multilevel system

Eva Thomann and Fritz Sager

ABSTRACT
The results of this collection allow for preliminary conclusions about the nuanced interplay between Europeanization and domestication forces in European Union (EU) implementation, which await testing in different contexts. Some policies lend themselves more to a strategy allowing for extensive domestication than others; but to be effective, decentralized implementing actors need both power and capabilities. Europeanization dynamics strongly influence the direction of domestication of EU policy, but if EU requirements are incompatible with national political preferences domestication trumps Europeanization. Domestication equally prevails if the relationship between EU and national policy is ambiguous and frontline implementers have high discretion. The trend toward the Europeanization of direct EU enforcement challenges its legitimacy. This has implications for EU researchers and practitioners, and suggests methodological challenges and future research trajectories for a performance perspective on EU implementation. More comparative research is needed about the trade-offs between conformance, diversity, and performance in EU multilevel governance.

What have we learned?

The contributions to this collection present findings and ideas that advance our knowledge of three aspects. First, they illuminate diverse responses to centrally decided policies within the European Union's (EU's) multilevel structure (Héritier 1999; Thomann 2015). Second, they provide valuable insights in the mechanisms underlying the application and enforcement of EU policies in practice (Versluis 2007). Third, they help us understand the motivations and roles of individual actors implementing EU policy (Tyler 1990; Woll and Jacquot 2010). We first summarize the findings and how they mutually contribute to answering these questions (see Table 1). These results bear concrete implications for Europeanization scholars and EU practitioners. We then

Table 1. Summary of results.

Contribution	Thomann & Zhelyazkova	Mastenbroek	Gollata & Newig	Dörrenbächer	Scholten	Heidbreder
Stage	Transposition	Legal compliance	Practical application	Practical application	Enforcement	Choice of implementation type
Unit of analysis	EU rules transposed in member states	Individuals in ministries	Programmes implemented at local level	Decision-making by frontline implementers	EU direct enforcement strategies	Policies
Actors	Member states	Legislative drafters	Municipalities	Case workers	EU agencies & networks	Policy-makers
Research interest	Customization: discretionary changes of EU policies during transposition • Conceptualization & measurement • Patterns across member states & policies • Relationship between customized density & restrictiveness	Frontline of EU compliance • Typology of dual roles: EU guardian vs politically loyal civil servant • Propensity of double-hatted actors to be guardians of EU law in the face of conflicting domestic political preferences	Conduciveness of multilevel governance (MLG) to effective policy implementation • Decentralization, spatial fit & participation • Collaboration & co-ordination among municipalities • Interaction between municipal & state levels	Motivations of street-level implementers • 'second frontline' between domestic & EU regulation creates new legal ambiguities • Instrumental motivations should discourage, normative motivations should generate uses of EU law	Role of EU in directly enforcing EU policy • Three enforcement strategies • Conditions for effectiveness of these strategies • Challenges posed by direct EU enforcement	Derive implementation strategies beyond conceptually limited compliance perspective • Combine top-down/bottom-up and vertical/horizontal MLG dimensions • Functional expectations about strategic choices
Policy area(s) / case(s)	21 environment directives (N = 894) 10 justice & home affairs directives (N = 750) 27 member states	Cross-sectoral 10 Dutch ministries	EU air quality policy 137 air quality and action plans in 16 German *Länder*	Migration policy 21 case workers of 10 *Ausländerbehörden* in North Rhine-Westphalia, Germany	EU-wide EU enforcement authorities, networks and soft, hard and case law	–

Methods	Manual coding of conformity reports Descriptive statistics	31 qualitative interviews	Quantitative & qualitative content analysis of documents Descriptive statistics	Qualitative interviews	Analysis of legal sources, official documents & multi-disciplinary literature	Literature review/ theory paper
Core findings	Considerable diversity of transposition beyond compliance Relationship between customized density & restrictiveness varies between policy areas Pronounced policy-specific logics	Legislative drafters recognize dual roles They employ interpretive techniques to bridge EU law with political preferences Political steering trumps EU requirements	Decentralization ineffective owing to lacking substantial enforcement capabilities of local administrations Planning remained tied to territorial jurisdictions Participatory planning voluntary & arbitrary	Different levels of law used to produce 'just' outcomes Instrumental motivations trigger limited use of EU law Substantive normative motivations trigger active use of EU law (procedural motivations are limited)	Proliferation of EU enforcement authorities and their direct enforcement powers Growing number of enforcement networks More hard, soft and case law regulating domestic enforcement	Four ideal-types of implementation: centralization, agencification, convergence, networking Only under certain conditions a particular strategy will lead to effective implementation
Europeanization dynamics	EU policy matters: Customization often follows direction of flexibility allowed for by EU provisions	Attempts to integrate EU legal requirements with national policy objectives whenever possible (escalation ladder)	Minimal compliance given (but air quality targets not met) Learning & capacity building	Implementers complement national law with EU law when the former is unclear Some implementers correct for missing transposition	Trend of enforcement moving to Brussels Direct enforcement by EU entity has greatest problem-solving potential Partly lacking juridical accountability/ legitimacy of EEAs	More constraining implementation types effective when little conflict/ ambiguity
Domestication dynamics	Domestic politics: Significant country differences in compliant customization	Role conflicts often lead to prioritization of national political preferences	Leeway led to German administration to keep with existing structures & procedures	Most implementers prioritize national guidance in their decision making	Member states retain some control over enforcement thanks to institutional choices (agencies, networks)	Less constraining implementation types effective when high conflict/ ambiguity

(Continued)

Table 1. Continued.

Contribution	Thomann & Zhelyazkova	Mastenbroek	Gollata & Newig	Dörrenbächer	Scholten	Heidbreder
Scope conditions	Policies represent regulatory logics of both positive and negative integration Comprehensive sample of old and new member states Limitations: Incomplete information Expert evaluations under-represent full extent of compliant customization, especially for ambiguous rules	Most different systems identifies varieties of strategies Likely case for a sense of EU loyalty Strong rule of law Limitations: Analytically representative but not statistically generalizable	Under-researched policy Policy lacks spatial fit Full sample of implementation in Germany Limitations: Contextually contingent	Normatively laden & client-intensive policy is crucial case for motivations High discretion & legal ambiguity Limitations: No statistical generalization May not apply to technical policy fields	Full sample Limitations: Causes and empirical consequences of trend mostly unknown	Strongly embedded in Europeanization & policy implementation literature Limitations: Empirical testing needed

discuss their implications in light of the central hypothesis we have put forward (Thomann and Sager 2017): that the interplay of Europeanization and domestication dynamics is a central explanation for implementation performance in the EU (Bugdahn 2005). Indeed, the findings allow for a preliminary identification of conditions that matter in this interplay. These insights lead us to outline the promise and limitations of a more performance-oriented perspective on EU implementation to complement established compliance perspectives. We discuss methodological considerations and future research trajectories in the quest to gradually gain a fuller picture of the EU's problem-solving capacity in practice.

Responses to EU law beyond compliance

The findings presented by Thomann and Zhelyazkova (2017) paint the first large-scale picture of the diverse legal interpretations of EU law by 27 member states across two policy areas. Their study empirically shows how 'member states simultaneously strive to achieve compliance, and adapt EU policies to their local contexts. The resulting diversity in compliant transposition remains concealed when only looking at legal compliance' (Thomann and Zhelyazkova 2017: 19). The authors measure and describe the patterns and extent of customization in its different directions (Bauer and Knill 2014), conceptually (not necessarily empirically) independent of the compliance question. This in turn paves the way for studying the reasons and implications of this diversity (Héritier 1999; Majone 1999) in a systematic, cumulative fashion.

Substantively, Thomann and Zhelyazkova (2017) provide evidence for two phenomena. First, the customization of EU provisions follows pronounced policy-specific logics; that is, the direction of flexibility indicated by EU rules. Conversely, contrary to previous case studies, their large-N approach does not offer evidence for distinct country-specific customization styles (Falkner *et al.* 2005; Thomann 2015; Thomson 2009; Toshkov 2007; Versluis 2007). Second, EU rules change along different dimensions that represent 'distinct aspects of state action and illuminate a differentiation of variation in national adaptation strategies that can be insightful' (Thomann and Zhelyazkova 2017: 7). The interplay of customized density and restrictiveness tells us about the problem-solving strategies of member states. For example, member states may differentiate EU rules in order to create exemptions, or they may do so in order to render EU rules more restrictive.

Thomann and Zhelyazkova (2017) do not shed light on the actual legislative mechanisms causing customization patterns. Mastenbroek partly fills this gap. She finds that most Dutch legislative drafters responsible for EU compliance try 'to integrate EU legal requirements with national policy demands' (Mastenbroek 2017: 4–5).

Similarly arguing that there is more to implementation than compliance, Heidbreder (2017) asks which implementation strategies appear most promising for achieving effective implementation in a multilevel setting. Her first theoretical contribution lies in deriving a typology of implementation strategies in the EU that overcomes the often criticized top–down versus bottom–up dichotomy, by linking it with Hooghe and Mark's (2003) two types of multilevel governance. She argues that in the EU, top–down and bottom–up elements are constantly intertwined, while the different levels of its system can also be in more vertical or more horizontal relationships. Based on these considerations, she identifies four strategies – centralization, agency, convergence and networks – for policy implementation in the EU, each with its unique characteristics, creation mechanisms, implementation logics and policy decision traits. A second contribution of Heidbreder's (2017) study lies in fleshing out expectations about the effectiveness of different implementation strategies based on Matland's (1995) two dimensions of ambiguity and conflict. By discussing several illustrations for her typology, Heidbreder (2017) convincingly demonstrates how this heuristic helps us understand why certain implementation strategies are successful in some contexts but not in others.

Taken together, the findings allow for a substantive conclusion: that characteristics of policies, in interaction with domestic political contexts, determine the responses of member states to EU policy – ultimately, the politics of implementation (Lowi 1972). Also in compliance research, patterns of EU implementation appear strongly policy- and country-specific (Mastenbroek 2005; Steunenberg 2007; Treib 2014). For researchers, this implies that diversity is inherent in EU implementation. A one-size-fits-all solution to effective policy implementation does not exist. While this may not be surprising, an important endeavour is still to gain a better understanding of the relevant properties of EU and domestic policies and institutions that trigger different implementation dynamics (see also Knill 2015). In the long term, such inquiries should be extended to include policy outcomes and impacts as the ultimate interest of a performance-oriented perspective (e.g., Skjærseth and Wettestadt 2008; Toshkov and de Haan 2013). Potentially relevant policy features include the direction of flexibility allowed by rules with different logics in contexts of positive or negative integration (Thomann and Zhelyazkova 2017), as well as the levels of ambiguity and conflict of a policy (Heidbreder 2017; Matland 1995).

These findings also provide insights for EU policy-makers. First, legal compliance is simply one of many possible transposition outcomes, and far from 'the end of the story'. Thus, if the interest lies in joint solutions to shared policy problems, then we need to consider the dynamics of customization (Thomann 2015) and performance in practice (Bondarouk and Liefferink 2016; Bondarouk and Mastenbroek 2017). Second, EU steering matters, as national deviations from EU rules relatively consistently follow the direction of flexibility indicated by EU legislation (Thomann and Zhelyazkova 2017). This then also means that such adaptations (e.g., gold-plating) often do not require regulatory action from a conformance perspective. Third, there are appropriate (and inappropriate) implementation strategies for different policies. Thus, it is worth considering the nature, ambiguity and regulatory logic of the policy under question, and the prevailing interest constellation on the ground. This should facilitate to identify appropriate venues for enabling discretionary adaptations, as well as situations in which more constraining steering instruments are more promising to ensure an effective Europeanization.

EU law 'in action'

In several respects, the comprehensive case study of all local air quality and action plans in Germany by Gollata and Newig (2017) sheds light on hitherto unknown aspects of EU law in action (Falkner *et al.* 2005; Versluis 2007). First, it empirically tests the claim advanced by polycentric governance theory (Hooghe and Marks 2003) that multiple levels of governance are conducive to effective implementation. Second, the study looks at patterns of collaboration, co-ordination and interaction between the municipal and state levels of governance. Their findings do not support the abovementioned assertion. While minimally complying with the EU requirement to establish air quality and action plans, municipalities continued to struggle to meet air quality targets – with significant variation between the German *Länder,* and some functionally more affected municipalities taking their implementation task more seriously than others.

The introduction of new functional governance layers and mandated planning (Newig and Koontz 2014) has not led to more effective implementation owing to lacking support by the national government in the German case. Specifically, it proved ineffective to decentralize decision-making to the local level because local administrations lacked substantial enforcement capabilities and were unable to obligate higher levels. Furthermore, spatial adaptation was scarce: planning remained largely tied to territorial jurisdictions, although some horizontal and vertical co-operation occurred. Finally, the process of air quality and action plan-making did involve non-state actors, but only on a voluntary and arbitrary basis. Overall, given the leeway conceded by the directives, the German Federal administration largely opted to keep with existing structures and procedures rather than engaging in the legal and institutional adaptation that would have been necessary for an actual rescaling of governance to the spatial level.

Dörrenbächer (2017) then shifts the focus to the individual motivations of caseworkers to use EU immigration law or domestic law respectively, to justify their decisions. Very little research has addressed how individuals implement EU policy (e.g., Gulbrandsen 2011; Versluis 2007). The study is an excellent example of how this micro-perspective helps us understand the mechanisms of putting EU policy into practice. Dörrenbächer argues that EU regulatory requirements put street-level bureaucrats at a 'second frontline' that can create considerable legal ambiguities: first, EU law often introduces fuzzy legal concepts. Second, the EU rules may have been transposed incorrectly or not at all. She finds that street-level implementers are aware of the multi-levelled nature of the legal framework they implement. Accordingly, they creatively and flexibly use legal tools from different origins. This leads to variation in implementation practices. Yet it also creates situations in which front-line implementers may correct for inadequate transposition.

While these two contributions illustrate the limits of Europeanization at the level of practical implementation, Scholten (2017) points to an important trend toward more direct enforcement activities in 'Brussels'. Accordingly, she asks what role is necessary for the EU to play in order to promote the implementation of EU policies. She provides original data to illustrate the growth of three intertwined strategies. First, in the past 15 years the number of EU enforcement authorities, with parallel, hierarchical or suppor-tive relationships with their national counterparts, has grown from one to seven (e.g., the European Medicines Agency [EMA]). Second, the number of EU enforcement networks bringing together relevant national authorities has increased to at least 20 entities. These networks include the Commission who can then influence national enforcement through co-ordination and data. Finally, enforcement standards laid down in EU hard, soft and case law increasingly prescribe procedural and substantive requirements for direct national enforcement.

Adopting a functional spillover perspective, Scholten (2017, see also Schol-ten and Scholten 2016) explains this trend by the desire to ensure the implementation of EU policies in light of the limits of indirect enforcement. She further argues that direct enforcement by European enforcement auth-orities has the greatest potential to resolve the problem of non-compliance; networks make EU influence possible by fostering mutual learning and co-operation (also see Mavrot and Sager 2016); while direct enforcement through EU norms still face the well-known danger of incorrect or non-trans-position, application and enforcement.

These results highlight the relationship between the implementation of EU law on paper and its subsequent implementation in practice. The study by Gollata and Newig (2017) is a striking illustration that conformance with EU requirements is often not enough to ensure appropriate policy performance (see also Versluis 2007; Zhelyazkova *et al.* 2016). So is Dörrenbächer's study, which points toward the potential of frontline implementation to correct for an inadequate legal transposition of EU policies. Scholten's findings reveal significant 'underground' efforts of the EU to overcome the separation between the two implementation stages. In this sense, the conclusion to be drawn is ambiguous: clearly, multilevel governance poses – perhaps inherent – challenges both for a uniform and an effective implementation of EU policies. Simultaneously, however, many local implementers do seem to care about correctly implementing EU policies whenever they can. They also use opportunities to – alone or collaboratively – achieve optimal policy outcomes, if they are capable of effectively doing so. Finally, the EU seems to have more possibilities to enforce member state compliance than we have traditionally assumed.

For researchers studying the practical implementation of EU law, these findings imply that we should tackle the theoretical and empirical relationship, or a lack thereof, between legal and practical implementation in the EU (Zhelyazkova *et al.* 2016). Second, it might be necessary to shift the focus to implementation levels below the member states (local as well as individual), if the goal is to gain a full picture of EU implementation. Conversely, Scholten (2017) invites:

> both academics and policy-makers at the EU and national levels to take a closer look at … the extent to which the EU's enforcement competences (direct and indirect) have been effective in promoting the implementation of EU law and policies … to determine what type of EU's enforcement competences should be desirable in specific circumstances.

Third, it seems warranted to address more systematically the conditions that lead implementers to refer to a correct and effective implementation of EU law in practice.

The results presented here suggest several relevant contextual features that affect these mechanisms – information that should also be useful for practitioners. First, Gollata and Newig (2017) show that it is not sufficient to confer implementation competencies to decentralized governance levels for effective implementation. Rather, these actors also need to be functionally affected and possess capacities of enforcement and obliging superordinate actors. Second, Dörrenbächer (2017) shows that the ambiguity and leeway engrained in both EU and domestic rules matter. More binding and clearer EU rules might lead implementers to weigh EU policy higher than domestic interests, especially when national policies are unclear or otherwise 'insufficient'. Finally, the individual motivations of implementing agents play a decisive role for the degree to which they implement EU policy and prioritize it *vis-à-vis* domestic policies.

Roles and motivations of implementing agents

Europeanization research has a long tradition of assuming different logics of action that guide actors implementing EU law. Accordingly, most prominent theoretical frameworks assume that there can be rationalist or norm-based paths toward Europeanization (Börzel and Risse 2003; Falkner *et al.* 2005; Jupille *et al.* 2003; March and Olsen 1998; Mastenbroek and Kaeding 2006; Michelsen 2008). This distinction has primarily been applied at the level of member states, while neglecting the variety of actors with diverging motivations in EU implementation (Mastenbroek 2010) and 'the study of individual action and its role in the transformation of the European political system' (Woll and Jacquot [2010: 1]; for a recent exception, see Bayram [2017]). Two contributions in this collection address this gap, both at the level of legislative drafters involved in processes of legal compliance (Mastenbroek 2017) and frontline implementers of EU policy (Dörrenbächer 2017). Parallel to a broader behavioural turn in public administration and public policy (Grimmelikhuijsen *et al.* 2017; John 2016), this approach is motivated by the insight that 'individual politicians and civil servants involved in processes of Europeanization may vary in their propensity to comply with the law' (Mastenbroek 2017). Fundamentally, 'street-level implementers at the 'frontline', between the laws in the books and actual practice crucially influence the final outcome of policies' (Dörrenbächer 2017; Lipsky 1980/2010). Accordingly, both studies analyse the reasons why and situations in which implementing actors give different relative weigh to EU and national policies when using their discretion.

The study by Mastenbroek (2017) illuminates the 'black box' of adaptation of national law to EU legislation. She criticizes rationalist accounts for neglecting the fact that individual administrators involved in compliance processes may differ in their propensity to comply with EU law (Mastenbroek 2017). She illustrates three roles of legislative drafters: that of 'guardians of EU law' striving for the best interpretation of EU law; the 'translator' as a politically loyal civil servant prioritizing national political demands; and the 'integrating professional' who seeks to reconcile EU law and domestic political demands, but ultimately should prioritize the former over the latter. By analysing how legislative drafters balance these roles with each other, she shows to what extent legislative actors play a role in effectively guarding EU law in the face of conflicting domestic political preferences.

Based on qualitative interviews with legislative drafters in ten Dutch ministries, Mastenbroek (2017) finds that her respondents are aware of this dual allegiance. Dutch legislative drafters reinterpret EU law and explore its limits in order to connect and reconcile EU law with national political demands. Sometimes, however, they cannot credibly do so, while staying within the bounds of EU law. In this case, they tend to prioritize political demands over EU legal requirements and go beyond the limits set by EU law. They do so even though they have received extensive training in the constitutive principles of EU law. Thus, legislative drafters tend to look for 'reasonable arguments' instead of working from 'the best view' of EU law.

Dörrenbächer's (2017) analysis additionally translates the idea of a logic of consequences and a logic of appropriateness into instrumental and normative motivations (Sunshine and Tyler 2003). Legal ambiguity for frontline workers prevails when EU law grants more discretion than national law, national law stands in tension EU law, or national law is even less explicit than EU rules (see Dörrenbächer and Mastenbroek 2017). In these situations, she expects that instrumental motivations will lead frontline bureaucrats to prioritize their national political principals' preferences over EU law. Frontline implementers motivated by a sense of EU loyalty should use EU law to resolve ambiguities. Finally, substantive normative motivations (personal feelings of justice) should lead implementers to 'pick and choose' between EU and national law.

Her findings indicate that the main situation in which frontline implementers explicitly refer to EU law is when national regulations are unclear or EU law is not transposed. Conversely, they do not use EU law in ways that run counter to or go beyond national law. In this sense, they mostly give priority to national guidance in their decisions. Instrumental motivations lead implementers to consider it risky to refer to EU law. Conversely, substantive (but not procedural) normative motivations can trigger an active use of EU law. In essence, '"double-hatted" street-level implementers (Egeberg and Trondal 2009) sometimes use the different levels of law to bring about policy outcomes they personally consider as just' (Dörrenbächer 2017). However, when national norms both conflict with EU norms and do not provide clear guidance, instrumental motivations lead frontline implementers to consider it risky *not* to rely on EU law.

From a strict conformance perspective, these findings may be rather sobering. However, they also provide extremely valuable lessons for EU researchers and practitioners. A first important insight is that individuals implementing EU policy are conscious of the content of these policies. They also make efforts to implement EU rules correctly. A factor consistently limiting these efforts is their loyalty to domestic policies and political principals, which they often prioritize over their EU loyalty. This suggests an important link between legal and practical implementation. A factor that can trigger their reference to EU rules, in turn, is their desire to bring about 'better' policy outcomes (Elmore 1979; Lipsky 1980/2010) – following normative, but sometimes also rationalist motivations. While the interplay between different logics of action has been subject to much dispute, these motivations do appear useful for studying Europeanization at the individual level. This, then, also implies that the behavioural components of EU policy implementation deserve further exploration, including possibilities of 'nudging' individual policy implementers (John 2016). Importantly, these findings considerably advance our understanding of patterns of and the interplay between Europeanization and domestication processes.

The interplay between Europeanization and domestication

Bugdahn (2005: 177–8) argues that 'the implementation of EU policies is best conceptualized as a blend of domestic choices of options in a policy area, only some of which have been determined by the EU'. In this vein, Europeanization – the EU influence over domestic policy choices in a given policy – is only one side of the coin. Simultaneously, 'member states can make choices of non-prescribed or non-recommended policy options that limit, mediate or accompany the Europeanization of the policy area in various forms' (Bugdahn 2005: 178). This complementary force of domestication poses a challenge for EU implementation research:

> instead of simply equating the implementation of EU policies with Europeanization scholars should develop and make use of concepts that (a) allow for the determination of the relative weight and importance of the EU in the national context and (b) capture the dual nature of the implementation process. (Bugdahn 2005: 179)

The contributions in this collection allow for preliminary conclusions about the complex interplay of Europeanization and domestication dynamics, and factors affecting it at different stages of the implementation cycle.

Choice of implementation type

According to Heidbreder (2017), the levels of *conflict and ambiguity* of the policy under question determine which implementation strategies promise to be effective (Matland 1995). Some strategies are less constraining for domestication, some more. When the different political actors have strong shared interests, then strategies emphasizing Europeanization over domestication come into play. If the policy is relatively unambiguous, implementation can be centralized in a top–down manner. If ambiguity is high, delegation to an agency is a likely option. Conversely, when there are conflicting interests, implementation strategies should allow for a high degree of domestication. If ambiguity is low, bottom–up implementation strategies can lead to 'voluntary' convergence. If ambiguity is high, policy-specific networks are a flexible strategy.

Legal transposition

The results presented by Thomann and Zhelyazkova (2017) illustrate that *Europeanization dynamics strongly influence the domestication of EU policy*. A large amount of domestication follows a direction that conforms to EU policy. Within this framework outlined by EU policy, the authors find evidence of a high diversity of domestication strategies, which they argue point to the importance of domestic politics. Mastenbroek (2017) confirms these insights by showing that legislative drafters interpret EU policy in order to reconcile

Europeanization with domestication. Yet, *if a reconciliation of EU requirements with the preferences of national political principals is not possible, then domestication trumps Europeanization.*

Practical application

The findings provided by Gollata and Newig (2017) suggest that *an implementation strategy aimed at capitalizing on domestication does not perform well in a context where decentralized implementing actors have discretion, but no power and capacity.* In such a situation, Europeanization may be limited to conformance, and domestication (here: non-adaptation) may not be conducive to performance. Dörrenbächer (2017) suggests that *domestication beats Europeanization, if the relationship between EU and national policy is ambiguous and frontline implementers have discretion.*

Enforcement

Scholten (2017) shows how the EU is in an ongoing process of countering the practical non-conformance with EU policy by *Europeanizing the enforcement of EU policy* – a domain which, with the exception of competition law, has traditionally been a central source of domestication (see also Jensen 2007; Kelemen 2012). Simultaneously, the institutional choices made allow member states to retain a certain amount of control over enforcement.

Scholten (2017) further discusses how the balance between Europeanization and domestication challenges the legitimacy of the EU governance structure. Essentially, she argues that the domestication of EU enforcement serves the system's input legitimacy (Scharpf 1999). The treaties do not foresee the shift of enforcement power to the EU. She also argues that accountabilities did not accommodate this power shift, since EU and national systems of judicial control over EU law enforcement remain strictly separated. This could result in blame avoidance (*cf.* Hinterleitner 2017; Hinterleitner and Sager 2016) and situations where member states cannot hold EU enforcement authorities accountable. In an EU with diverse legal cultures, shared enforcement also requires institutional, procedural and substantive adaptations that can pose their own legitimacy problems. Scholten concludes that the Europeanization of enforcement would have to be more effective in order to compensate for this lack of input legitimacy with increased output legitimacy. However, there is no empirical proof of this yet.

In a similar vein, Thomann and Zhelyazkova 2017) highlight how bottom–up implementation theory assumes that discretion for implementers

> can facilitate context-sensitive solutions of the original policy problem at stake and increase the likelihood of effective and broadly accepted policy solutions at

the point where the problem is most immediate. ... European integration is increasingly perceived as a loss of sovereignty over national policies. The customization phenomenon ... illuminates how member states use transposition as an opportunity to modify EU law and regain control.

These comments suggest that the 'optimal' balance between Europeanization and domestication fundamentally depends on the capacity of the configuration of these two forces to resolve joint policy problems effectively in the EU. In this respect, a performance-oriented perspective on EU implementation can make a viable contribution.

Directions for a performance perspective on EU implementation

Considerations of legitimacy and acceptance are not merely of academic interest. Rothstein (2014) argues that political science tends not to put enough focus on the state machinery and its performance or lack thereof. As Héritier (2016: 17) points out, 'this argument is particularly interesting in the light of empirical findings which indicate that in public opinion good governance of the state is a more important source of democratic legitimation than the correct and fair democratic procedures as such'. Prominent politicians like Martin Schulz have argued that the acceptance of EU decisions can be enhanced by bringing them closer to the citizens – by deciding globally, but decentralizing as much implementation power as possible to local actors who know how to best resolve the problem.[1] A crucial advantage of a performance perspective on EU implementation is that it complements a conformance approach to emphasize domestication dynamics in the analysis of Europeanization. Thereby, it allows for putting assertions as the ones above to empirical scrutiny.

A performance-oriented perspective on EU implementation can add significantly to our theoretical understanding of multilevel and particularly EU implementation, and move the latter forward in the direction of implementation as problem-solving (Elmore 1979). By shedding light on the complex interplay between Europeanization and domestication, such a perspective can reveal conditions under which this interplay can foster effective policy solutions (see also Knill and Tosun 2012; Richardson 2012; Richardson and Mazey 2015). Doing so is important to better understand the link between legal and practical implementation, and the situations in which conformance is or is not enough to achieve good policy performance (Keman 2000). This in turn should stimulate the further exploitation of synergies between differing analytic lenses. For example, analysing the process of interpretation of EU law by individual implementers helps understand the conditions under which compliance with EU law is improbable. Analytically, it helps us to conceptualize and operationalize the complex mechanisms and outcomes of multilevel implementation systems. Researchers may identify which properties of EU and domestic policies and institutions trigger different implementation dynamics, and accordingly, appropriate implementation strategies; or which enforcement strategies are warranted in specific circumstances.

Methodological considerations

An analytic focus on complexity, processes, individual interpretations and motivations, and policy outcomes also bears methodological challenges that have more broadly been associated with bottom–up implementation studies (e.g., Hupe and Hill 2016). The high internal validity aspired by such research questions often implies an in-depth focus and considerable efforts of primary data collection and analysis, resulting in research designs that do not allow for representative and generalizable insights (Hartlapp and Falkner 2009; see scope conditions in Table 1). Such studies then sometimes have a descriptive character and often do not allow for disentangling parsimonious explanations from purely context-dependent (e.g., policy-specific) patterns (Goertz and Mahoney 2012; Treib 2014). However, Héritier (2016: 11) also rightly points out that the 'rigour versus relevance question is not a question of quantitative or qualitative research but rather a question of … opting for substantive problem oriented, methodologically stringent research in a limited-scope theoretical context'.

In this vein, several methodological strategies appear promising to obtain, in a cumulative manner, a more complete picture of policy implementation and effectiveness in the EU (see Toshkov 2016). First, qualitative implementation studies should explicitly formulate scope conditions for their findings; that is, the analytically relevant properties of their case(s) that influence what answers they find to their research question (Mahoney and Goertz 2004). Second, comparative Europeanization research needs systematic, theoretically grounded conceptualizations of core concepts that capture diversity and performance in EU implementation beyond compliance, which allow for their application in diverse research contexts while preserving the equivalence of concept meaning and measurement (Adcock and Collier 2001; for examples, see Bondarouk and Liefferink 2016; Bondarouk and Mastenbroek 2017; Thomann and Zhelyazkova 2017: Online Appendix; Tummers *et al.* 2012). This way, the results of different studies can more directly speak to each other. Third, the best research arguably combines 'the best of both worlds', for example, through mixed-methods research involving collaborations with colleagues with different methodological skills (Héritier 2016). Nested designs identify patterns across large sets of cases and then select analytically relevant cases for in-depth analyses of underlying mechanisms (Lieberman 2005; Schneider and Rohlfing 2013).

Finally, while ready-made databases on EU implementation are biased toward certain aspects of legal compliance (Hartlapp and Falkner 2009), alternative options for data collection and analysis in less 'optimal' data contexts do exist. For example, survey pools in bureaucracies or experimental designs are useful to analyse the motivations of policy implementers (Grimmelikhuijsen *et al.* 2017; Tummers *et al.* 2012). Innovative techniques of quantitative text analysis can systematically extract information from large amounts of EU conformity and evaluation reports (Grimmer and Stewart 2013; Klüver 2009). Finally, set-theoretic methods such as qualitative comparative analysis (Rihoux and Ragin 2009; Schneider and Wagemann 2012) or explanatory typologies (Møller and Skaaning 2015) model several of the causal patterns identified in this collection. For example, they assume that 'many ways can lead to Rome', that configurations of factors matter, and that the same factor may not always have the same effect, depending on the context (Exadaktylos and Radaelli 2012; Thomann and Maggetti 2017; e.g., Cacciatore *et al.* 2015; Di Lucia and Kronsell 2010; Maatsch 2014; Schmälter 2017; Sager and Thomann 2016; Thomann 2015).

Ways ahead

Given their limited generalizability, the findings of this collection call for more comparative research, channelling efforts and resources to go beyond the 'usual suspects' of countries and policies traditionally studied in EU implementation research. To conclude, we outline three core features of a promising research agenda for testing the applicability of our conclusions about the interplay between Europeanization and domestication in other contexts.

First, more research is needed that addresses the practical effectiveness of EU policy, while accounting for context-specific patterns from a performance perspective (e.g., Skjærseth and Wettestadt 2008; Toshkov and de Haan 2013). In particular, the results of this collection encourage us to explore the relevant properties of policies and institutions creating different implementation dynamics, as well as the conditions under which implementers implement EU law correctly and effectively. As outlined above, such a comparative ambition has both conceptual and methodological implications. The question of actual performance also requires a more evaluative perspective, raising challenges regarding data availability and the quality of legislative *ex-post* evaluation in the EU (Mastenbroek *et al.* 2016).

In this vein, the contributions of this collection highlight many open research questions about the EU's practical problem-solving capacity. For instance, Heidbreder (2017) calls for more research on the conditions under which particular implementation strategies prove effective, and the role of the factual and normative ambiguity of policies therein (Matland 1995; Schmidt 2008). Thomann and Zhelyazkova (2017) suggest to strive for a more in-depth and improved coding of customization especially in the face of legal ambiguity. They propose to analyse its empirical relevance so as to systematically compare discretionary freedoms across different member states and issue areas. This paves the way for identifying the conditions under which national authorities increase or decrease the leeway of domestic implementing actors; how member states make use of different dimensions of customization to satisfy domestic interests during implementation; and to what extent more or less restrictive interpretations of EU rules enhance the legitimacy and acceptance of EU law 'on the ground' (see Dörrenbächer and Mastenbroek 2017). Gollata and Newig (2017) call for a more thorough analysis of rationales and institutional prerequisites that drive the choice of governance approaches, such as diverging 'governance cultures'. We must disentangle the effect of the governance model from that of contextual factors in order to assess the usefulness of policy implementation through multilevel governance.

Second, we need to gain a better understanding of the processes, mechanisms and motivations underlying patterns of compliance and diversity. To this end, it is crucial that Europeanization research focuses more explicitly on individuals implementing EU law, connecting the micro level with meso level and macro level variables. In this regard, EU implementation research can benefit from integrating recent theoretical and methodological developments in behavioural public administration and policy research (e.g., Grimmelikhuijsen *et al.* 2017; John 2016; Tummers *et al.* 2012) and drawing from the literature on social psychology and socialization processes (e.g., Bayram 2017; Beyers 2010; Sunshine and Tyler 2003; Tyler 1990). Such an approach facilitates a deeper understanding of the organizational and national structures, cultures and institutions involved in EU implementation. For example, it can lend empirical substance to recurring arguments such as Falkner *et al.*'s (2005) 'worlds of compliance', or Gibson and Caldeira's (1996) legal cultures of Europe.

Our collection points to several research gaps in this respect. Mastenbroek (2017), for example, proposes to carry out comparative large-N explanatory research on the roles chosen by EU-involved drafters or other civil servants (Bayram 2017; Egeberg 1999; Sager and Overeem 2015), taking into account background variables such as age and seniority, but also more theoretically informed variables such as instrumental and normative considerations. Dörrenbächer (2017) poses two crucial questions for future research: what role does EU law play for implementers who operate under less discretion (Trondal 2011; Wockelberg 2014), and what is the relationship between normative and instrumental motivations and the use of EU law?

Third, a thorough understanding of the effects and acceptance of EU policies requires researchers to tackle the challenging task of linking different stages of the policy cycle in the EU multilevel system. For example, the present collection advances our knowledge of the relationship between the EU implementation on paper and in practice (Versluis 2007; Zhelyzkova *et al.* 2016). Beyond the implementation stage, more research should scrutinize how EU policy-making interacts with implementation (e.g., Thomson

2010; Zhelyazkova 2013). Next to the question of how member states regain control over EU policies during implementation (Thomann and Zhelyazkova 2017), we also know very little about how implementation decisions are reloaded into decision-making in order to optimize EU policies. In this regard, the interplay between implementation and legislative design deserves more attention. How do EU institutions try to 'stack the deck' of EU implementation by installing and stimulating checks and balances on non-compliance (Kelemen 2012)?

In this latter vein, Scholten (2017) stresses the importance of investigating the extent to which different EU enforcement strategies have been effective in addressing certain non-implementation problems of EU law and policies, and subject to which conditions. As she notes:

> such studies could contribute to building a model, which would also be useful for policy-makers, to determine what type of EU's enforcement competences should be desirable in specific circumstances ... The findings on effectiveness could also inform researchers investigating the legitimacy of the EU and the 'underground' method of expanding power. ... future studies also need to consider whether, in light of these challenges [in terms of legitimacy, accountability and the organization of shared enforcement], this 'solution' is indeed worthy. (Scholten 2017)

This collection illustrates that research tackling such questions benefits from complementing a compliance perspective with a performance perspective. This implies a procedural view on EU implementation as an act of interpretation of EU policy by actors who operate within multiple (policy and domestic) contexts, characterized by a complex interplay between Europeanization and domestication dynamics (Bugdahn 2005). We argue that such research should strive for more cumulativeness and integrate insights from neighbouring literatures. More comparative approaches require systematic conceptualizations and innovative data collection strategies and methodologies. Jointly, such research efforts will increase our understanding of the inherent trade-offs between conformance, the diversity of member-state legislation, and efficient and effective problem-solving (Scharpf 1997) in the EU multilevel system.

Note

1. Martin Schulz, 2 July 2016, programme conference 'Europe' of the German Social Democratic Party, Berlin.

Disclosure Statement

No potential conflict of interest was reported by the authors.

Funding

This work was supported by Schweizerischer Nationalfonds zur Förderung der Wissenschaftlichen Forschung: [Grant Number P2BEP1-162077,P300P1_171479].

References

Adcock, R. and Collier, D. (2001) 'Measurement validity: a shared standard for qualitative and quantitative research', *American Political Science Review* 95(3): 529–46.

Bauer, M.W. and Knill, C. (2014) 'A conceptual framework for the comparative analysis of policy change: measurement, explanation and strategies of policy dismantling', *Journal of Comparative Policy Analysis: Research and Practice* 16(1): 28–44.

Bayram, A.B. (2017) 'Good Europeans? How European identity and costs interact to explain politician attitudes towards compliance with European Union law', *Journal of European Public Policy* 24(1): 42–60.

Beyers, J. (2010) 'Conceptual and methodological challenges in the study of European socialization', *Journal of European Public Policy* 17(6): 909–20.

Bondarouk, E. and Liefferink, D. (2016) 'Diversity in sub-national EU implementation: the application of the EU Ambient Air Quality directive in 13 municipalities in the Netherlands', *Journal of Environmental Policy & Planning*, doi:10.1080/1523908X.2016.1267612

Bondarouk, E. and Mastenbroek, E. (2017) 'Reconsidering EU compliance: implementation performance in the field of environmental policy', *Environmental Policy and Governance*, online first.

Börzel, T.A. and Risse, T. (2003) 'Conceptualizing the domestic impact of Europe', in K. Featherstone and C.M. Radaelli (eds), *The Politics of Europeanization*, Oxford: Oxford University Press, pp. 57–82.

Bugdahn, S. (2005) 'Of Europeanization and domestication: the implementation of the environmental information directive in Ireland, Great Britain and Germany', *Journal of European Public Policy* 12(1): 177–99.

Cacciatore, F., Natalini, A. and Wagemann, C. (2015) 'Clustered Europeanization and national reform programmes: a qualitative comparative analysis', *Journal of European Public Policy* 22(8): 1186–211.

Di Lucia, L. and Kronsell, A. (2010) 'The willing, the unwilling and the unable–explaining implementation of the EU Biofuels Directive', *Journal of European Public Policy* 17(4): 545–63.

Dörrenbächer, N. (2017) 'Europe at the Frontline: analyzing street-level motivations for the use of European Union migration law', *Journal of European Public Policy*, doi:10.1080/13501763.2017.1314535

Dörrenbächer, N. and Mastenbroek, E. (2017) 'Passing the Buck? Analysing the delegation of discretion after transposition of European Union law', *Regulation & Governance*, doi:10.1111/rego.12153

Egeberg, M. (1999) 'Transcending intergovernmentalism? Identity and role perceptions of national officals in EU decision-making', *Journal of European Public Policy* 6(3): 456–74.

Egeberg, M. and Trondal, J. (2009) 'National agencies in the European administrative space: government driven, commission driven or networked?', *Public Administration* 87(4): 779–90.

Elmore, R.F. (1979) 'Backward mapping: implementation research and policy decisions', *Political Science Quarterly* 94(4): 601–16.

Exadaktylos, T. and Radaelli, C.M. (2012) *Research Design in European Studies: Establishing Causality in Europeanization*, Chippenham: Palgrave Macmillan.

Falkner, G., Treib, O., Hartlapp, M. and Leiber, S. (2005) *Complying with Europe: EU Harmonisation and Soft Law in the Member States*, New York: Cambridge University Press.

Gibson, J.L. and Caldeira, G. (1996) 'The legal cultures of Europe', *Law & Society Review* 30(1): 55–86.

Goertz, G. and Mahoney, J. (2012) *A Tale of Two Cultures: Qualitative and Quantitative Research in the Social Sciences*, Princeton, NJ: Princeton University Press.

Gollata, J.A.M. and Newig, J. (2017) 'Policy implementation through multi-level governance: analysing practical implementation of EU air quality directives in Germany', *Journal of European Public Policy*, doi:10.1080/13501763.2017.1314539

Grimmelikhuijsen, S., Jilke, S., Olsen, A.L. and Tummers, L. (2017) 'Behavioral public administration: combining insights from public administration and psychology', *Public Administration Review* 77(1): 45–56.

Grimmer, J. and Stewart, B.M. (2013) 'Text as data: the promise and pitfalls of automatic content analysis methods for political texts', *Political Analysis* 21(3): 267–97.

Gulbrandsen, C. (2011) 'The EU and the implementation of international law: the case of 'sea-level bureaucrats', *Journal of European Public Policy* 18(7): 1034–51.

Hartlapp, M. and Falkner, G. (2009) 'Problems of operationalization and data in EU compliance research', *European Union Politics* 10(2): 281–304.

Heidbreder, E.G. (2017) 'Strategies in multilevel policy implementation: moving beyond the limited focus on compliance', *Journal of European Public Policy*, doi:10.1080/13501763.2017.1314540

Héritier, A. (1999) *Policy-making and Diversity in Europe: Escape from Deadlock*, Cambridge: Cambridge University Press.

Héritier, A. (2016) 'Rigour versus Relevance'? Methodological discussions in political science', *Politische Vierteljahresschrift* 57(1): 11–26.

Hinterleitner, M. (2017) 'Policy failures, blame games and changes to policy practice', *Journal of Public Policy*, doi:10.1017/S0143814X16000283

Hinterleitner, M. and Sager, F. (2016) 'Anticipatory and reactive forms of blame avoidance: of foxes and lions', *European Political Science Review*, doi:10.1017/S1755773916000126

Hooghe, L. and Marks, G. (2003) 'Unraveling the central state, but how? Types of multilevel governance', *American Political Science Review* 97(2): 233–43.

Hupe, P. and Hill, M. (2016) *Understanding Street-level Bureaucracy*, Bristol: Policy Press.

Jensen, C.B. (2007) 'Implementing Europe: a question of oversight', *European Union Politics* 8(4): 451–77.

John, P. (2016) 'Behavioral approaches: how nudges lead to more intelligent policy design', in B.G. Peters and P. Zittoun (eds), *Contemporary Approaches to Public Policy. Theories, Controversies and Perspectives*, London: Palgrave Macmillan UK, pp. 113–31.

Jupille, J., Caporaso, J.A. and Checkel, J.T. (2003) 'Integrating institutions: rationalism, constructivism, and the study of the European Union', *Comparative Political Studies* 36(1–2): 7–40.

Kelemen, R.D. (2012) 'Eurolegalism and democracy', *JCMS: Journal of Common Market Studies* 50(s1): 55–71.

Keman, H. (2000) 'Federalism and policy performance. A conceptual and empirical inquiry', in U. Wachendorfer-Schmidt (ed.), *Federalism and Political Performance*, London: Routledge, pp. 196–227.

Klüver, H. (2009) 'Measuring interest group influence using quantitative text analysis', *European Union Politics* 10(4): 535–49.

Knill, C. (2015) 'Implementation', in J. Richardson and S. Mazey (eds), *European Union: Power and Policy-making*, London: Routledge, pp. 371–97.

Knill, C. and Tosun, J. (2012) 'Governance institutions and policy implementation in the European Union', in J. Richardson (ed.), *Constructing A Policy-Making State? Policy Dynamics in the EU*, Oxford: Oxford University Press, pp. 309–33.

Lieberman, E. (2005) 'Nested analysis as a mixed-method strategy for comparative research', *American Political Science Review* 99(3): 435–52.

Lipsky, M. (1980/2010) *Street-Level Bureaucracy: The Dilemmas of the Individual in Public Services*, New York: Russell Sage Foundation.

Lowi, T.J. (1972) 'Four systems of policy, politics, and choice', *Public Administration Review* 32(4): 298–310.

Maatsch, A. (2014) 'Are we all austerians now? An analysis of national parliamentary parties' positioning on anti-crisis measures in the eurozone', *Journal of European Public Policy* 21(1): 96–115.

Mahoney, J. and Goertz, G. (2004) 'The possibility principle: choosing negative cases in comparative research', *American Political Science Review* 98(4): 653–69.

Majone, G. (1999) 'Regulation in comparative perspective', *Journal of Comparative Policy Analysis: Research and Practice* 1(3): 309–24.

March, J.G. and Olsen, J.P. (1998) 'The institutional dynamics of international political orders', *International Organization* 52(4): 943–69.

Mastenbroek, E. (2005) 'EU compliance: still a 'black hole'?', *Journal of European Public Policy* 12(6): 1103–20.

Mastenbroek, E. (2010) 'EU compliance. Towards a procedural logic of appropriateness', Paper presented at ARENA, Oslo, 30 November.

Mastenbroek, E. (2017) 'Guardians of EU law? Analysing roles and behavior of Dutch legislative drafters involved in EU compliance', *Journal of European Public Policy*, doi:10.1080/13501763.2017.1314537

Mastenbroek, E. and Kaeding, M. (2006) 'Europeanization beyond the goodness of fit: domestic politics in the forefront', *Comparative European Politics* 4(4): 331–54.

Mastenbroek, E., van Voorst, S. and Meuwese, A. (2016) 'Closing the regulatory cycle? A meta evaluation of ex-post legislative evaluations by the European Commission', *Journal of European Public Policy* 23(9): 1329–48.

Matland, R.E. (1995) 'Synthesizing the implementation literature: the ambiguity-conflict model of policy implementation', *Journal of Public Administration Research and Theory* 5(2): 145–74.

Mavrot, C. and Sager, F. (2016) 'Vertical epistemic communities in multilevel govern-ance', *Policy & Politics*, doi:10.1332/030557316X14788733118252.

Michelsen, J. (2008) 'A Europeanization deficit? The impact of EU organic agriculture regulations on new member states', *Journal of European Public Policy* 15(1): 117–34.

Møller, J. and Skaaning, S.E. (2015) 'Explanatory typologies as a nested strategy of inquiry: combining cross-case and within-case analyses', *Sociological Methods & Research*, doi:0049124115613778

Newig, J. and Koontz, T.M. (2014) 'Multi-level governance, policy implementation and participation: the EU's mandated participatory planning approach to implementing environmental policy', *Journal of European Public Policy* 21(2): 248–67.

Richardson, J. (2012) *Constructing a Policy-making State? Policy Dynamics in the EU*, Oxford: Oxford University Press.

Richardson, J. and Mazey, S. (2015) *European Union: Power and Policy-making*, London: Routledge.

Rihoux, B. and Ragin, C.C. (2009) *Configurational Comparative Methods. Qualitative Comparative Analysis (QCA) and related techniques*, Thousand Oaks, CA: Sage.

Rothstein, B. (2014) 'Human Well-being and the Lost Relevance of Political Science', *Max Weber Lecture No. 2014/03*, Florence: European University Institute.

Sager, F. and Thomann, E. (2016) 'Multiple streams in member state implementation: politics, problem construction and policy paths in Swiss asylum policy', *Journal of Public Policy*, doi:10.1017/S0143814X1600009X.

Sager, F. and Overeem, P. (eds) (2015) *The European Public Servant: A Shared Administrative Identity?*, Colchester: ECPR Press.

Scharpf, F. (1997) 'Introduction: the problem-solving capacity of multilevel govern-ance', *Journal of European Public Policy* 4(4): 520–538.

Scharpf, F. (1999) *Governing in Europe: Effective and Democratic?*, Oxford: Oxford University Press.

Schmälter, J. (2017) 'Willing and able? A two-level theory on compliance with civil lib-erties in the EU', *Journal of European Public Policy*, doi:10.1080/13501763.2016.1268192.

Schmidt, S.K. (2008) 'Beyond compliance: the Europeanization of member states through negative integration and legal uncertainty', *Journal of Comparative Policy Analysis: Research and Practice* 10(3): 299–308.

Schneider, C.Q. and Rohlfing, I. (2013) 'Combining QCA and process tracing in set-the-oretic multi-method research', *Sociological Methods & Research* 42(4): 559–97.

Schneider, C.Q., and Wagemann, C. (2012) *Set-Theoretic Methods for the Social Sciences. A Guide to Qualitative Comparative Analysis*, New York: Cambridge University Press.

Scholten, M. (2017) 'Mind the trend! Enforcement of EU law has been moving to 'Brussels'', *Journal of European Public Policy*, doi:10.1080/13501763.2017.1314538

Scholten, M. and Scholten, D. (2016) 'From regulation to enforcement in the EU policy cycle: a new type of functional spillover?', *JCMS: Journal of Common Market Studies*, doi:10.1111/jcms.12508

Skjærseth, J.B. and Wettestad, J. (2008) 'Implementing EU emissions trading: success or failure?', *International Environmental Agreements: Politics, Law and Economics* 8(3): 275–90.

Steunenberg, B. (2007) 'A policy solution to the European Union's transposition puzzle: interaction of interests in different domestic arenas', *West European Politics* 30(1): 23–49.

Sunshine, J. and Tyler, T.R. (2003) The role of procedural justice and legitimacy in shaping public support for policing, *Law & Society Review*, 37(3): 513–48.

Thomann, E. (2015) 'Customizing Europe: transposition as bottom-up implementation', *Journal of European Public Policy* 22(10): 1368–87.

Thomann, E. and Maggetti, M. (2017) 'Designing research with Qualitative Comparative Analysis (QCA): approaches, challenges, tools', Paper presented at the 2017 ECPR Joint Sessions of Workshops, Nottingham, 25–30 April.

Thomann, E. and Sager, F. (2017) 'Moving beyond legal compliance: innovative approaches to EU multilevel implementation', *Journal of European Public Policy*, doi:10.1080/13501763.2017.1314541

Thomann, E. and Zhelyazkova, A. (2017) 'Moving beyond (non-)compliance: the customization of European Union policies in 27 countries', *Journal of European Public Policy*, doi:10.1080/13501763.2017.1314536

Thomson, R. (2009) 'Same effects in different worlds: the transposition of EU directives', *Journal of European Public Policy* 16(1): 1–18.

Thomson, R. (2010) 'Opposition through the back door in the transposition of EU Directives', *European Union Politics* 11(4): 577–96.

Toshkov, D. (2007) 'In search of the worlds of compliance: culture and transposition performance in the European Union', *Journal of European Public Policy* 14(6): 933–59.

Toshkov, D. (2016) *Research Design in Political Science*, London: Palgrave Macmillan.

Toshkov, D. and de Haan, L. (2013) 'The Europeanization of asylum policy: an assessment of the EU impact on asylum applications and recognitions rates', *Journal of European Public Policy* 20(5): 661–83.

Treib, O. (2014) 'Implementing and complying with EU governance outputs', *Living Reviews in European Governance* 9(1): 1–47.

Trondal, J. (2011) 'An emergent European executive order', *Journal of European Integration* 33(1): 55–74.

Tummers, L., Steijn, B. and Bekkers, V. (2012) 'Explaining the willingness of public professionals to implement public policies: content, context, and personality characteristics', *Public Administration* 90(3): 716–36.

Tyler, T.R. (1990) *Why People Obey the Law*, Princeton, NJ: Princeton University Press.

Versluis, E. (2007) 'Even rules, uneven practices: opening the "black box" of EU law in action', *West European Politics* 30(1): 50–67.

Wockelberg, H. (2014) 'Political servants or independent experts ? A comparative study of bureaucratic role perceptions and the implementation of EU law in Denmark and Sweden', *Journal of European Integration* 36(7): 731–47.

Woll, C. and Jacquot, S. (2010) 'Using Europe: strategic action in multi-level politics', *Comparative European Politics* 8(1): 110–26.

Zhelyazkova, A. (2013) 'Complying with EU Directives' requirements: the link between EU decision-making and the correct transposition of EU provisions', *Journal of European Public Policy* 20(5): 702–21.

Zhelyazkova, A., Kaya, C. and Schrama, R. (2016) 'Decoupling practical and legal compliance: analysis of member states' implementation of EU policy', *European Journal of Political Research* 55(4): 827–46.

Index